Many Moons

Many Moons

Reflections on Departed Vaiṣṇavas

Giriraj Swami

TorchLight Publishing
shifting the paradigm

Design by Māyāpriyā dāsī
Bhakti Tirtha Swami's cover and *kīrtana* photos courtesy of Lakṣmīvān dāsa

Printed in the United States of America
Published simultaneously in the United States of America and Canada by Torchlight Publishing

Library of Congress Cataloging-in-Publication Data

Giriraj, Swami, 1947-
Many moons : reflections on departed Vaisnavas / Giriraj Swami.
p. cm.
Includes index.
ISBN 978-1-937731-01-4
1. Vaishnavites--Biography. I. Title.
BL1170.G57 2012
294.5'5120922--dc23
[B]

2012002834

Readers interested in the subject matter of this book or wishing to correspond with the author are invited to write to:
Varsabhanavi.GRS@pamho.net or Damodar.GRS@pamho.net

Torchlight Publishing
shifting the paradigm

PO Box 52, Badger CA 93603
Phone: (559) 337-2200 Fax (559) 337-2354
torchlightpublishing@yahoo.com www.torchlight.com

To the moonlike followers of Śrīla Bhaktivedanta Swami Prabhupāda and Śrī Kṛṣṇa Caitanya Mahāprabhu. May they illuminate the sky in the darkness of night— and fill my heart with their light.

Regarding serving your godbrothers, this is a very good practice. The spiritual master is never without his followers, so to serve the spiritual master also means to be the servant of his disciples. When you want to serve the king, you must also serve his minister, secretary, and everyone who serves him. And to serve his servants may please him more than to serve the king personally. So the spiritual master is not alone. He is always with his entourage. We are not impersonalists. We take care of every part of the whole, as much as one should take care of his hat as well as his shoes. Both are equally important for the upkeep of the body. I hope that you will understand this rightly.

—Śrīla A.C. Bhaktivedanta Swami Prabhupāda

Contents

Appendixes 307

Acknowledgments

I would like to thank the following persons who contributed to the publication of this book:

Bhakti Bhṛṅga Govinda Swami, Bhūrijana dāsa, Bhakta Carl Herzig, Ekavīra dāsa and Vraja-līlā dāsī, Guṇagrāhī dāsa Goswami, Guru-bhakti dāsī, Kuntīdevī dāsī, Māyāpur dāsa, Rasikendra dāsa, Ṛtadhvaja Swami, and Sārvabhauma dāsa for their written and oral offerings.

Bhakta Carl Herzig for revising and editing the text and for encouraging and advising me at every stage of production;

Viśākhā Priyā and Bhaktin Mira for editing and proofreading;

Vārṣabhānavī for transcribing, formatting, and other aspects of production;

Nikuñja Vilāsinī, Ṭhākura Haridāsa, and others too numerous to mention by name who have helped directly or indirectly.

I pray that Śrīla Prabhupāda will continue to inspire them in their service to *guru* and Gaurāṅga—and bless me with their continued association.

Hare Kṛṣṇa.

Foreword

A Vaiṣṇava feels joy when he sees the Lord bestow His grace upon another devotee. We can see this in the meeting of Śrīla Rūpa Gosvāmī and Śrīla Sanātana Gosvāmī with Śrī Caitanya Mahāprabhu. The brothers opened their hearts, which were melting with love and humility, and were accepted by the Lord. Śrī Caitanya requested the Vaiṣṇavas present to bless the two so they would attain perfection in the execution of devotional service. And upon hearing this request and seeing the brothers' qualities, the devotees felt joy and blessed them abundantly.

Similarly, we experience great joy when in *Many Moons* we hear and recall—and celebrate—the wonderful lives, qualities, and activities of remarkable devotees who have passed beyond the scope of our vision. Their lives—both what they gave and what they accomplished—were themselves celebrations of the mission of Śrīla Prabhupāda, Śrī Caitanya Mahāprabhu, and Śrī Kṛṣṇa, and we pray for their blessings, that hearing about them may inspire us with a mood of gratitude and obligation.

Śrī Kṛṣṇa informs us that we are His *sac-cid-ānanda* parts and parcels. Due to our misidentification with the body and association with this material world, we continually undergo a hard struggle with our minds and senses. The same Śrī Kṛṣṇa, in His golden form of Śrī Caitanya, gave us the process of spiritual awakening by cultivating a taste for topics of Śrī Kṛṣṇa and sincerely chanting His holy names. And beyond that, Śrī Caitanya ordered that we share the philosophy, pastimes, and pure holy names with everyone we meet.

The great souls described in these pages are bright, full moons of Śrīla Prabhupāda's, Śrī Caitanya's, and Śrī Kṛṣṇa's mercy. Their lives are living instructions, their activities *candrikās*—cooling, illuminating moonbeams of Vaiṣṇava sharing, teaching, and realization.

They all, in their own special and uniquely beautiful ways, were instruments of Vaiṣṇava love, charity, faith, hope, and determination. Each assisted in easing the tribulations of many embodied souls. Thus they all performed the sacred mission requested by Śrī Caitanya Mahāprabhu, and we are confident that the benediction moons of Śrīla Prabhupāda, Śrī Caitanya Mahāprabhu, and Śrī Kṛṣṇa have bestowed their love and grace upon them.

Alas, I am bereft of such mercy. Therefore I approach these Vaiṣṇavas, who have it in their grasp. In gratitude and love I fall to the ground and call out:

"Please, just once, cast your sidelong glance of Vaiṣṇava compassion upon me. Please bless me to follow your examples so that my heart will change and I may become a useful tool in the service of my spiritual master. And please bless me that I may one day chant the name of God with purity and love."

My sincere appreciation, thanks, and prayers for mercy go to my dear friend Giriraj Swami Mahārāja for having undertaken the effort of compiling this touching memorial to these departed Vaiṣṇavas. O Vaiṣṇava, I beg your mercy.

Dāso 'smi—I am your servant.

With much love, in Kṛṣṇa consciousness,
Bhakti Bhṛṅga Govinda Swami

Preface

durgame pathi me 'ndhasya
skhalat-pāda-gater muhuḥ
sva-kṛpā-yaṣṭi-dānena
santaḥ santv avalambanam

"My path is very difficult. I am blind, and my feet are slipping again and again. Therefore, may the saints help me by granting me the stick of their mercy as my support."

—*Śrī Caitanya-caritāmṛta, Antya-līlā* 1.2

All of us, as we endeavor to progress on the spiritual path, need the association—the knowledge, experience, and affection—of those more advanced than we. The association of such devotees is one of the most potent factors in the development of Kṛṣṇa consciousness. In his *Bhakti-rasāmṛta-sindhu*, known as "the complete science of *bhakti-yoga*," Śrīla Rūpa Gosvāmī recommends:

śrīmad-bhāgavatārthānām
āsvādo rasikaiḥ saha
sajātīyāśaye snigdhe
sādhau saṅgaḥ svato vare

"One should taste the meaning of *Śrīmad-Bhāgavatam* in the association of pure devotees, and one should associate with the devotees who are more advanced than oneself and who are endowed with a similar type of affection for the Lord." (*Brs* 1.2.91)

How to find—or recognize—and appreciate and avail oneself of such association is often a question, and in *Many Moons* I present recollections of nine great souls no longer physically with us who have given me and many others strength and inspiration on our spiritual journeys.

Vedic authorities inform us that there are two means of association: by *vapuḥ*, physical presence, and by *vāṇī*, transcendental sound, or words. "Physical presence is sometimes appreciable and sometimes not, but *vāṇī* continues to exist eternally. Therefore we must take advantage of the *vāṇī* . . ." (Cc "Concluding Words")

The first of these great souls, Jayānanda dāsa, was known to me mainly through my hearing about him. When Jayānanda Prabhu was physically present, he was stationed on the West Coast of the United States and I on the East Coast and in India, so we had little chance to meet personally. Still, what I heard and read about him, to some extent when he was present and even more so after he departed, inspired me to want to follow his wonderful example of humility, dedication, and service. The other eight—Gour Govinda Swami, Tamal Krishna Goswami, Sridhar Swami, Bhakti Tirtha Swami, Bhaktisvarūpa Dāmodara Swami, Arcā-vigraha dāsī, Abhirāma Ṭhākura dāsa, and Kīrtidā dāsī—were devotees with whom I was blessed to have more personal association. Whether personal or indirect, however, association can always be enhanced through discussion of the person's exemplary behavior and character, teachings and instructions.

In the *Bhagavad-gītā* (10.9), Lord Kṛṣṇa says,

mac-cittā mad-gata-prāṇā
bodhayantaḥ parasparam
kathayantaś ca māṁ nityaṁ
tuṣyanti ca ramanti ca

"The thoughts of My pure devotees dwell in Me, their lives are fully devoted to My service, and they derive great satisfaction and bliss from always enlightening one another and conversing about Me." Such discussion of Kṛṣṇa includes discussion of Kṛṣṇa's devotees. Śrīla Rūpa Gosvāmī says that all the processes of devotional service performed in relation to Lord Kṛṣṇa can also be applied to His pure devotees.

This volume contains discussions about many wonderful

devotees, and by reading it one can gain their beautiful association.

Śrīla Prabhupāda, the founder-*ācārya* of the International Society for Krishna Consciousness (ISKCON), formed the society in order to afford people the opportunity to associate with pure devotees, and within the society one will find many devotees like the ones mentioned in this book. Other great souls, not described in this book, have also left us, and we honor them all. Those described are not necessarily greater than other devotees; they are just devotees who by some divine arrangement or mercy came into my life, played significant roles in it, and occupy special places in my heart.

In describing the devotees of Lord Caitanya, Śrīla Kṛṣṇadāsa Kavirāja Gosvāmī, the author of *Śrī Caitanya-caritāmṛta*, wrote:

yata yata mahānta kailā tāṅ-sabāra gaṇana
keha karibāre nāre jyeṣṭha-laghu-krama

"All the great personalities in the line of Lord Caitanya enumerated these devotees, but they could not distinguish between the greater and the lesser.

ataeva tāṅ-sabāre kari' namaskāra
nāma-mātra kari, doṣa nā labe āmāra

"I offer my obeisances unto them as a token of respect. I request them not to consider my offenses.

vande śrī-kṛṣṇa-caitanya-
premāmara-taroḥ priyān
śākhā-rūpān bhakta-gaṇān
kṛṣṇa-prema-phala-pradān

"I offer my obeisances to all the dear devotees of Śrī Caitanya Mahāprabhu, the eternal tree of love of Godhead. I offer my respects to all the branches of the tree, the devotees of the Lord who distribute the fruit of love of Kṛṣṇa." (Cc *Ādi* 10.5–7)

To external vision some pure devotees may appear greater

or lesser than others, but we should learn to recognize and appreciate them all, and respect and serve them all. As Śrīla Prabhupāda wrote in his purport to this last verse, "Śrī Kṛṣṇa-dāsa Kavirāja Gosvāmī sets the example of offering obeisances to all the preacher devotees of Lord Caitanya, without distinction as to higher and lower. . . . [He] offers equal respect to all the preachers of the cult of Śrī Caitanya Mahāprabhu, who are compared to the branches of the tree. ISKCON is one of these branches, and it should therefore be respected by all sincere devotees of Lord Caitanya Mahāprabhu."

Elsewhere, Kavirāja Gosvāmī compares the devotees of Lord Caitanya to moons:

jaya śrī-caitanyacandrera bhakta candra-gaṇa
sabāra prema jyotsnāya ujjvala tri-bhuvana

"All glories to the moons who are devotees of the principal moon, Lord Caitanyacandra! Their bright moonshine illuminates the entire universe." (Cc *Ādi* 13.5)

Such devotees are moons because they can illuminate the darkness of the night. But how? By reflecting the light of the sun—Kṛṣṇa and His associates. As Śrīla Prabhupāda explains, "The sun has the ability to shine powerfully, and the moons reflect the sunshine and therefore look brilliant. In the *Caitanya-caritāmṛta* Kṛṣṇa is described to be like the sun. The supreme powerful is the Supreme Personality of Godhead Śrī Kṛṣṇa, or Lord Śrī Caitanya Mahāprabhu, and His devotees are also bright and illuminating because they reflect the supreme sun. The *Caitanya-caritāmṛta* (*Madhya* 22.31) states:

kṛṣṇa—sūrya-sama; māyā haya andhakāra
yāhāṅ kṛṣṇa, tāhāṅ nāhi māyāra adhikāra

'Kṛṣṇa is bright like the sun. As soon as the sun appears, there is no question of darkness or nescience.' " (Cc *Ādi* 13.5 purport)

In prosecuting the Kṛṣṇa consciousness movement all over the world, Śrīla Prabhupāda was looking for just one moon—one devotee to be trained and engaged in dissipating the darkness of the Age of Kali, the darkness in people's hearts—in accordance with the Sanskrit maxim:

varam eko guṇī putro
na ca mūrkha-śatair api
ekaś candras tamo hanti
na ca tārā-gaṇair api

"It is better to have one qualified son than a hundred foolish ones. Innumerable stars cannot dissipate the darkness, but one moon can illuminate the night."

He taught his new devotees *Śrīmad-Bhāgavatam*, which is meant to give people light in this age:

kṛṣṇe sva-dhāmopagate
dharma-jñānādibhiḥ saha
kalau naṣṭa-dṛśām eṣa
purāṇārko 'dhunoditaḥ

"This *Bhāgavata Purāṇa* is as brilliant as the sun, and it has arisen just after the departure of Lord Kṛṣṇa to His own abode, accompanied by religion, knowledge, etc. Persons who have lost their vision due to the dense darkness of ignorance in the age of Kali shall get light from this *Purāṇa*." (*SB* 1.3.43)

He instructed them in the offenseless chanting of the holy name, which can dissipate the world's darkness:

aṁhaḥ saṁharad akhilaṁ sakṛd
udayād eva sakala-lokasya
taraṇir iva timira-jaladhiṁ
jayati jagan-maṅgalaṁ harer nāma

"As the rising sun immediately dissipates all the world's darkness, which is deep like an ocean, so the holy name of the Lord, if chanted once without offenses, dissipates all the reactions of a living being's sinful life. All glories to that holy name of the Lord, which is auspicious for the entire world." (*Padyāvalī* 16)

In sum, he trained them in Lord Caitanya's service. By bringing the knowledge of *Śrīmad-Bhāgavatam* and the holy name of Śrī Kṛṣṇa—the mission of Lord Caitanya—to the fallen souls, a moonlike devotee can, like Śrī Caitanya Mahāprabhu Himself, illuminate people's hearts.

anarpita-carīṁ cirāt karuṇayāvatīrṇaḥ kalau
samarpayitum unnatojjvala-rasāṁ sva-bhakti-śriyam
hariḥ puraṭa-sundara-dyuti-kadamba-sandīpitaḥ
sadā hṛdaya-kandare sphuratu vaḥ śacī-nandanaḥ

"May the Supreme Lord who is known as the son of Śrīmatī Śacī-devī be transcendentally situated in the innermost chambers of your heart. Resplendent with the radiance of molten gold, He has appeared in the Age of Kali by His causeless mercy to bestow what no incarnation has ever offered before: the most sublime and radiant mellow of devotional service." (Cc *Ādi* 1.4)

When Śrīla Prabhupāda began his mission, everyone wondered whether he would be able to bring even one soul to pure devotional service, Kṛṣṇa consciousness. And we, his followers, had the same question, or doubt. *Śrīmad-Bhāgavatam* (2.4.18) states,

kirāta-hūṇāndhra-pulinda-pulkaśā
ābhīra-śumbhā yavanāḥ khasādayaḥ
ye 'nye ca pāpā yad-apāśrayāśrayāḥ
śudhyanti tasmai prabhaviṣṇave namaḥ

"Kirāta, Hūṇa, Āndhra, Pulinda, Pulkaśa, Ābhīra, Śumbha, Yavana, members of the Khasa races, and even others addicted to sinful acts can be purified by taking shelter of the devotees of the Lord, due to His being the supreme power. I beg to offer my respectful obeisances unto Him." This verse refers specifically to fallen souls in Russia, Germany, Greece, Turkey, Afghanistan, Pakistan, Mongolia, and China, and to aboriginal tribes in India. Yet although such statements were there in scripture, and although histories described isolated cases of powerful sages like Nārada delivering greatly sinful people within India, there was no record of anyone venturing outside India to deliver souls habituated to gross sinful acts. So people wondered whether it was really possible.

In spite of a great many difficulties and disappointments, Śrīla Prabhupāda persisted in his mission—to get one moon. In a talk in New York he said, "We don't want numerical strength. We want one sincere person who has learned to love God, Kṛṣṇa. That's all. I have come to your country with this mission, and if I find one or two boys or girls have sincerely learned how to love God, Kṛṣṇa, then my mission is successful. I'm not after any number of . . . Because if I can turn one soul to Kṛṣṇa consciousness, he'll do tremendous work, because he'll be fire. You see? He can do tremendous work. *Ekaś candras tamo hanti na ca tārāḥ-sahasraśaḥ*. One moon is complete to drive away the darkness of night, not millions of stars required. What these millions of stars can do? One moon is sufficient."

That was Śrīla Prabhupāda's mission and desire. But would it be fulfilled? And if he did get such a moon, would we even be able to recognize it? Only Śrīla Prabhupāda himself could tell us definitively.

He continued, "So our propaganda is to create one moon. You see? But fortunately, by Kṛṣṇa's grace, many moonlike boys and girls have come to me. You see? Many moons. [chuckles] I was thinking of having only one moon, but Kṛṣṇa . . . I am hopeful that there are many moons, and in the future they'll be doing very nice. This is *para-upakāra*. To spread this Kṛṣṇa consciousness movement is the best service to the humanity. Please try to understand this. It is not a bluffing thing. To love God, *premā pumartho mahān* . . . Caitanya Mahāprabhu said that the highest achievement in the human form of life is to attain the perfectional stage to love God. That is the highest."

We were not sure of even one moon, but Śrīla Prabhupāda, out of his extraordinary mercy and power—and by Kṛṣṇa's grace—created many.

Now, one may argue that Śrīla Prabhupāda was speaking in such terms just to encourage us, that these devotees were not yet actually moons but that he was calling them moons in the hope that one day they would become so. And that may be true too. But when Jayānanda Prabhu left this world in Kṛṣṇa consciousness and Śrīla Prabhupāda wrote that "he has been transferred to Vaikuṇṭha [the spiritual abode]" and that "in all of our temples a day may be set aside for holding a festival in his honor, just as we do on the disappearance day of the other great Vaiṣṇavas," there could be no doubt. In Jayānanda Prabhu, Śrīla Prabhupāda had a moon—one of many.

In fact, Śrīla Prabhupāda wanted us all to be moons, to dissipate the darkness of the Age of Kali in the world. As he wrote in the same purport quoted above, "By the illumination of all the moons, brightened by the reflection of the Kṛṣṇa sun, or by the grace of all the devotees of Caitanya Mahāprabhu, the entire world will be illuminated, despite the darkness of Kali-yuga. Only the devotees of Lord Caitanya Mahāprabhu can dissipate the darkness of Kali-yuga, the ignorance of the population of this age. No one else can do so. We therefore wish that all the devotees of the Kṛṣṇa consciousness movement may reflect the supreme sun and thus dissipate the darkness of the entire world." (Cc *Ādi* 13.5 purport)

By associating with Śrīla Prabhupāda and his moonlike devotees, we, too, can become moons. Or, as Śrīla Prabhupāda often said, "By serving the great, one becomes great."

mahat-sevāṁ dvāram āhur vimuktes
tamo-dvāraṁ yoṣitāṁ saṅgi-saṅgam
mahāntas te sama-cittāḥ praśāntā
vimanyavaḥ suhṛdaḥ sādhavo ye

"One can attain the path of liberation from material bondage only by rendering service to highly advanced spiritual personalities. . . . The *mahātmās* are equipoised. They do not see any difference between one living entity and another. They are very peaceful and are fully engaged in devotional service. They are devoid of anger, and they work for the benefit of everyone. They do not behave in any abominable way." (*SB* 5.5.2)

We develop the qualities of those whom we serve, and by serving great souls, *mahātmās*, we become great. By serving Śrīla Prabhupāda, so many devotees have developed his mood of service, and by serving them, we can also develop their qualities, in service to Śrīla Prabhupāda. That has been my principle in my spiritual life, and that has been my principle in writing this book. "A *mahātmā*, or great soul, develops through association with other *mahātmās*, pure devotees." (*Bg* 9.13 purport) "The servants of God come to propagate God consciousness, and intelligent people should cooperate with them in every respect. . . . By serving the servants of the Lord, one gradually gets the quality of such servants, and thus one becomes qualified to hear the glories of God." (*SB* 1.2.16 purport)

Such servants are always meek and humble, considering themselves puppets in the hands of their spiritual master and Kṛṣṇa, and they give all credit for their success to their superiors—the spiritual master, the disciplic succession, and the Supreme Personality of Godhead. And in this regard (as in all others), Śrīla Prabhupāda was exemplary. He gave all credit to his *guru mahārāja*, thinking that whatever light he brought to the world was reflected from the sun of Kṛṣṇa and His associates, and he showed us the mood we should have in his—their—service, as exemplified in a letter he wrote to one disciple: "You have written so many nice things in praise of me, but I think that my *guru mahārāja* is great. I am not great; he is great. Sometimes, by the association of the great, one appears great. Just like the sun is great heat and light, and by reflecting the greatness of the sun's light the moon in the dead of night also appears great, but actually the moon is by nature dark and cold, but in association with the sun it has become accepted as great. This is the real position. So I thank you very much that you are appreciating my *guru mahārāja*, who wanted to preach Kṛṣṇa consciousness all over the world. He is so great." (*SP* letter dated August 1, 1973)

Much more could be said and written about the moonlike devotees featured in *Many Moons*, but I have not attempted here to give a full history or biography of each. Other devotees have already written biographies of some, and I hope and expect that more will be written in the future. What I have tried to present here, through my own words and the words of others, is the essence—the heart—of these great souls and how they were able to touch the hearts of those who knew them and loved them and served them.

In appreciating the essence of devotees, we consider their mood of devotion and service to Kṛṣṇa. We are not so concerned with their external status in *varṇāśrama*, the Vedic system of social and spiritual orders. The great Vaiṣṇava saint and poet Narottama dāsa Ṭhākura prayed, *gṛhe vā vanete thāke, 'hā gaurāṅga' bale ḍāke/ narottama māge tāra saṅga*: "Whether you are a householder or a renunciant, if you are a devotee of Lord Caitanya, I desire your company." And in another song he prayed, *doyā koro śrī-ācārya prabhu śrīnivāsa/ rāmacandra-saṅga māge narottama-dāsa*: "O Śrīnivāsa Ācārya, please be merciful to me. O Rāmacandra, I always desire your company." Śrīnivāsa was Narottama's colleague, or peer, yet Narottama, as a humble Vaiṣṇava, prayed for his mercy. And Rāmacandra

Kavirāja was Śrīnivāsa's disciple, whom Śrīnivāsa placed under Narottama's tutelage, yet Narottama accepted him as his intimate friend and prayed for his association, which he valued more than practically anything.

Of course, in our personal dealings we must observe the standard etiquette in terms of *varṇa* (social order) and *āśrama* (spiritual order), spiritual seniority, and gender, but anyone who surrenders to Kṛṣṇa can achieve Him, the supreme destination, and we can gain from his or her association (*māṁ hi pārtha vyapāśritya ye 'pi syuḥ pāpa-yonayaḥ/ striyo vaiśyās tathā śūdrās te 'pi yānti parāṁ gatim* [Bg 9.32]).

Some readers, like me, personally knew devotees featured in this book, and reading it will bring them—us—to appreciate these great souls even more and to experience, even in their physical absence, their spiritual presence and blessings. Some readers may wish that they had recognized the greatness of these devotees earlier—or known how soon they would leave us—so that they could have made more of an effort to serve and associate with them. And some readers may resolve to appreciate and serve the great souls still with us, not knowing how long we will have the opportunity.

All the devotees described in *Many Moons* reflect some of the light, some of the greatness, of Śrīla Prabhupāda, and we hope that by reading about them and thus associating with them we will also get some of their light—the light coming from Śrīla Prabhupāda, Lord Caitanya, Śrī Kṛṣṇa, and their servants—and become glorious moons ourselves. Thus we can all realize the potential we have within us and fulfill the mission for which we all were born. As stated in the Vedic aphorism (*Bṛhad-āraṇyaka Upaniṣad* 1.3.28), *tamaso mā jyotir gamaya*: "Do not stay in darkness; go to the light." *Asato mā sad gamaya*: "Do not stay in illusion; go to the eternal reality." *Mṛtyor mā amṛtaṁ gamaya*: "Do not keep taking material bodies; become immortal!"

Hare Kṛṣṇa.

Aindra Dāsa

When this book was almost finished, I received news of the sudden departure from this world of Śrīla Prabhupāda's disciple Aindra dāsa, who for many years had headed the 24-hour *kīrtana* in Vṛndāvana. When I heard, I spontaneously prayed to him, "My dear Aindra Prabhu, your sudden departure is a great loss for us all. Your *kīrtanas* and words gave shelter and enlightenment to devotees and ultimately the whole world. We have lost a dear friend and well-wisher. I shall try to follow in your mood of service. Kindly bless me."

Aindra's internal meditation was in the mood of Vraja, *mādhurya*—the sweet pastimes of Rādhā and Kṛṣṇa and Their associates. And his external activities were an expression of the mood of Caitanya Mahāprabhu, *audārya*—the generous distribution of Kṛṣṇa consciousness—especially through *nāma-saṅkīrtana* and transcendental literature. His separation enhanced our appreciation of both him and the practices of devotional service—*hari-pūjā*, *hari-kathā*, and *hari-nāma-saṅkīrtana.*

Although deadlines did not allow me to devote a section to him in this book, I hope that my readers will take full advantage of his association through his *vāṇī*—his words and his *kīrtanas.* I also hope that other devotees will write more about him, for us all to read. And I pray for his mercy upon us.

Jayānanda Dāsa

A Successful Life, a Glorious Death

The following letters were written by Śrīla Prabhupāda shortly before and after Jayānanda's death.

To Jayānanda dāsa, February 26, 1977:

This body is today or tomorrow finished. We should not be very much bothered about the body. Trees also live for thousands of years, but that does not mean a successful life. A successful life is one of Kṛṣṇa consciousness. By the grace of Kṛṣṇa, from the very beginning you are a devotee, and that is the real profit of your life.

About a *sādhu* it is said, *jīva vā māra vā*—a *sādhu* may live or die, it doesn't matter. While living he is engaged in Kṛṣṇa conscious business, and when dying he goes back home, back to Godhead.

To Jayānanda dāsa, May 5, 1977:

I am feeling very intensely your separation. In 1967 you joined me in San Francisco. You were driving my car and chanting Hare Kṛṣṇa. You were the first man to give me some contribution ($5,000) for printing my *Bhagavad-gītā*. After that, you have rendered very favorable service to Kṛṣṇa in different ways. I so hope at the time of your death you were remembering Kṛṣṇa and as such, you have been promoted to the eternal association of Kṛṣṇa. If not, if you had any tinge of material desire, you have gone to the celestial kingdom to live with the demigods for many thousands of years and enjoy the most opulent life of material existence. From there you can promote yourself to the spiritual world. But even if one fails to promote himself to the spiritual world, at that time he comes down again on the surface of this globe and takes birth in a big family like a *yogī's* or a *brāhmaṇa's* or an aristocratic family, where there is again chance of reviving Kṛṣṇa consciousness. But as you were hearing *kṛṣṇa-kīrtana*, I am sure that you were directly promoted to Kṛṣṇaloka.

janma karma ca me divyam
evaṁ yo vetti tattvataḥ
tyaktvā dehaṁ punar janma
naiti mām eti so 'rjuna
[*Bg* 4.9]

Kṛṣṇa has done a great favor to you, not to continue your diseased body, and has given you a suitable place for your service.

Thank you very much.

To Rāmeśvara dāsa, May 11, 1977:

Jayānanda's death is glorious. It is very good that he had stated, "What is the use of such a useless body? Better to give it up." He has left his body very wonderfully, and he has been transferred to Vaikuṇṭha. I have already sent a condolence letter for publication in *Back to Godhead*. Everyone should follow the example of Jayānanda. I am very proud that I had such a nice disciple. If possible, Jayānanda's picture should be hung in the *ratha* of Lord Jagannātha, and in all of our temples a day may be set aside for holding a festival in his honor, just as we do on the disappearance day of the other great Vaiṣṇavas.

Remembering Jayānanda Prabhu

Reflections from Guṇagrāhī dāsa Goswami, October 2009.

I loved Jayānanda Prabhu's association. Around 1975, when I was the temple president in San Diego, I needed to take a break, so I went to join one of the Radha-Damodara bus parties. I thought I would try Gurudas's bus in Oregon. But he, along with Parivrājakācārya Mahārāja, left the party, and when I went up there, to my surprise Jayānanda Prabhu was the *saṅkīrtana* leader.

I was amazed by Jayānanda Prabhu's attitude. He would always clean up after all the young men and was constantly serving them. He was very kind to everybody, very compassionate, and enthusiastic about every service he rendered. He never found fault with anyone and never complained about anything or anybody.

We would all go out on book distribution every day. Jayānanda was not only the *saṅkīrtana* leader but also the driver of the van. One day I was the last to get out and was sitting with him, talking for a while before leaving. He took out a big bowl of *halavā* and began eating—and eating. Then he said to me, "I always get a little nervous before I go out on *saṅkīrtana*, and this *halavā* really calms me down and relaxes me. I really love this *halavā*." It was very sweet to see how he so unabashedly took shelter of *prasāda*.

That same day, I was the first to get picked up, and again Jayānanda and I spent some time talking. He confided in me, "You know, this *saṅkīrtana* is just so wonderful, so enlivening; it is the most enlivening thing I have ever experienced. I have finally found a service I can see myself doing for the rest of my life." I was really struck by that, because he was older, very mature, and qualified in so many ways. He could have assumed any number of leadership positions but was completely happy serving Prabhupāda by living a simple life preaching alongside the *brahmacārīs* and helping them grow in spiritual life.

One weekend afternoon while in Eugene doing *saṅkīrtana*, one of the devotees heard that there was a Mind Body Spirit Festival going on and informed us all when he returned to the bus. Although the festival was due to wind down soon, when Jayānanda heard the news he immediately lit up and sprang into action. "Quick, we need to make lots of sweetballs and distribute *prasāda* to everybody."

I remember thinking, as we mixed, mashed, and mushed together all the ingredients for the sweetballs, that I had never in my life seen so many opulent ingredients in one preparation—cream cheese and walnuts and dates and almonds and figs and dried pineapple and dried papaya and . . . The devotees became really fired up seeing the sweetballs take shape and were rolling them frantically to get them finished before the festival ended. Finally we had a few hundred made, offered them, and then sped off. The festival was in a big gymnasium and had just begun to wind down when we got there. I felt a little intimidated by all the stares as we walked in but had not even a minute to wallow in my fears before I heard the next command from our *saṅkīrtana* general: "Okay, *prabhus*, *hari-nāma!* Follow me!" Jayānanda then started chanting and dancing with the greatest enthusiasm, and we all found ourselves swept up right behind him.

We circumambulated along the perimeter of the gym where the booths were set up, and Jayānanda was chanting and dancing like a madman. The sweetballs were going out as fast as we could distribute them, and all the people, who moments before were looking at us like, "Who the heck are these guys?" began chanting and dancing along with us. I still remember the smiles on their faces as many of them joined our transcendental parade. It was an experience to behold and one that I often remember:

in just a few minutes Jayānanda had completely transformed that gymnasium into Vaikuṇṭha and given everyone a taste of the spiritual realm they had spent all day long futilely trying to grasp.

Either later that year or during the next year, we found out that Jayānanda had cancer and had been receiving various allopathic treatments. However, they were not helping very much, he was averse to spending so much money on them, and most important, they were affecting his ability to think clearly and meditate on Kṛṣṇa. Thus he decided to try a natural cure and found out that in Tijuana, Mexico, right across the border from San Diego, there was a facility that administered one with considerable success.

We helped Jayānanda Prabhu get set up in the clinic, and I started going down weekly to see him. On my first visit I saw he was really ecstatic. He said, "This is fantastic! I am reading the *Bhagavad-gītā* daily. I have never been able to absorb myself as much as I can now. I am getting so many realizations, and every day I give classes to the other patients. I am so enlivened. I have never done anything like this before. It is giving me so much life. Plus, the laetrile seems to be helping, so I am really satisfied being here."

The following week, I returned, but this time when I asked him how things were going, he said, "I'm leaving. Let's get out of here!" Surprised at the drastic change, I asked him what had happened. He said, "They told me I couldn't give classes anymore, that it was against their rules to preach the *Bhagavad-gītā* or teach religion of any kind." He continued, "What's the use of being here if I can't preach? What's the use of living if I can't preach? Let's go." I was amazed, truly amazed. I had never seen him so grave and determined, and while on one hand I was extremely disappointed at the turn of events, I became very much enlivened to witness the fearlessness, detachment, and

Jayānanda dāsa at the Los Angeles temple in the spring of 1977.

Gour Govinda dāsa with Śrīla Prabhupāda in Māyāpur, 1973.

Gour Govinda Swami with his disciple Mādhavānanda dāsa in Bhubaneswar, 1994 or '95.

Tamal Krishna with Śrīla Prabhupāda in London, late 1969 (top), and in Māyāpur, early 1973 (bottom).

Tamal Krishna Goswami and Giriraj Swami carrying the small Rādhā-Śyāmasundara Deities into the ISKCON Vṛndāvana temple, Rādhāṣṭamī 1994.

Sridhar Brahmacārī and Giriraj Brahmacārī with Śrīla Prabhupāda on Juhu Beach, Bombay.

Sridhar Swami's return to Māyāpur, February 13, 2004.

Ghanaśyāma dāsa distributing books in the US in the summer of 1973.

Bhakti Tirtha Swami at the ISKCON Potomac temple, near Washington DC, May 2004.

Bhaktisvarūpa Dāmodara Swami, known by scholars as Dr. Thoudam Singh, addressing scientists and religionists in San Francisco, February 1990.

Bhaktisvarūpa Dāmodara Swami leading Maṇipuri devotees in a *kīrtana* performance, January 2001.

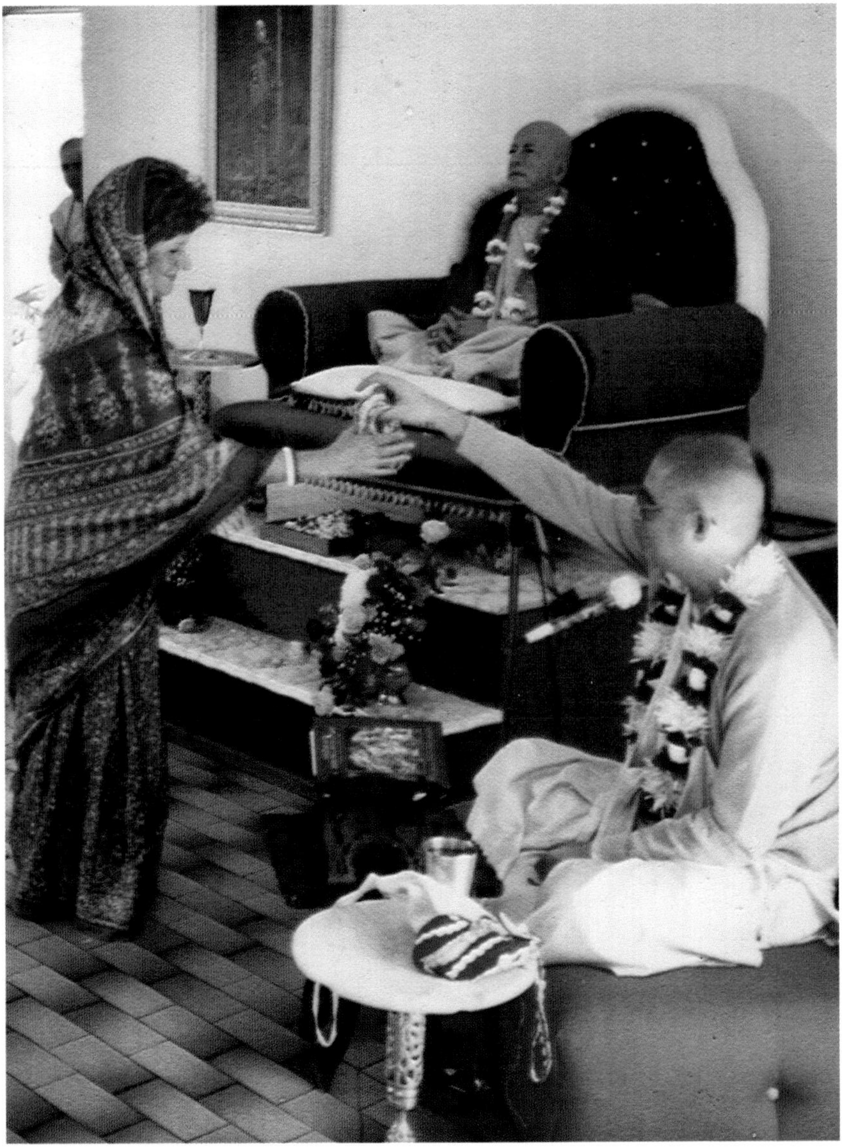

Arcā-vigraha dāsī at her initiation in Muldersdrift, Johannesburg, May 1987.

Mother Arcā-vigraha in Ramaṇa-reti, Vṛndāvana, in 1992 or '93.

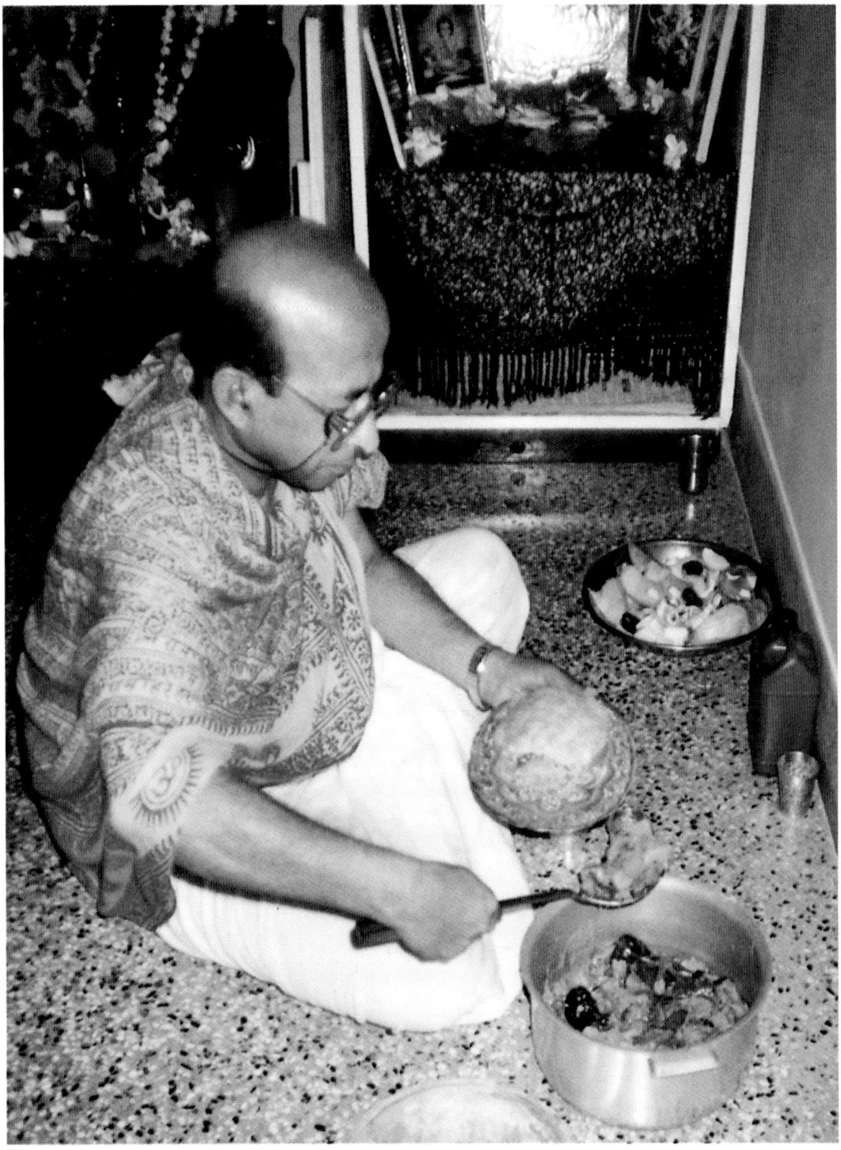

Abhirāma Ṭhākura dāsa preparing an offering for his Deities,
Karachi, Janmāṣṭamī 1988.

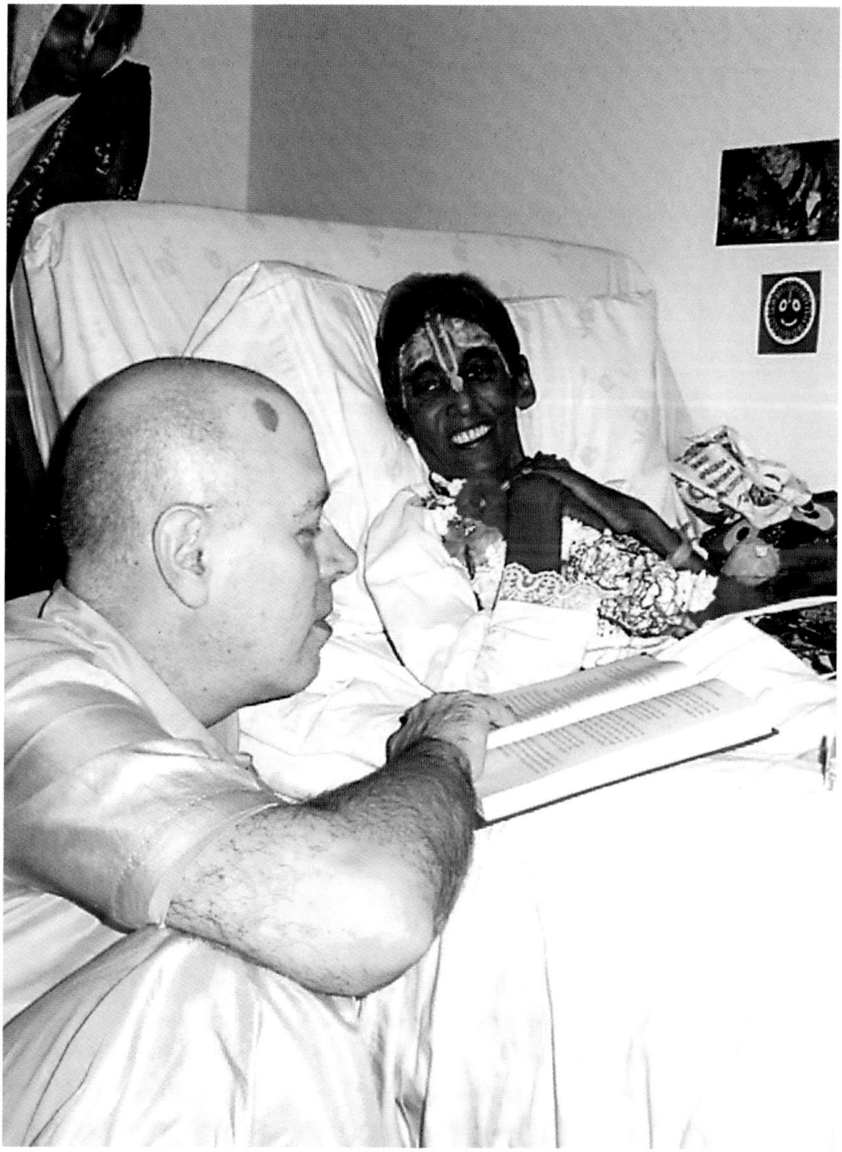

Kīrtidā dāsī with Tamal Krishna Goswami in her Dallas room,
June 11, 2001.

Mother Kīrtidā at the Temple of Heaven Park in Beijing, late 2000.

utter resolve of this great devotee who wanted nothing more than to live the rest of his life preaching, no matter how short a time that might wind up being.

Jayānanda Prabhu had already packed his belongings, and we immediately headed back to San Diego. He remained there for a while, giving classes and constantly commenting on how amazing the *Bhagavad-gītā* was and how many realizations one could get by reading it. After a few weeks he decided to go to Los Angeles, as his health had started deteriorating again and he would get much better attention and facilities there and have much more senior association.

I continue to meditate on Jayānanda Prabhu quite often, especially when in need of the tolerance, enthusiasm, and compassion necessary to push on and to please Śrīla Prabhupāda the way I know he always did.

Prabhupāda's Son, Prabhupāda's Moon

A haiku written for Jayānanda dāsa's disappearance day in 1982.

Prabhupāda's full moon
Beams upon my heart's lotus—
Guru's service blooms

Gour Govinda Swami

Gour Govinda Swami's Kindness

A letter written for Gour Govinda Swami's Vyāsa-pūjā celebration in Mumbai on September 6, 2002.

My dear devotees,

Please accept my humble obeisances. All glories to Śrīla Prabhupāda.

Yesterday His Holiness Sridhar Swami phoned and told me that His Holiness Gour Govinda Swami Mahārāja's Vyāsa-pūjā was around the same time as ours, and he wanted to know if I would approve of keeping a *vyāsāsana* for him at our celebration. I welcomed the opportunity to glorify His Divine Grace Śrīpāda Gour Govinda Swami Mahārāja, especially because I had not had the opportunity to properly glorify him after his departure.

In 1996, in Māyāpur, some days before Śrīla Bhaktisiddhānta Sarasvatī Ṭhākura's appearance day, I received a telegram from my father saying that he had had a stroke and that although he was apparently out of danger he still would like me to come. In the twenty-five years since I had joined, my father had never really asked me for anything, and after consulting some of my close godbrothers, I decided I should go. I got my reservation to leave on Śrīla Bhaktisiddhānta Sarasvatī Ṭhākura's appearance day, but before I left I wanted to see Ravindra Svarūpa Prabhu, who happened to be upstairs in the GBC conference room with the educational sub-committee. As I entered, I saw, seated at the table just to my left, His Holiness Gour Govinda Swami Mahārāja. He had come late for the meetings and had just arrived in Māyāpur the night before. As I had not seen him since he had arrived, I took the opportunity to bow down and place my head at his lotus feet, and in his affectionate way he rubbed my back. He smiled at me warmly and looked at me with his eyes full of love and brightness and bliss. I explained to Ravindra Svarūpa Prabhu that I would be leaving, and again I looked at Mahārāja. We exchanged happy glances and smiles, and I left.

Only some weeks later did I find out that on the very day I had left Māyāpur His Divine Grace Śrīpāda Gour Govinda Swami Mahārāja had left his body. From Māyāpur I had gone to Miami, where my father was in the hospital, and there I had not had any chance to get the news. Only after I accompanied my father to Chicago and spoke to the devotees there did I learn of Mahārāja's departure. At first I couldn't believe it, but then His Holiness Radhanath Swami came to visit me, and he confirmed the news.

My association with His Holiness Gour Govinda Mahārāja goes back many years. I first heard of him from Bhāgavata dāsa Prabhu, a friend of mine who had served with me in Bombay and with Mahārāja in Bhubaneswar. He told me about the saintly person who lived in a grass hut and was translating Śrīla Prabhupāda's books into Oriyā. So even before I got to know His Holiness, I had a very favorable impression of him from Bhāgavata dāsa.

But I really got to know Mahārāja when he came to Mauritius. Mauritius is a small island in the Indian Ocean, between India and Africa. At its widest it is forty miles across—at its longest, sixty. At that time Mahārāja was very seriously translating Śrīla Prabhupāda's *Śrīmad-Bhāgavatam* into Oriyā to have it ready in time for Śrīla Prabhupāda's Centennial. Still, we got the opportunity to have many wonderful exchanges. Whenever he drove from the temple in the town of Phoenix to the temple at the farm in Bon Accueil, we would ride in the car together and discuss. So I had many opportunities to speak with him. Also in the classes—he would give very long classes, and at the end I would ask questions. Once, at the farm in Bon Accueil, I referred to the verses in *Śrī Caitanya-caritāmṛta* (*Madhya* 22.128–129) about the five most potent forms of devotional service:

sādhu-saṅga, nāma-kīrtana, bhāgavata-śravaṇa
mathurā-vāsa, śrī-mūrtira śraddhāya sevana

"One should associate with devotees, chant the holy name of the Lord, hear *Śrīmad-Bhāgavatam*, reside at Mathurā, and worship the Deity with faith and veneration.

sakala-sādhana-śreṣṭha ei pañca aṅga
kṛṣṇa-prema janmāya ei pāṅcera alpa saṅga

"These five limbs of devotional service are the best of all. Even a slight performance of these five awakens love for Kṛṣṇa."

I told him how much I cherished *mathurā-vāsa*, residing in Mathurā (or Vṛndāvana). Mahārāja replied, "Kaṁsa also resided in Mathurā, but still he was a demon." He spoke these words to me with great love and compassion. And I felt that he was seeing straight into my polluted heart and acting to purify it. He instructed me that the goal was not to reside in Mathurā but to actually develop the consciousness of a devotee.

Anyway, we discussed so many things. Even at the airport before he left, we spoke for an hour and a half, very intimately. He mentioned the predicted ten-thousand-year golden age within Kali-yuga, giving some reference for it and expressing his hope that ISKCON would usher it in. And he told me about himself also. He told me about his first meeting with Śrīla Prabhupāda, how Śrīla Prabhupāda had engaged him, and how later he had brought Śrīla Prabhupāda to Orissa. He also told me how he had found guidance after Śrīla Prabhupāda left, how he had developed the notebooks he kept with various verses, and how he would quote from the notebooks when he gave class. He told me so many things.

I remember his eyes—they always seemed moist with tears of love, tears of joy, and his voice was always full of affection and enthusiasm and the ecstasy of realization. In my mind's eye, even now, I can see his eyes and his smile—his head slightly nodding, his eyes looking into mine, blinking, and his face smiling.

The other opportunities we had to meet and discuss came mainly in Juhu. Mahārāja would often leave India from Bombay, and when he returned from his tours abroad he would also come through Bombay and stay in the Juhu guesthouse. There, too, we had many wonderful discussions. One evening, I had a preaching program, but before leaving the temple I wanted to visit him in his room and just offer my respects. When I did, he suddenly began to describe a most wonderful pastime of Rādhā and Kṛṣṇa and how They were assisted by Vṛndādevī. Once, when Kṛṣṇa failed to meet Rādhārāṇī at the appointed time and place, She sent Her girlfriends (*sakhīs*) to investigate. And when they reported that they had found Him at the secret grove of Her rival Candrāvalī, Rādhā manifested the ecstasy of transcendental loving jealous anger (*māna*), and thereafter She refused to meet Him. Distraught, Kṛṣṇa tried in so many ways to break Her *māna*, but nothing He said or did would pacify Her. Finally, Vṛndādevī came to Him and advised Him to disguise Himself as a *sannyāsī* and beg some charity from Her. When He did, Śrī Rādhā could not refuse, and She gave Him what He asked—*prema*. And thus the Divine Couple was happily reunited. I had heard and read many pastimes, but I had never heard this particular one—and he was narrating it in such an animated way. I was just enchanted and did not want to leave. But time was passing, and it was getting later and later for the program. Still, I could not tear myself away. Finally he concluded, and I told him I had to go for a preaching program. And so I left, feeling very enlivened by the *kṛṣṇa-kathā* he had so kindly narrated.

His Holiness Gour Govinda Swami Mahārāja was—and is—a most extraordinary devotee. Although his health was fragile and his age advanced, he took the trouble to travel all over the world like a young man, preach the message of Śrī Caitanya Mahāprabhu and Śrīla Prabhupāda, and enliven the devotees. He was a great and magnanimous soul. Other devotees have documented his purity, his presentation of the philosophy, and his achievements and contributions to the movement. Here I just wanted to relate my own experiences with him—and feelings for him.

We miss him now. Such souls are rare indeed. He was a great source of strength to the movement. But although he has left, I do feel that his legacy continues. Just last week I received a copy of *Śrī Kṛṣṇa Kathāmṛta*. The whole issue was dedicated to the subject of *vaiṣṇava-aparādha*, "the mad elephant offense," and from the quality of *kṛṣṇa-kathā* in the magazine, the intelligence with which the articles were conceived and arranged, I felt, "Yes, his legacy is continuing. His disciples and followers are continuing his mission." I felt very enlivened by the purity of the *kathā* in the magazine. I felt both chastened and inspired.

Mahārāja himself assured us that we can get association and guidance even after the spiritual master leaves this world. How? Through the *guru's* instructions and through the instructions of *śāstra* and *sādhu*—by the *guru's* mercy. He said, "The instruction of *guru* is also *guru*. You'll get *guru-kṛpā*, the mercy of the *guru*, through his instructions, *vāṇī*. One who is very, very eager and very, very inquisitive will pray to his spiritual master, 'O spiritual master, you are not physically present, so I cannot understand. I am such an ignorant fool. I have no qualification. Though your instructions are there, I cannot understand what you have said. Please help me.' The *guru* will come, but not in the same form. He may come in the form of a *sādhu*, a very dear devotee, who is also very dear to your spiritual master. Through him, knowledge will be revealed. Doubts will be cleared. Through him, you will be able to understand *tattva*, purport. You should think, 'My *guru* is teaching me, speaking to me in this form.' Don't think, 'My *guru* is not here. He has departed. What shall I do?' Pray fervently to your spiritual master. He must help you. We have personal experience. We have been helped in this way. Also, the great *mahājanas*, *ācāryas*, have said this. It is an eternal process. Kṛṣṇa is eternal, and His teachings are eternal. The process is also eternal. But we should be very, very inquisitive. One should not feel desperate. There is no reason to be pessimistic. We should be full of optimism in this process."

We conclude with the immortal words of Śrīla Bhaktivinoda Ṭhākura inscribed at the tomb of Ṭhākura Haridāsa in Jagannātha Purī:

> He reasons ill who says that Vaiṣṇavas die,
> When thou art living still in sound!
> The Vaiṣṇavas die to live, and living try
> To spread the holy name around.

I never fully realized until now how much I love Mahārāja. It is certainly his kindness upon me, and I pray that he, from his position, will bless me that I may be a good servant of my spiritual master, Śrīla Prabhupāda, and ultimately become qualified to serve Śrī Śrī Rādhā-Govinda (Gopal Jiu).

Thank you very much. Hare Kṛṣṇa.

Your servant,
Giriraj Swami

A Lifetime in Service

A talk given on Gour Govinda Swami's disappearance day and Śrīla Bhaktisiddhānta Sarasvatī Ṭhākura's appearance day, on February 26, 2008, in Santa Barbara, California.

Today is Śrīla Bhaktisiddhānta Sarasvatī Gosvāmī Prabhupāda's appearance day, as well as the disappearance day of Śrīla Gour Govinda Swami Mahārāja, who left on Śrīla Bhaktisiddhānta Sarasvatī Ṭhākura's appearance day on February 9, 1996, in Māyāpur.

The first time I celebrated Śrīla Bhaktisiddhānta's appearance day I was a new devotee in the Boston temple in early 1970, and Śrīla Prabhupāda instructed us to observe his spiritual master's appearance day with the ceremony called Vyāsa-pūjā. Apart from the offering of *bhoga*, *puṣpāñjali*, and *guru-pūjā*, Śrīla Prabhupāda instructed us to write appreciations, or homages, for his *guru-mahārāja*. I was so new in Kṛṣṇa consciousness that I didn't know much about His Divine Grace Śrīla Bhaktisiddhānta Sarasvatī Ṭhākura, but I thought about him deeply and had two thoughts, or realizations. One, he must have been a most wonderful personality, because someone as great as Śrīla Prabhupāda surrendered to him. And two, it is by his mercy that we came in touch with Śrīla Prabhupāda and Kṛṣṇa consciousness. He gave Śrīla Prabhupāda the instruction to preach Kṛṣṇa consciousness in the English language in the Western world, and in accordance with his divine instruction Śrīla Prabhupāda came to America to deliver us all. So I felt great appreciation for His Divine Grace Śrīla Bhaktisiddhānta Sarasvatī Ṭhākura, and deep gratitude to him.

Today I will focus on His Holiness Śrīla Gour Govinda Swami Mahārāja, who may be less known to many of you. Śrīla Gour

Govinda Swami Mahārāja was born in a Gauḍīya Vaiṣṇava family in Orissa on September 2, 1929. His family members were followers of Śrīmān Mahāprabhu and worshipers of Lord Kṛṣṇa from the time of Śyāmānanda Paṇḍita in the seventeenth century, and they served their family Deity, Gopal Jiu. As a child, Gour Govinda Mahārāja was always very serious. He didn't play with the other children and engaged his free time from school either in serving Gopal Jiu or in performing *kīrtana* with his uncles. So Gour Govinda Mahārāja grew up in that atmosphere—reading *Śrīmad-Bhāgavatam* and *Śrī Caitanya-caritāmṛta*, chanting the Hare Kṛṣṇa *mahā-mantra*, singing the songs of Narottama dāsa Ṭhākura and Bhaktivinoda Ṭhākura, and worshiping Gopal Jiu.

He was educated in Hindi, Bengali, Sanskrit, and English and in various other subjects. In due course, as was customary, he married. And to maintain his family he worked in government service as a school teacher.

But within his heart, his desire to serve the Lord fully grew stronger and stronger, and he prayed to his Deity to relieve him of family responsibilities, as recorded in his diary: "O Prabhu Gopal, please make me a *yogī sannyāsī*. I do not need anything, Prabhu. I am not asking You for material opulence, respect, glory, or anything else. You may give those things to my younger brother Kripa-sindhu. Let him maintain Your [my] family. Make me a *saṁsāra-vairāgī-yogī*, a renunciate of family life. Let me beg that *prema-dhana*, that wealth of love of Godhead. Let me distribute *prema* and *ānanda*. Let me serve You. Please shower this mercy on me, Prabhu! Please bless me with *prema-bhakti*, ecstatic love for You!"

In response to his sincere desire and prayers, he was enabled to leave his family. He adopted the name Gour Gopal and began to travel like a *sannyāsī*, although officially he was not initiated into the renounced order. He traveled as a mendicant *sādhu* and at the same time was looking for a spiritual master who could properly enlighten him and engage him in devotional service. Eventually, in September of 1974, he decided to go to Vṛndāvana, and ultimately he came to the ISKCON property there. He wanted to meet Śrīla Prabhupāda, that great person who had spread Kṛṣṇa consciousness all over the world and converted persons from outside India into pure Vaiṣṇavas. He did meet His Divine Grace, and at their first meeting Śrīla Prabhupāda offered to give him *sannyāsa*. At that moment Gour Gopal realized that Śrīla Prabhupāda was his spiritual master, that Prabhupāda knew his heart and could help him to realize his spiritual aspirations. As he commented later, "I could then understand, 'He is a genuine *guru*, because he knows my heart. He is *caitya-guru*.' I was in search of such a person under whom I could find shelter. I took shelter of him. My heart was naturally attracted toward him. I had full faith in Kṛṣṇa and Caitanya Mahāprabhu, and They helped me."

Thus he accepted Śrīla Prabhupāda as his spiritual master, and soon thereafter Śrīla Prabhupāda initiated him. Śrīla Prabhupāda gave him first and second initiation at one time, and then, at the grand opening of the Kṛṣṇa-Balarāma temple, on Śrī Rāma-navamī, April 20, 1975, he gave him *sannyāsa*. Because Gour Govinda Mahārāja was educated, Śrīla Prabhupāda asked him to translate his books into Hindi, and later into Oriyā. Gour Govinda Mahārāja took that service very seriously. He was translating regularly, but for Śrīla Prabhupāda's Centennial in 1996 he took a vow not to eat until he had translated his quota for the day—a certain number of verses, which would take at least an hour. And he was so strict that even when he couldn't translate because of circumstances—he would sometimes travel on long flights overseas—he would still fast until he had done his quota, even if it was late at night. He took that order to translate very seriously. On one occasion, in Gita Nagari, his servant locked up his books in his suitcase and lost the key. They left Gita Nagari that day, flew to Delhi on an overnight flight, and then flew from Delhi to Bhubaneswar. Mahārāja refused to take *prasāda* during this whole time, until they managed to open his bags and he was able to get to his books and meet his quota of translating.

Śrīla Prabhupāda also asked Gour Govinda Mahārāja to establish a temple in Bhubaneswar. A donor had given ISKCON some land that at the time was outside the city, in the wilderness. The place then was nothing more than a jungle full of snakes, scorpions, mosquitoes, and other creatures. (To this day there are still wild elephants living in a reserve only a twenty-minute walk from the temple.) Gour Govinda Mahārāja took up the challenge, the order, the service, and lived in extremely austere conditions.

He decided to start staying at the property even before there were any buildings on it. The only shelter he was able to manage at first was to stay with some of the road workers (who were working on National Highway Number 5) in a tent. Road workers in India are not exactly *sāttvika*, and they probably were smoking, chewing pan, and using foul language. A student who sometimes came and assisted Mahārāja was shocked when he saw where he was living. "Mahārāja, how can you stay in such a nasty place?" he asked. "No," Mahārāja replied. "This is a very nice place. This is what my *guru mahārāja*, Śrīla Prabhupāda, has given to me."

Śrīla Prabhupāda predicted that one day that area would become the center of the city. When the temple started, there were no buildings as far as the eye could see. Today the area is densely populated and is the fastest growing in Bhubaneswar. A major highway runs right past our property, and shops and offices and residences have developed on all sides. It is a major location.

In 1977, after the Mahā-kumbha-melā in Allahabad, Śrīla Prabhupāda himself went to Bhubaneswar. Gour Govinda Mahārāja, Pradyumna Prabhu, and Hari-śauri Prabhu stayed together in the mud-and-thatch hut where Gour Govinda Mahārāja had been doing his *bhajana* and translation work. And for seventeen days Śrīla Prabhupāda stayed in an attached hut. When Śrīla Prabhupāda was translating, they could hear him through the connecting wall, dictating the purports. Gour Govinda Mahārāja continued to live there after Śrīla Prabhupāda left, and after Gour Govinda Mahārāja's departure from this world his body was placed there in *samādhi*.

On the auspicious occasion of Śrī Nityānanda-trayodaśī in 1977, Śrīla Prabhupāda laid the cornerstone for the Kṛṣṇa-Balarāma temple to be developed there. He also completed an important phase of his own writing, the Ninth Canto of *Śrīmad-Bhāgavatam*, and began working on the Tenth Canto. In time, Gour Govinda Swami Mahārāja raised the funds and built a beautiful temple on the land.

After Śrīla Prabhupāda left this world, Gour Govinda Mahārāja was ready to execute another important instruction that Śrīla Prabhupāda had given him, that he should travel and help Prabhupāda's devotees. So he began to travel overseas and preach. Seeing the needs of the society and the devotees, he evolved his mission, in pursuance of Śrīla Prabhupāda's instructions to him, which was, by his own account:

1. to show that everything is in Śrīla Prabhupāda's books,
2. to show that you can get everything within ISKCON and need not go outside, and
3. to "preach to the preachers"—to maintain and encourage the devotees so that they don't fall down or go away.

As for the books, Gour Govinda Mahārāja said that Śrīla Prabhupāda's books are like an ocean filled with gems and that in order to gather those gems one must dive very deep. Gour Govinda Mahārāja's own books—compiled from his talks by his disciples, especially Mādhavānanda dāsa—are mainly classes based on Śrīla Prabhupāda's books. And in them he reveals just what gems there are in Śrīla Prabhupāda's books and how one can get from the books the highest realizations of Kṛṣṇa consciousness—*sambandha*, *abhidheya*, and *prayojana*: what our relationship with Kṛṣṇa is, how to act in that relationship, and how to actually realize the ultimate goal of life, pure love for Kṛṣṇa, *kṛṣṇa-prema*.

He also showed that you can get everything within ISKCON. He himself gave much to the society of devotees in ISKCON, mainly through his *kṛṣṇa-kathā*, which was filled with his realization of Kṛṣṇa consciousness. He was an example of a pure devotee who had ecstatic love for Kṛṣṇa and direct perception of Kṛṣṇa. From his liberated platform of pure devotional service he could guide and encourage and enlighten devotees, and give them hope that if they followed the same process—as followers of Śrīla Prabhupāda—they could also attain the same result.

I have heard advanced Gauḍīya Vaiṣṇavas outside of ISKCON speak about Kṛṣṇa (*kṛṣṇa-kathā*), and I can honestly say that the *kṛṣṇa-kathā* spoken by Gour Govinda Swami Mahārāja appeals to me as much as any of theirs. But hearing from Gour Govinda Mahārāja is different because he is a disciple of Śrīla Prabhupāda and a member of ISKCON. So we are getting it in our line, in the line of Śrīla Bhaktisiddhānta Sarasvatī Ṭhākura and Śrīla Prabhupāda. So it is more congenial for advancement in Kṛṣṇa consciousness in ISKCON. Hearing from Gour Govinda Swami Mahārāja or reading his books, one can get everything that one could ever want, right within ISKCON. And by his association, through his talks or books or even followers, one can feel very enlivened in Kṛṣṇa consciousness; one can be greatly nourished and make tangible progress—what to speak of not falling down or going away. One can get a glimpse of the perfection of Kṛṣṇa consciousness and have hope that we can actually reach the ultimate goal in this lifetime by following the same process of *bhakti-yoga* as given to us in our line, from Śrīla Bhaktisiddhānta Sarasvatī Ṭhākura to Śrīla Prabhupāda and then to his followers.

So Śrīla Gour Govinda Mahārāja has significance not only for those who knew him personally or served him in Orissa, where he had his base, given to him by Śrīla Prabhupāda as his *prabhu-datta deśa*, but also for all of us—for everyone associated with ISKCON. His instructions and mercy are available to all of us, even now.

His strong faith in and intense dedication to *guru* are expressed in a talk on *Śrīmad-Bhāgavatam* 8.14.6, which he gave in Bhubaneswar on April 7, 1992:

"The teachings coming from Mahāprabhu through our *paramparā* are true. They are our *sadācāra*, our regulative principles. They are laws for all humanity, coming through *paramparā*. If we disrespect them, not executing them in our lives, if we impose any deliberation on them or twist them, we become offenders. We commit *nāmāparādha* by not obeying the orders of *guru*. Then we are far away from his lotus feet.

"To become a true follower of *guru* one should never hesitate to carry out his orders. If to obey the order of *guru* it is necessary to become very proud, I should never hesitate to become so. If it means becoming an animal, I should never hesitate to become one. Even if it is necessary to go to hell for *guru*, I should never hesitate. I should never hear from anyone but my *guru*. We should never listen to those who say something different from the teachings of Mahāprabhu coming through bona fide *paramparā*. If somebody says something different, then like Bhīmasena I will crush it with my fist. I will destroy it. I will defeat it. I am that proud.

"With just one speck of dust from the lotus feet of my *guru*, crores and crores of people can be delivered. There is no such a scholar as my *guru*. I will never accept anyone else as a scholar.

There are no teachings like those that my *guru* has imparted to be found in any human being or demigod. No one else can give such teachings. Nothing in this world is as heavy as a tiny speck of dust from his lotus feet. This is the mood of the follower of true *paramparā*. I am proud to be associated with such a *paramparā*."

Now we come to his disappearance pastime. It was on Śrīla Bhaktisiddhānta Sarasvatī Ṭhākura's appearance day in Māyāpur, on February 9, 1996. I was obliged to leave Māyāpur early that day to fly to America for some urgent business. Still, in the morning I met him (he had arrived in Māyāpur only the night before) and was fortunate to be able to offer my obeisances to him. I placed my head on his feet, and out of his mercy and kindness he affectionately rubbed my head and back. And that was the last time I saw him. After offering my obeisances and packing and getting ready to leave, I went to the temple hall for the *puṣpāñjali* and *guru-pūjā* for Śrīla Bhaktisiddhānta Sarasvatī Ṭhākura's Vyāsa-pūjā, took *darśana* of the Deities, blessings from the Deities, and intended to depart immediately. But some devotees prevailed on me to first honor the feast offered to Śrīla Bhaktisiddhānta Sarasvatī Ṭhākura, which I did with the other devotees, and I still reached the Calcutta airport with time to spare. But it wasn't until much later—because where I was in America I had no opportunity to get news about ISKCON and I was just starting to use a computer, but not regularly—when I met His Holiness Radhanath Swami in Chicago, that I received the news that Śrīla Gour Govinda Swami Mahārāja had left this world.

It so happened that in the afternoon of Śrīla Bhaktisiddhānta Sarasvatī Ṭhākura's appearance day, two senior devotees came to meet Gour Govinda Mahārāja in his room, and they enquired of him about Kṛṣṇa—why Lord Caitanya made His base in Purī, what was the relationship between Lord Jagannātha and Vṛndāvana. Mahārāja began to narrate the pastimes of Kṛṣṇa and how Kṛṣṇa, having been in separation from Rādhārāṇī, assumed the form of Jagannātha. It was a very ecstatic description. Because of Gour Govinda Swami's advanced stage of Kṛṣṇa consciousness, he felt transcendental ecstasy remembering the pastimes of Kṛṣṇa. And in this case, he became overwhelmed; he excused himself, saying he was unable to speak more. He lay back on his bed and, gazing at a picture of his worshipable Deity Gopal Jiu, while devotees chanted the holy names, in a very deep state of Kṛṣṇa consciousness, he left this world.

His disciples of course were greatly aggrieved, feeling intense separation from him. They decided to bring his body to Bhubaneswar to place him in *samādhi* at the site of his *bhajana-kuṭīra*, near the Rādhā-Gopīnātha temple that he had established on the ISKCON land in Bhubaneswar.

So, the disappearance day of an *ācārya* is a sad occasion because we think of him and his wonderful association and we miss him. But from another point of view, it is not only a glorious occasion but also a jubilant one, because the pure soul has been reunited with the Supreme Soul as His eternal servant, has returned to his eternal service to Kṛṣṇa. Certainly, it is an occasion of great jubilation in the spiritual world. On the absolute platform, as Śrīla Prabhupāda explained, there is no difference between meeting and separation—both are occasions of ecstasy. Once, on his *guru mahārāja* Śrīla Bhaktisiddhānta's disappearance day in Surat, Śrīla Prabhupāda said that on the absolute platform the spiritual master's appearance and disappearance are the same—both are beautiful. Just like the sunrise and the sunset—both are beautiful.

Now, there is a very specific connection in service between Śrīla Gour Govinda Swami Mahārāja and Śrīla Bhaktisiddhānta Sarasvatī Ṭhākura. Of course, there is a connection in terms of the general mission, which is to distribute books, establish temples, and make devotees. Śrīla Bhaktisiddhānta Sarasvatī

Ṭhākura did all three, and Śrīla Prabhupāda also did all three, and he wanted ISKCON to do all three. In his "Concluding Words" to *Śrī Caitanya-caritāmṛta* he wrote, "Our society, the International Society for Krishna Consciousness, has been formed to execute the order of Śrī Caitanya Mahāprabhu and His Divine Grace Śrīla Bhaktisiddhānta Sarasvatī Ṭhākura." So all followers of Śrīla Prabhupāda within ISKCON, whatever their particular service may be, are furthering that mission, which ultimately results in the publication and distribution of books, the establishing and maintaining of temples, and the making and maintaining of devotees. But Śrīla Gour Govinda Mahārāja served Śrīla Bhaktisiddhānta Sarasvatī Ṭhākura in a very special way as well. And that relates to the Deity and temple of Ālālanātha, or Alarnath, in Brahmagiri, outside Jagannātha Purī.

When Śrī Caitanya Mahāprabhu was residing in Purī during the last eighteen years of His manifest pastimes, He would daily go to the temple of Lord Jagannātha for *darśana.* He would see Jagannātha not as we may see Him but as Kṛṣṇa Himself, Śyāmasundara, in His beautiful threefold-bending form (*śyāmaṁ tri-bhaṅga-lalitaṁ*). But every year, fifteen days before the Ratha-yātrā festival, Lord Jagannātha is bathed in the *snāna-yātrā* ceremony and thereafter taken into seclusion for two weeks, for repairs, or to recover from having caught a cold. During that period, called *anavasara*, Śrī Caitanya Mahāprabhu and all the other devotees would not be able to see Lord Jagannātha. So, feeling separation from Jagannātha, Śrī Caitanya Mahāprabhu would walk fourteen miles to the temple of Alarnath. The deity of Alarnath is a four-handed Viṣṇu form, installed by Lord Brahmā many millennia ago, on the top of a hill—Brahmagiri. So, Śrī Caitanya Mahāprabhu would pass the *anavasara* period with Lord Alarnath.

In the course of time, the Alarnath temple became dilapidated. And when Śrīla Bhaktisiddhānta Sarasvatī Ṭhākura visited in 1929 and saw the poor conditions, he undertook to build a boundary wall and repair the main temple. He was so keen on finishing the project expeditiously that he personally rolled *bīḍīs* (cigarettes) for the workers so that they wouldn't stop their work. That is how sincere and intent he was in his purpose. During some excavation work in the temple compound, one of the priests discovered an ancient *utsava* deity, which looked exactly like the large deity of Alarnath in the temple. All major temples with large deities also have small *utsava* deities that are used for festivals. The large deities are never moved, but the *utsava* deities can be moved, conveniently brought forward for *abhiṣekas*, taken on processions, placed on swings and in boats, and served in ways that cannot be done with the large deities. So, the *pūjārī* put the *utsava* deity on the altar, but one night the Deity came to him in a dream and told him, "I want to be worshiped by My dear devotee Bhaktisiddhānta Sarasvatī."

The next morning the *pūjārī*, in obedience to the order of the Deity in his dream, searched for the saintly person named Bhaktisiddhānta Sarasvatī, and when he found him, he presented him the small deity of Alarnath. And Śrīla Bhaktisiddhānta installed the deity in the Brahmā Gauḍīya Maṭha established by him near the original Alarnath temple.

For Śrīla Prabhupāda's Centennial, Śrīla Gour Govinda Swami Mahārāja also took up service for Lord Alarnath at Brahmagiri. He began renovations on the ancient temple, including the construction of a new deity kitchen, a hall for *kīrtana* and *prasāda*, and a small temple for Lord Śiva, the protector of the *dhāma*, within the temple compound. And on January 1, 1996, just weeks before he left this world in Māyāpur, Mahārāja inaugurated the project. Thus, Śrīla Gour Govinda Swami Mahārāja continued the line of service to Lord Alarnath begun by Śrīla Bhaktisiddhānta Sarasvatī Ṭhākura.

Another service that His Holiness Gour Govinda Swami Mahārāja took up was to develop a plantation of *phasi* trees to be used to build Lord Jagannātha's Ratha-yātrā chariots. Lord Jagannātha's chariots are huge, and their construction requires a huge amount of wood—more than six hundred trees per year. According to *śāstra* and tradition, the wood must come from only certain species of trees. Those trees grow slowly, and as Kali-yuga has progressed, the natural forests of those trees, which belong to Lord Jagannātha, have been encroached upon, and the supply of *phasi* wood has been depleted to such an extent that it appeared that in a few years there wouldn't be enough to build Lord Jagannātha's chariots. So His Holiness Gour Govinda Swami Mahārāja took up the cause. In December of 1995, the Government of Orissa allocated 150 acres of Lord Jagannātha's traditional jungle for this project. And now, with the help of Gour Govinda Mahārāja's followers and supporters, 70,000 young *phasi* trees are growing in the Orissan jungle, under the supervision of Lord Jagannātha's devotees. This is the Śrī Jagannātha Forest Project.

Śrīla Gour Govinda Swami Mahārāja is a great personality, a munificent personality. He did great service not only for Śrīla Prabhupāda and ISKCON and its devotees in a limited sense, but also for the entire *sampradāya* and for the larger cause of Kṛṣṇa consciousness—devotional service to Lord Kṛṣṇa, to Lord Jagannātha. Through his talks and writings he explained the esoteric significance of Jagannātha Purī, of Alarnath, of Lord Jagannātha—that Jagannātha Purī is a place of separation. Lord Jagannātha feels separation from Śrīmatī Rādhārāṇī and His other friends in Vṛndāvana, and Śrī Caitanya Mahāprabhu, in the mood of Rādhārāṇī after Kṛṣṇa left Vṛndāvana for Mathurā and Dvārakā, also feels separation. Jagannātha is feeling separation from Śrīmatī Rādhārāṇī, and Śrī Caitanya Mahāprabhu, in the mood of Rādhārāṇī, is feeling separation from Kṛṣṇa, Lord Jagannātha. So Jagannātha Purī is *vipralambha-kṣetra*, a sacred land where ecstatic separation is relished. As Śrīla Prabhupāda taught us and as Śrīla Gour Govinda Swami Mahārāja has explained, service in separation is the highest ecstasy of love of God. Once, Mahārāja said of his work in Orissa, "We are opening a school for crying."

Now we too are feeling separation, from Śrīla Gour Govinda Swami Mahārāja. We miss him—his personal *darśana*, his merciful glance, his affectionate touch. We miss sitting at his lotus feet and hearing *kṛṣṇa-kathā* from his lotus mouth. At the same time, we know that he is present; we know that he is pleased when we diligently chant the holy name, earnestly discuss *kṛṣṇa-kathā*, and enthusiastically serve Śrīla Prabhupāda and ISKCON and endeavor to spread Kṛṣṇa consciousness, following in the footsteps of our *guru-paramparā*, Śrīla Bhaktisiddhānta Sarasvatī Ṭhākura, Śrīla Prabhupāda, and Śrīla Prabhupāda's exalted followers. So on this auspicious occasion we pray to Śrīla Bhaktisiddhānta Sarasvatī Ṭhākura and Śrīla Gour Govinda Swami Mahārāja that we may serve them eternally, as they desire. This is *paramparā*—serving Śrīla Prabhupāda and his predecessors and followers. We pray for their mercy that we may relish the internal moods of Kṛṣṇa consciousness and at the same time fulfill their compassionate desire to bring others to Kṛṣṇa consciousness—by their divine grace.

Tamal Krishna
Goswami

Appreciating Tamal Krishna Goswami—in Service and Separation

A talk given two days after Goswami Mahārāja's departure, on March 16, 2002, in Dallas.

Śrīla Prabhupāda said that when a Vaiṣṇava departs we feel simultaneously happy and sad. We feel happy because we know the Vaiṣṇava has gone to Kṛṣṇa, but we feel sad because we will miss the Vaiṣṇava's association. I have no doubt that Śrīla Tamal Krishna Goswami Mahārāja has gone both to the lotus feet of Śrīla Prabhupāda and to the lotus feet of Śrī Śrī Rādhā-Kālachandjī. By such service as he offered to Śrīla Prabhupāda for so many years, one is naturally promoted to Their service.

The last time I spoke here, Goswami Mahārāja was in his quarters, and as I recall, he sort of tricked me into giving the class. I think he said he had to do some service in his quarters, so I gave the class. And remembering that incident, it is easy for me now to imagine that I am giving class and he is in his quarters and that we are all together. Before that class I'd had a very significant talk with Goswami Mahārāja in which he gave me some important instructions.

The discussion had actually begun the night before, when I'd first arrived. We were both sitting on the floor, and he was saying how people thought that he was such a senior devotee, that he had been practicing Kṛṣṇa consciousness for so many years, that he was a direct disciple of Śrīla Prabhupāda, and that he'd had so much of Śrīla Prabhupāda's association. But, he said, in spite of his *hari-nāma*, Gāyatrī, and *sannyāsa* initiations from Śrīla Prabhupāda and all his association with Śrīla

Prabhupāda and his practice of Kṛṣṇa consciousness, he still felt he needed guidance from other devotees. He said that he took their guidance and that he considered some of these guides to be *śikṣā-gurus*. And then he listed the names of godbrothers whom he considered to be his *śikṣā-gurus*.

At the time, I was being refused a visa to enter India, where I had served for many years—the first few with Goswami Mahārāja. Being unable to return to India, I based myself first in Mauritius and then gradually divided most of my time between Mauritius and South Africa. So I was pretty isolated from my godbrothers. And historically at that time in the movement some of the biggest leaders had fallen down, and I was in such a state of shock that I had resolved within my heart that I would never take shelter of anyone else again—except Śrīla Prabhupāda. So when Goswami Mahārāja spoke to me as he did, I had to consider what he said. I always took what he said seriously, but at the same time I had vowed never again to place my faith in anyone except Śrīla Prabhupāda.

The next morning while we were chanting our rounds in the temple, somehow the feeling, or realization, came in my heart that actually what Goswami Mahārāja had said was true: we do need guidance; we do need a *śikṣā-guru* or *śikṣā-gurus*. And it became equally clear that the person who was meant to be my *śikṣā-guru* was Goswami Mahārāja himself. So when I had such a clear realization, such a strong realization, I became very excited and approached him. In general I wouldn't have wanted to disturb him while he was chanting his rounds, but I couldn't help myself. I told him that I had just had the realization that what he had said was true: despite all our association with Śrīla Prabhupāda, we still need the guidance of other devotees. He nodded his head knowingly, in agreement and approval. Finally I had realized what he already knew.

Then I said, "And I have also been inspired with the

conclusion that you should be my *śikṣā-guru*." I don't remember if physically I actually did it, but my mood was to throw myself at his lotus feet and beg him to be my *śikṣā-guru*. And I don't remember exactly what he said, but in effect he agreed. So I was very happy.

Some years earlier, when I had been feeling especially wretched and miserable, Śrīla Prabhupāda had discussed one verse on a morning walk on Juhu Beach. It comes originally from *Stotra-ratna* by Śrī Yāmunācārya, but Śrīla Rūpa Gosvāmī and Śrīla Sanātana Gosvāmī addressed it to Lord Caitanya when they met Him for the first time:

bhavantam evānucaran nirantaraḥ
praśānta-niḥśeṣa-manorathāntaraḥ
kadāham aikāntika-nitya-kiṅkaraḥ
praharṣayiṣyāmi sanātha-jīvitam

"By serving You constantly, one is freed from all material desires and is completely pacified. When shall I engage as Your permanent eternal servant and always feel joyful to have such a perfect master?"

Śrīla Prabhupāda had elaborated especially on the word *sa-nātha*. *Nātha* means "master," and *sa* means "with." He said that the goal of life is to become *sa-nātha*, "with master," not *a-nātha*, "without master," or "orphan." Then he pointed to the dogs on Juhu Beach. The dogs with masters—he pointed to one who was really stout and strong, just like its master—were as confident as their masters. "I have my master," Śrīla Prabhupāda said they felt. "I have a home, a place to go at night. I will have food. If there is any difficulty, my master will protect me and take care of me."

And then he pointed to some stray dogs. They were skinny and scraggly, and he said that without masters they were *anātha*; other dogs would bark at them and children would throw stones at them. They didn't know where they would sleep or how they would get food. They were always in anxiety.

So our goal of life is to become *sanātha*, with master, protected. And the supreme master is Kṛṣṇa, the Supreme Personality of Godhead. Here Rūpa Gosvāmī and Sanātana Gosvāmī were appealing to Lord Caitanya to become their master and allow them to become His servants.

Sometimes, even having been initiated by Śrīla Prabhupāda and having had so much association with him, I still felt like an *anātha*, an orphan, especially after some of the leaders whom I had respected so much left. And then I made my resolution. But after I approached Goswami Mahārāja and he accepted me, I felt I was again *sanātha*: I had a master. Not that he took the place of Śrīla Prabhupāda, but he helped me in my relationship with Śrīla Prabhupāda, in my service to Śrīla Prabhupāda. He helped me to approach Śrīla Prabhupāda.

As the years passed, I saw Goswami Mahārāja in different situations. There was a time when he was staying in an apartment in the lower part of New York, writing one of his dramas, either *Jagannātha-priya Nāṭakam* or *Prabhupāda Antya-līlā*. He had entered a new field of service. He was studying Sanskrit drama and writing plays. At the same time he had even been reading some Western dramas, and he wasn't sure if what he was doing was correct, so he wanted to consult his godbrothers.

After that, I saw that whenever he had to make an important decision, he would always consult his godbrothers. He had special friends whom he consulted on specific points, but when he had to make a major decision, or a difficult decision, he would consult many godbrothers. He might consult them individually, but when he had the chance he would have them all come together, and he would present his thoughts and doubts to them, the different points in favor of and the different points against the idea, and basically he would accept their decision.

Śrīla Prabhupāda also said that when the Vaiṣṇavas—the right devotees in the right atmosphere—consider and all agree, we should take their conclusion as Kṛṣṇa's conclusion.

In any case, Goswami Mahārāja always consulted his godbrothers. He had faith in their association, and he loved their association. And for important decisions, he had faith in the conclusions that would arise from their association. He was a very honest person. He spoke according to his realization, and he acted as he spoke.

Now coming to the reality of the present situation, Goswami Mahārāja himself was an extraordinary person. His insight, his intelligence, and his association with Śrīla Prabhupāda made him uniquely qualified to answer questions and give guidance. It is extremely rare to find someone who is so spiritually attuned and at the same time so astute in worldly matters, so conscious of an individual's mentality and psychology and mood and sincerity.

In the last few days we have received so many phone calls. Many have come from Goswami Mahārāja's godbrothers. One, Bharadvāja Prabhu, who lives in Los Angeles now, told me how much Goswami Mahārāja had helped him over the years. Bharadvāja Prabhu is an artist, and Śrīla Prabhupāda had engaged him in artwork, first in painting for his books and then in learning the art of doll making in Bengal. Later, Bharadvāja Prabhu came to lead the FATE project, the museum in Los Angeles. He told me of an incident when he was very sick in a Calcutta hospital. He was so sick and the situation seemed so hopeless that he had almost given up the will to live. Then Tamal Krishna Goswami came to visit him, and he spent two hours with him in the hospital. Bharadvāja Prabhu's real desire was to preach in Russia. At the time, no one had gone to Russia, and Bharadvāja Prabhu was born in part of the USSR. Goswami Mahārāja understood what was in his heart and encouraged him to go to

Russia to preach—how important it would be and how good it would be. And just by that talk with Goswami Mahārāja, Bharadvāja Prabhu developed the will to live again. He felt he had something to live for, and he got better.

Once, Goswami Mahārāja himself needed an operation in Bombay. He had gone to Jaslok Hospital, the best in Bombay at the time. But when Śrīla Prabhupāda heard about it, he wanted to stop the operation. So he got into our jeep, the only vehicle we owned, and rode all the way to central Bombay, to the hospital. But when he got there it was too late. Goswami Mahārāja had just come out of the operation theater, and when he opened his eyes and saw Śrīla Prabhupāda, he told him that he had just had a dream: Śrīla Prabhupāda had been giving a report to the previous *ācāryas* about his work on the planet earth, and Śrīla Prabhupāda had said that people basically had no spiritual assets—no knowledge, no austerity, practically no good qualities at all. But in the dream Śrīla Prabhupāda had said that they did have one qualification: "Their one qualification is that they have faith in me, and they do whatever I say." Then Goswami Mahārāja looked up at Śrīla Prabhupāda to see his response. And Śrīla Prabhupāda agreed, "Yes, it is true."

Actually, we have no qualification except our faith in Śrīla Prabhupāda as spiritual master. And Goswami Mahārāja was the epitome of such faithful and devoted service. In fact, he acted like an extension of Śrīla Prabhupāda. The way he took care of Śrīla Prabhupāda at the end, the way he rendered such intimate service to him—sometimes it seemed like he could read Śrīla Prabhupāda's mind, which was a great asset for a personal servant. (Of course, Goswami Mahārāja was so perceptive he could practically read anyone's mind.)

After Śrīla Prabhupāda left, Goswami Mahārāja took complete charge of the ceremonies. He made the arrangements for Śrīla Prabhupāda to visit the deities of Vṛndāvana, the arrangements for Śrīla Prabhupāda to be placed in *samādhi*, the arrangements for the festival, and the invitations to the Vaiṣṇavas of Vṛndāvana—the senior Vaiṣṇavas associated with the different temples and *maṭhas*. Another thing that impressed me was how Goswami Mahārāja took possession of some of Śrīla Prabhupāda's personal effects and then gave them to individual devotees as *mahā-prasāda*, as remnants of Śrīla Prabhupāda's to keep Śrīla Prabhupāda near to them, as a remembrance to sustain them in separation. He was so perceptive that he seemed empowered to give just the right item to the specific individual.

Recently, I was recalling the history of ISKCON, looking at pictures of the history of ISKCON, and there was Goswami Mahārāja—everywhere. It is inconceivable how one person could have done so much to spread Kṛṣṇa consciousness, to serve Lord Caitanya and Śrīla Prabhupāda. Anyway, I could go on, but maybe . . .

DEVOTEES: Please do!

GIRIRAJ SWAMI: But where would I stop? There would be no end.

DEVOTEES: Don't stop.

GIRIRAJ SWAMI [laughing]: All right, I'll continue. I'll talk about the academy.

At the end of November 2000, Goswami Mahārāja came to visit me in Carpinteria, California, near Santa Barbara. He had been presenting papers at the AAR, the American Academy of Religion. There he had noticed a lady professor, Barbara Holdrege; he had been struck by her and impressed by her, and had developed the desire to meet her. At the same time, she had been observing him and hearing him deliver papers, and she had also been impressed and had developed the desire to meet him. So on the last day of the AAR meeting, they had been introduced to each other. He had told her that he was going to be visiting Santa Barbara, where she is a scholar and Professor of Religious Studies at the University of California, and she had said, "All right, when you come to Santa Barbara, please phone me and we'll get together."

So he phoned her and arranged for her to come to my place for lunch. Goswami Mahārāja and I actually walked down the driveway—a long driveway—to wait for her. She was late to arrive, but Goswami Mahārāja saw the positive opportunity and said, "Well, we can walk up and down the driveway and get in a little walk." So we walked up and down the driveway, and eventually she came.

He had meticulously planned the whole meeting. He met with her first without me, and then he brought her to the temple room, where I was waiting and chanting. She sat down right in front of our Deities Śrī Śrī Gāndharvikā-Giridhārī. And we discussed Gauḍīya Vaiṣṇava *siddhānta*.

Then we all had lunch together, and I thought, "Wow! When I was at college we never had professors like her!" And I started to see that there was a whole new field in academia. Until then, I had not had any idea of what the field was like. My knowledge of the academy was from back in 1969, when I had graduated from Brandeis and joined Śrīla Prabhupāda. But Goswami Mahārāja had told me that many people of our generation who were spiritually inclined either joined religious movements—like we did—or went into Religious Studies.

Anyway, Professor Holdrege was extraordinary, and of course Goswami Mahārāja was extraordinary, and the discussion between them was wonderful. It really gave me a glimpse into the field. I had heard a lot from Goswami Mahārāja, but until I met her I really didn't have a sense of what the field was actually like. In the end she stayed for seven hours. By the time she phoned her husband she was well overdue, but it was okay. And afterwards I was completely enlivened.

The temple room was on the way to the guestroom where

Goswami Mahārāja stayed, so we stopped there on the way back after she left, at around ten o'clock at night. Suddenly, I remembered a letter that Śrīla Prabhupāda had written to me when I first joined in 1969. Śrīla Prabhupāda's letter revealed that my father had written to him, and so Śrīla Prabhupāda wrote: "I have received one letter from your father. It appears that you are a good scholar and have a taste for psychology and divinity studies. Of course, Kṛṣṇa consciousness is on the line of divinity. If you make a thorough study of all theological schools and explain Kṛṣṇa consciousness as the post-graduate presentation of all theological theses, it will be a great accomplishment."

As I was reading the letter with Goswami Mahārāja, I was thinking of Professor Holdrege. She had studied all religions. She had gone most deeply into Judaism and Hinduism, and her great work was called *Veda and Torah*. She said that after going through all the different literatures and all the different traditions, she had become particularly interested in Gauḍīya Vaiṣṇavism and planned to make Gauḍīya traditions a focus of her research.

Now it has been a year and a half since Goswami Mahārāja introduced me to her, and she has been working on a research project on holy places in India that features a section on Vraja. Last January, she and Tripurāri dāsa came for dinner, and we discussed the project. All that time, she had kept in communication with Goswami Mahārāja. One of the last times I spoke to him by phone we spoke of her.

I mention her—she is like a grain from the pot—because the combination of meeting her, and seeing how Goswami Mahārāja dealt with her, and rereading the letter from Śrīla Prabhupāda all convinced me of the importance of the work in the academic field. And Goswami Mahārāja definitely emerged as the leader in the field. He showed that one could be a devotee and at the same time an excellent scholar and writer. And he has already published so many articles and collections and established so many deep relationships with people in the academy.

On Thursday, when we received the news about Goswami Mahārāja, Professor Holdrege also heard and phoned me at ten o'clock at night. She didn't have much personal association with Goswami Mahārāja—the main times they were together were at my place for lunch and then again at the last AAR conference—but she was deeply moved when she heard what had happened. But she was also very concerned about the project she was working on, and although she intimated that she wanted to discuss it with me, she felt reluctant because of my own state after hearing the news. Somehow, I got the idea that Goswami Mahārāja would want me to discuss it with her, and knowing that I would be leaving for Dallas, I said, "No, it's all right. We can discuss." And when we began, I felt that Goswami Mahārāja was pleased; I felt some presence in the room, a brightness, and actually a blissfulness, as we were talking.

After the conversation, around eleven at night, I went out of my room into the temple room, and I really felt Goswami Mahārāja's presence, just as if he were with me. Not only was he with me, but I felt he was—I guess among family we can speak openly—I felt he was indicating that not only was he with me then but that now he could be with me always, and intimately, without being hampered by the trappings of having a body in the world and a role in society. And that was very encouraging. So I felt very bright and blissful and wonderful, although since then I have felt much separation.

Here I may also mention one other phone call, from one of Goswami Mahārāja's disciples in Los Angeles named Balarāma Prabhu, from the Philippines. Balarāma phoned and began asking about what had happened, and he was very controlled. Most of the people who phoned began very controlled, and then, somewhere between three seconds and three minutes later, they would break down and start to cry. Anyway, Balarāma went on for one or two minutes and then said, "I have to tell you about a dream I had the night before Śrīla Gurudeva left." And he began to sob uncontrollably. He wanted to tell me, but it was almost impossible for him to get it out because he was crying so much.

He said that Śrīla Gurudeva had come to him the night before, flanked by two devotees in saffron, and said, "I have to leave now." In the dream Balarāma became a little angry and asked, "Why? Why do you have to leave?" Śrīla Gurudeva replied, "I just have to leave now." Then Balarāma said that Śrīla Gurudeva told him, "I will always be with you . . ." And then Balarāma managed to get out the next few words: "with my godbrothers." So I thought he meant that Śrīla Gurudeva would always be with him and always be with his godbrothers too. Then Balarāma indicated that Gurudeva meant that he would always be with Balarāma when Balarāma was with Gurudeva's godbrothers, because Gurudeva was always with his godbrothers. So Balarāma said he wanted to come and spend some time with me because I was "the closest," and of course he also mentioned Giridhari Swami. I said, "Well, I am leaving for Dallas, but when I come back you can come and we can meet."

When I heard Balarāma's dream, I thought there was definitely some plan. Then Professor Holdrege phoned the next morning and said that she hadn't been able to sleep the previous night, because she had been thinking of Tamal Krishna Goswami and felt enlivened by his presence. So we can imagine how much effect Goswami Mahārāja has had on people, both in his manifest presence and now.

When I speak of "Śrīla Gurudeva," I really feel that Goswami Mahārāja is an expansion of *guru-tattva*. Devotees may not be able to articulate the feeling in the same terms, but whether one is a disciple, a godbrother, a spiritual niece or nephew, or a university professor who may have only had a few encounters with Goswami Mahārāja, anyone can experience Śrīla Gurudeva's presence. Feeling Śrīla Gurudeva's presence may take some time, depending on the individual, but all categories have certainly been deeply influenced by Śrīla Gurudeva.

So this is *guru-tattva*. Therefore, whatever our external relationship might have been, the scriptures' teachings about the relationship with the spiritual master still hold: "He lives forever by his divine instructions, and the follower lives with him." Thus, whatever the official relationship may be, the follower of Śrīla Gurudeva's instructions will live with him. Or, Śrīla Gurudeva will live with the follower.

Of course, the challenge now is to keep that memory alive, to keep that relationship alive. And the community here will be a great support. I have seen many disciples, even of Śrīla Prabhupāda, fall away from the strict practices of devotional service as time has passed. Of course, many of them had bad experiences in the movement and became discouraged. But if the community remains united and the devotees remain strong in their spiritual practices and association, and keep Śrīla Gurudeva's memory alive, not in a sentimental way but in a real way—that "I had a real, tangible relationship with him; he gave me so many instructions, which I must follow"—there is no doubt we will feel Śrīla Gurudeva's presence.

Still, we should not act as fanatics or sentimentalists. Even Śrīla Prabhupāda's disciples sometimes quote Śrīla Prabhupāda in a fanatical way and do things in his name that we know he would not condone. So we must always beware of *niyamāgraha*, following the rules and regulations fanatically without really understanding the purpose behind them, or disregarding the rules and regulations and acting independently or whimsically. But if we keep our association strong, if our community is strong and our practice is strong, then there is no doubt that we will feel Śrīla Prabhupāda's and Śrīla Gurudeva's living presence, even now.

Of course, I am saying, "even now." Twenty-four years have passed since Śrīla Prabhupāda left. It took me time. When Śrīla Prabhupāda left, I was just crying. It took me time before I could actually feel his presence. And even then it has been a gradual process, an incremental process of feeling Prabhupāda's presence. At the time, I was just crying, feeling separation. But, having gone through the experience with Śrīla Prabhupāda and having some experience of it even now with Śrīla Gurudeva, I know that it is possible to have that relationship even without the physical presence. And I also know the conditions that are conducive to maintaining the relationship and developing it further—we should associate with other devotees who have similar faith and whose association will be conducive to our faith, conducive to our practice, and conducive to our service. If we can keep such association we can blossom spiritually—individually and collectively.

Now we are thinking that Śrīla Gurudeva was so young, which is true. But when Prabhupāda left, we were thinking that we were so young. We were thinking, "How could Kṛṣṇa take Śrīla Prabhupāda when we're so young? How can we live without him?" And some of the devotees who were cast into the role of *gurus* then had been devotees for only seven years. Many of you have been devotees for fifteen, or even twenty, years. So I think your own spiritual maturity and the strength of the community will serve you well—along with Śrīla Gurudeva's example. After Prabhupāda left, Goswami Mahārāja commented that Śrīla Prabhupāda, as the *ācārya*, had shown us the example of how to do everything, except for one thing: how to relate to godbrothers. Prabhupāda didn't have any godbrothers who were ready to join with him. So we had no experience of godbrothers who had disciples—how they would relate to each other, how their disciples would relate to each other—because in ISKCON there was just Śrīla Prabhupāda. He was the *guru*, and we all were his disciples. Śrīla Prabhupāda invited his godbrothers to cooperate with him; it's not that he wanted to be the only disciple of Śrīla Bhaktisiddhānta Sarasvatī Ṭhākura who was preaching the message of Caitanya Mahāprabhu in the West. But no one came at the time. So that was the one example we didn't have from Śrīla Prabhupāda.

But we do have that example from Śrīla Gurudeva—how he associated with his godbrothers; how he consulted with his godbrothers; how he loved them; how he opened his heart to them; how they opened their hearts to him; and how they enjoyed *kīrtana* together, reading and discussing together, and serving Śrīla Prabhupāda together. And that example can be a real inspiration and guide us. So now everything is complete. We have the instructions, we have the examples, we have the community, we have the Deities—we have everything. And if we just stick to the principles and stay together, stay united, with Śrīla Prabhupāda and his beloved and trusted servant Śrīla Gurudeva in the center, we can continue, and continue to make progress.

When I think back on my last talk with Goswami Mahārāja before he went to India (and I feel glad in retrospect that we had the talk—it probably lasted an hour and a half or more), I see it came at a time when certain things in my own service to Śrīla Prabhupāda were becoming clarified and facilitated. So I went over my service with Goswami Mahārāja and he commented on it, and I feel that in relation to my service to Śrīla Prabhupāda, what he said then can serve to guide me for the rest of my life. I had hoped to discuss more of the details with him as the service evolved, but now I can't speak to him like I used to, by dialing his number on the telephone. Still, the basic plan is there, the basic instructions are there, the important confirmations are there, and I have faith that by the process of chanting and hearing and praying and consulting other devotees—mainly godbrothers, though there are also many other qualified devotees who are competent to respond wisely to questions and problems—we can get the answers we need in order to progress in our service.

I was thinking how in 1976, when Śrīla Prabhupāda was in New York, already ill and aged, he wanted the benediction to go on fighting for Kṛṣṇa. Thinking of the circumstances of Goswami Mahārāja's last manifest service, I was reminded of Śrīla Prabhupāda's statement. Tripurāri dāsa told me about Goswami Mahārāja's mood in Oxford before leaving for India. Tripurāri used to visit Goswami Mahārāja's house at least five times a week to do some service, and he also spent time with him just talking and doing things together. He said that Goswami Mahārāja was very focused and very disciplined, and that for five hours every day he would work on his dissertation. Immovable. His routine was fixed. But he said that in the last two days Goswami Mahārāja was so excited about the prospect of going to India that he couldn't work on his dissertation. He was too excited. And then in Māyāpur he immersed himself in hearing and chanting about Kṛṣṇa—every evening there would be *bhajanas* and *kīrtanas* in his quarters for hours.

So Goswami Mahārāja was very happy in Māyāpur. He was pleased with the association of his godbrothers, pleased with the *bhajanas*, the *sat-saṅga*, the *kīrtanas*. He was completely immersed in Kṛṣṇa consciousness. And, of course, just being in the *dhāma* has its own value. Probably all of us—what to speak of Goswami Mahārāja—have experienced, when we leave the *dhāma*, being absorbed in thoughts of the *dhāma*, with memories of our experiences there and appreciation for the personalities who gave us mercy. But at the same time, when we leave, we leave for a purpose; we leave on a mission. We feel sad to leave the *dhāma*, and we are still relishing the association of the *dhāma* and the mercy of the higher personalities, but at the same time we know we have our mission—we are going to serve our spiritual master. I can imagine that Goswami Mahārāja would have been in the same type of mood. And, transcendental as he was, the mood would have been even more heightened, more glorious—going out to fight for his spiritual master, for Śrīla Prabhupāda.

From the point of view of the Society, also, I thought it was so appropriate and so auspicious; I could think of no better time or place for him to leave. So many devotees and leaders were there in Māyāpur, the meetings had just ended and the festival had just begun, and practically the whole Society and its leadership were there and could worship and glorify His Holiness Tamal Krishna Goswami Mahārāja.

I felt that it was an occasion when the Society could come closer together, become more united in appreciation of Śrīla Prabhupāda's right-hand man. Time will reveal more about Kṛṣṇa's plan, but I do feel that Goswami Mahārāja's departure has provided us an opportunity and an occasion to come closer together. For the sincere, openhearted, pure-hearted devotees, it is an occasion to regroup our forces and appreciate each other more, appreciate the value of each other's presence on the planet, and at the same time recognize the tenuousness of our existence in the body and realize that any one of us could go at any time. And therefore, with whatever time we have left, we should do the best we can for each other, and for Śrīla Prabhupāda, for the mission, and give up petty thoughts, petty preoccupations, petty grudges—just let it all go and fix our vision on Kṛṣṇa, Śrī Śrī Rādhā-Kālachandjī; Śrī Caitanya Mahāprabhu; the Six Gosvāmīs; the previous *ācāryas*; Śrīla Prabhupāda; and Śrīla Prabhupāda's intimate associates, including Śrīpāda Tamal Krishna Goswami—and group together under their shelter and serve them, exalt them, and glorify them. And that will make us exalted and glorified too.

Serving with Goswami Mahārāja

A talk at Tamal Krishna Goswami's Vyāsa-pūjā celebration in Dallas on June 25, 2005.

As we were waiting to greet the Deities, Śrī Śrī Rādhā-Kālachandjī, some of my godbrothers pushed me forward to be the first in line. I suppose this was correct according to etiquette, from their point of view, but I felt that something was wrong—His Holiness Tamal Krishna Goswami Mahārāja should have been there, first in the line, as he had been so many other times when I had stood to greet the Deities here, and in Houston, Bombay, Vṛndāvana, and other places. Reflecting on that sentiment, I thought of my relationship with him and my relationship with Śrīla Prabhupāda in relation to him, and I would say that clearly, he helped me in my relationship with Śrīla Prabhupāda. So I thought to discuss that idea, because I feel that it is a principle that applies to all of us here, whether we are godbrothers and godsisters or disciples, whether he was acting as an older brother helping us in our service to our spiritual father, Śrīla Prabhupāda, or as a spiritual father bringing his spiritual children to their spiritual grandfather. As the founder-*ācārya*, Śrīla Prabhupāda is more than just a spiritual grandfather, but he is a spiritual grandfather nonetheless. In all our cases, Tamal Krishna Goswami Mahārāja is helping us in our relationship with Śrīla Prabhupāda.

I first met His Holiness Tamal Krishna Goswami in Boston in 1969. Goswami Mahārāja was already a legend, and we had heard much about him even before he came. Brahmānanda Prabhu was also in Boston then. He was the biggest leader on the East Coast, and Goswami Mahārāja managed the West Coast. The two of them met and spent almost all their time together, and practically the whole time they were talking about Śrīla Prabhupāda. That really struck me. They would talk for hours and hours about Śrīla Prabhupāda. One evening, a few of us were standing in line for *prasāda*, and Brahmānanda Prabhu suddenly said, "Everyone wants love. So the simple solution is that we should love each other, we should just give each other a lot of love." It was a striking statement. Our understanding then was that we should just love Kṛṣṇa, just focus on Kṛṣṇa. And that is true, of course. We direct our love to Kṛṣṇa, and by loving Kṛṣṇa we automatically love all living entities. But the idea of making a conscious effort to love each other seemed different from our understanding at the time.

Anyway, Tamal Krishna Goswami continued his travels. He went to Europe, and the next time I met him was in 1970, in Bombay. He was my authority then, the GBC for India. And during the first Bombay *paṇḍāl* program at Cross Maidan he was my immediate authority. I was like the temple commander for the *paṇḍāl*, and he was like the temple president. Working with him was very instructive. Then, after the success of the Bombay program, Śrīla Prabhupāda sent the two of us to Calcutta to organize the first *paṇḍāl* there, and on the way we spoke on the train. That was when Goswami Mahārāja first really opened up to me. But it was what I learned from him one night in Calcutta that became my guiding principle in Kṛṣṇa consciousness.

I was a new devotee and had heard about the importance of chanting. I had heard about the importance of studying scripture. I had heard about the importance of Deity worship. And to me, everything was important. I didn't distinguish between one process and another. They all were important, and I was meant to do all of them. So, one night—it must have been after nine o'clock, because everyone else was already asleep—the two of us, somehow, were still up, standing alongside each other on the balcony of the Calcutta temple on Albert Road.

Suddenly Goswami Mahārāja started speaking to me confidentially about his relationship with Śrīla Prabhupāda. He said that Śrīla Prabhupāda had a few disciples who were quite intimate with him and that he was one of them. This was a revelation to me because at that stage in my spiritual development I did not distinguish. I saw them all as senior devotees whom Prabhupāda loved, and I did not make such distinctions. Then Goswami Mahārāja started to glorify Śyāmasundara Prabhu, saying that he was one of the biggest preachers in ISKCON. In fact, Śyāmasundara Prabhu was the one who had conceived of the Bombay *paṇḍāl* and organized us all in its execution. Further, Śyāmasundara Prabhu was very instrumental in developing the life membership program. He designed the life membership form and wrote an appeal that was very well done; even today I doubt there is an appeal that surpasses the one he wrote then. But the whole time I was working with him he had never given a class. So I asked Goswami Mahārāja, "What do you mean 'one of the biggest preachers'? I don't think I have ever heard him give class." And Mahārāja replied, "Preaching does not just mean speaking about Kṛṣṇa. Preaching ultimately means engaging people in Kṛṣṇa's service." By developing the life membership program, by staging the first *paṇḍāl* program, and through so many other programs, Śyāmasundara Prabhu had engaged so many people in Kṛṣṇa consciousness—this too was preaching. That, for me, was an important instruction.

Then Goswami Mahārāja came back to himself and his relationship with Śrīla Prabhupāda. He told me about the incident in 1970 when Śrīla Prabhupāda felt that there was an attempt by some of his disciples to wrest control of the movement from him, how Śrīla Prabhupāda had called Mahārāja to Los Angeles and confided in him. One of the problems at the time was that some of the leaders were very preoccupied with collecting money and engaging the devotees to collect money. So the spiritual lives of the devotees were being hampered. I remember that in Boston we had to go out early in the morning and just stay out all day and come back late at night. I was the type that if I did not chant my rounds in the morning, at least twelve rounds, I would feel uneasy during the day. And the way things were going then, day after day I was falling behind on my rounds. So one morning I decided, "I am just going to sit in the temple room and chant my rounds; that's it." I had not chanted more than two or three rounds when one of the leaders came in and said, "Come on, you can't just sit here and chant. You have to go out." So it was a difficult period.

Śrīla Prabhupāda had become aware of what was happening, and he confided in Tamal Krishna and discussed with him what to do. Soon thereafter, back in Boston, we received the word: "Śrīla Prabhupāda wants us to do this and this and this and not that and that." But now, on that special night in Calcutta, Tamal Krishna Goswami was explaining to me that Śrīla Prabhupāda had asked him, "What do we do?" And Goswami Mahārāja had suggested many of the measures that Śrīla Prabhupāda ultimately implemented. The measures were that the devotees should come back at five o'clock in the evening, attend the program in the temple, take rest early, get up early, and attend *maṅgala-ārati* and the morning program. And on *saṅkīrtana* we should just give people the magazine. At that time we basically distributed only *Back to Godhead* magazines, BTGs. "Just give them the magazine and ask for a donation," Śrīla Prabhupāda had said. "Any gentleman will give a quarter." A quarter was a pretty good amount in those days, and the cost of BTG at the time was maybe ten or twelve cents. So a quarter was good enough, more than good enough. But the idea was to make us more regulated, to have us spend enough time in the morning and evening programs, to have us do enough hearing and chanting and worshiping and associating with devotees in the temple, and then on *saṅkīrtana* to be more detached, not too greedy or aggressive, and just give people the literature and depend on Kṛṣṇa.

So I was struck. I had not realized that Goswami Mahārāja had played such an important role in these events. I had thought that everything just issued forth from Śrīla Prabhupāda without any discussion, coming straight from Kṛṣṇa. And I am sure that in an ultimate sense it all was coming from Kṛṣṇa, but in practical terms Śrīla Prabhupāda consulted with trusted disciples.

Then Goswami Mahārāja told me (and this is really the basic point), "The essence of spiritual life is service to the spiritual master." That was the part that really struck me and entered deep. There was chanting the holy names, reading the scriptures, worshiping the Deities, and doing service—that much I knew. But he said, "The essence of spiritual life is service to the spiritual master." And I had never thought of that. Like I said, the process was all there, and I knew that we had to do all of it, but I did not see how the different practices related to each other. And Tamal Krishna Goswami's realization, which I accepted at the time and still do now, was that service to the spiritual master is the essence.

From then on, my approach to devotional service—even chanting—changed. I liked to chant, and I still do, but I began to chant more in the mood of service to the spiritual master. When we were in Calcutta, Goswami Mahārāja used to get annoyed because I wouldn't want to go out until I had finished at least twelve rounds. He used to say, "Oh, you just want to avoid work. That's why you are standing in front of the Deities and chanting." [laughter] Still, he let me. Some times he would get more annoyed than other times, but ultimately he let me, because I needed that. But my mood had become a little different. Yes, I was chanting, and I enjoy chanting, but I was also thinking, "I need to chant to do my various duties for Śrīla

Prabhupāda. If I chant, my consciousness will be purified. Kṛṣṇa will guide me what to do and when. And I will be better able to deal with people. I will be able to preach better if I chant and purify my consciousness."

From then on we were close friends. I did not really have . . . In a way I had friends, but not like that. Our friendship was deeper, because we had the common focus of service to Śrīla Prabhupāda.

The first Calcutta *paṇḍāl* was a great success. More people came than even to the first Bombay *paṇḍāl*. Goswami Mahārāja had said, "You collect the money and I'll spend it." [laughter] I was fine with that. I knew I could not manage the way he could, but I could convince people to give. So that worked well.

Of course, we had so many experiences together, but I'd like to speak a little about our service in Bombay and again, the idea of cooperation. During that period in Bombay we were struggling to get the Juhu land, so we could not really collect much for the Juhu project; it just wasn't the right time. But the Vṛndāvana temple construction needed funds, so Goswami Mahārāja and I formed a team to collect for it. One devotee suggested that it would be most effective if two preachers went together, one heavy and the other soft. I don't know which one I was. [laughter] Anyway, we went along with the idea. And there were two instances in particular when it really worked well. In the first case we went to meet Natvarlal Jivanlal Gandhi in the spice market. The spice market was in the old section of Bombay—Bombay-2, Bombay-3, Bombay-9—the cloth market, the spice and grain market, and the iron market. That time of the year was especially hot and humid, and Old Bombay was really congested. You had all these people pulling these carts, long platforms on wheels, loaded with big bags of grains and spices and sugar. The streets were so narrow and crowded with carts and cars and people that you could hardly move. Goswami

Mahārāja had been a bit annoyed from the beginning that I had made an appointment down there. On the way, he said, "You know I don't like appointments down here." He wanted the appointments to be in places like Churchgate and Flora Fountain, the newer and, you know, more congenial parts of town.

Anyway, we found the address, climbed up the rickety wood stairs in the old frame building, and found a big bare room, and at one end, to one side, sitting at a desk, a simple man in white *khādī* cloth. And this simple man, we discovered, was Mr. Gandhi. The large room was not air conditioned, and Mr. Gandhi didn't even have his own private office. It was very basic. Goswami Mahārāja murmured, "Oh God, why did you bring me here?" So, we sat down, but I had hardly opened up my briefcase before Goswami Mahārāja turned to me again and said, "We're just wasting our time. Let's get out of here!" "We have come all this way," I suggested. "Let's just take a chance. We are already here. It won't take much longer."

So, we sat down at the gentleman's desk and began our appeal. We took out our book of photos and showed the pictures of our preaching around the world. And then we started to talk about Vṛndāvana—how due to Śrīla Prabhupāda's preaching, devotees from all over the world now wanted to come to Vṛndāvana but how there was no proper place to receive them. I told the story of my parents, how they came to visit me in Vṛndāvana and how there was no place we could go even to eat. There were two or three eating-places, but they were all dirty, with flies everywhere. So then we decided, "Okay, let's try Mathurā." But even in Mathurā there was nothing. Finally we went to Agra, and there we found some decent hotels. So, we told Mr. Gandhi, as we had told others, "There is no proper place for Westerners in Vṛndāvana. Therefore Śrīla Prabhupāda wants to build a temple with a guesthouse and restaurant to international standards." That was a very strong argument.

Then Goswami Mahārāja said, "We could have been like you. We could have gone into business and made lots of money, but then who would preach this message? We need preachers. So we have dedicated our lives to preach, and you, in your position, can help by giving money." And that also made perfect sense. It was a strong presentation.

In the end, Mr. Gandhi really surprised us. He donated for the biggest room. People would sponsor rooms in the guesthouse, and he took the biggest. It was twenty-nine thousand rupees or so, really a lot then. And that was a big surprise. So it was good, that there was that cooperation.

Another vivid example of how well our cooperation worked was when we went to see Bhogilal Patel. Seth Bhogilal was a most devotional man. He was highly cultured and aristocratic, and so pious and softhearted. The first devotee to meet him was Gargamuni. When Gargamuni started to tell him how Śrīla Prabhupāda was spreading Kṛṣṇa consciousness all over the world and how people all over the world were chanting Hare Kṛṣṇa, Bhogilal began to weep. He literally shed tears.

He had become a life member, and we made an appointment to see him. At that point, we were collecting for Juhu. We made our presentation, and Bhogilal said that he would really like to give much more but that his son had taken charge of the business and was not so devotionally inclined, so all he could give was x amount. Goswami Mahārāja, sitting next to me, poked me in the side and whispered, "That's not enough; that's not enough—he can give much more!" I just did not have the heart to ask for more. But Goswami insisted: "You have to. You have to do it. It's not enough. He's a rich man." So, I don't remember if I was the one who finally did it or if in the end he took over, but based on his determination we said it: "You have to give more than that. We need funds, and you have to give more." And Seth Bhogilal doubled the figure. So it was definitely Goswami

Mahārāja's insistence that brought about that increased service. And that is the idea: cooperation—"You make the money and I will spend it."

Over the years, our friendship deepened. And the basis, of course, was service to Śrīla Prabhupāda, though it was not that our service to Śrīla Prabhupāda was always the explicit topic of discussion or focus of every interaction. At the same time, there was so much affection between us.

In November of 1977, shortly before he ultimately left this material world, Śrīla Prabhupāda wanted to form the Bhaktivedanta Swami Charity Trust to give grants to support projects in Gauḍa-maṇḍala-bhūmi that could not be completed without financial assistance—those of his godbrothers and even those undertaken by devotees not in the line of Bhaktisiddhānta Sarasvatī.

It was hot—although it was November, it was very hot—and Goswami Mahārāja sent me to Mathurā with Bhagatji to get the document typed up and registered. It was a big challenge for me, and I was quite bewildered. I didn't know Mathurā at all, and I had never worked with Bhagatji, who was an older, local devotee and a friend of Śrīla Prabhupāda's. But I tried my best. We took a bus to Mathurā, found some typist outside the courthouse, got him to type up the document, fought through the chaos inside, and finally got it registered. It was all quite an endeavor. Then we rode back to Vṛndāvana, handed the document over, and as it was pretty late and I was tired, I took rest. About ten minutes after I turned out the lights, I was awakened by loud banging on the door—repeated loud banging. So I opened the door and there was Goswami Mahārāja. He was fuming. He was furious. He told me that Śrīla Prabhupāda had seen the document and was very upset, because instead of "Bhaktivedanta Swami Charity Trust" we had put "Bhaktivedanta Charitable Trust," and "Bhaktivedanta"—there could be so many "Bhaktivedantas"; it had to be "Bhaktivedanta Swami." Then Goswami said, with great intensity, "You blew it!"

Actually, however, as a result of that interaction with Goswami Mahārāja I felt very elated. I felt elated because Śrīla Prabhupāda really was the center of our relationship. It was not a mundane friendship. Goswami Mahārāja was not going to compromise on Śrīla Prabhupāda's service for the sake of so-called friendship or keeping our relationship congenial in a mundane way. So that was very enlivening, very encouraging. No matter what, Śrīla Prabhupāda's service comes first, and that was the basis of everything: our friendship, our good times together—everything.

So, we miss him, though at the same time, in such wonderful association with devotees who also appreciate him and love him, by thinking of him and speaking about him and trying to execute his will and serve in his mood—the mood of surrendered service to the spiritual master—we do experience his presence and guidance.

And we should know, as well, that along with so much practical service, Tamal Krishna Goswami was also very intent on his internal spiritual development. Not everyone had the opportunity to witness this directly, but we did. There were periods when he would get up very early. He would chant, offer prayers, and read *śāstra*. He was very intent on his spiritual practice. And I think that is also very important to note, along with that mood of selfless service to the spiritual master in the field of practical activity.

Here I call to mind our dear godbrother His Holiness Bhakti Tirtha Swami. After a long discussion with Bhakti Tirtha Mahārāja over the phone, some months ago now, I wrote him and asked if he had any other instructions, any final instruction for me. As you may know, he was very concerned about the welfare of the devotees, and he was already pleased that we had taken up the project for senior ladies in Vṛndāvana, Kirtan Ashram, and were working to create a hospice for devotees, also in Vṛndāvana. So, I wrote and asked if he had any further instructions. He encouraged me to continue along the same lines but added: "We need simultaneously to go deeper in our consciousness. Śrīla Bhaktivinoda Ṭhākura says that inoffensive chanting naturally brings forth the compassion in a *sādhu* and that this compassion should manifest externally in ways to protect the devotional service of as many devotees as possible, through tangible projects. So these two parallel activities must go on: our own diving into deeper, richer, internal devotional consciousness, and, inspired by this effort, our work on greater projects and arrangements."

That was an important instruction, and I think it exemplifies His Holiness Tamal Krishna Goswami's method of devotional service—that along with our practical service we should dive deeply into our internal practice of Kṛṣṇa consciousness. By going deeply we will develop the mood of compassion, and that compassion will be expressed in projects that will protect and nurture the devotional service of others. So, that is something we all have to balance. Sometimes the circumstances are such that we have more facility to chant and hear and remember, and sometimes the circumstances are such that we have to be more engaged in external activities. But overall, we want to do both. And although the external results of Tamal Krishna Goswami's service are more visible, we know that he was also very serious about his internal cultivation of Kṛṣṇa consciousness, and that is something we all should try to emulate.

Lessons in Love

A talk by Ṛtadhvaja Swami at Tamal Krishna Goswami's Vyāsa-pūjā celebration in Dallas on June 25, 2005.

Hare Kṛṣṇa. Śrīla Tamal Krishna Goswami Mahārāja *ki jaya!* Śrīla Prabhupāda *ki jaya!*

It's nice to see everybody. This is one of the great parts of this festival, that we all come together and have this opportunity for association. So many devotees here have so many wonderful things to say. I wrote something a while back and had wanted to read it on this occasion. I did not get a chance to read it to the devotees before and was waiting for an opportunity. But now I am really moved and impressed by all your realizations and by the sentiments you have expressed for a devotee. As one devotee said, sometimes we have to wait for people to depart before we can tell them that we love them and that we want to be with them more.

So I feel that this is an opportunity for us to overcome that part of ourselves that does not open up to others and allow ourselves to freely love one another as devotees need to love one another. I know that our dear friend Bhakti Tirtha Swami has been pushing this for some time. Recently I have had a little time off, believe it or not—something that has not happened to me since I joined—and have had time to reflect on devotee relationships and deepen my appreciation for what Śrīla Prabhupāda has given us, what this Hare Kṛṣṇa movement is. Out of all the things we have, we have each other, and I think this is practically the most important thing we have. We have buildings. We have this. We have that. But we really have each other, and this is becoming so clear as we see some of our devotees leaving this world. We are coming to understand the value of this association.

I just wanted to mention—everybody is telling these wonderful stories—that I met Tamal Krishna Goswami, the first time, without meeting him. When I read his book *Servant of the Servant* I learned that he was once in Minot, North Dakota. I am from there. Now you know somebody from North Dakota. [laughter] It is rare to know somebody from North Dakota. It is even rarer to be somebody from North Dakota. [laughter] There are plenty of devotees that came out of there; you don't have many choices there. So, there are funny stories, amazing stories of his preaching and his association with Rādhā-Dāmodara, and to my understanding, the first devotional service I rendered was to the Radha-Damodara party.

I was a musician. I had been out on tour, and I got back home about six o'clock in the morning. At around eight there was a knock on the door. There was a guy on my porch in pink pajamas, a pink sweatshirt, pink shoes, pink socks—everything pink. I was a person of an "alternative lifestyle"—that's a polite way of saying it—and I had decided that I would just plant flowers in my yard, because flowers were more beautiful than grass. So I had thousands of flowers growing—no grass, just flowers. So, this person said, "We would like some flowers for our altar. Would you mind if I take some?" I said, "No, take what you want. Whatever is mine is yours. Whatever is yours is mine." You know our old philosophy. So, he said, "Thank you." And I went back to sleep. Then about fifteen minutes later he knocks on the door and says, "Do you have a knife?" I remember thinking, "There are no weirdos in North Dakota." And I thought, "Well, my dog weighs 190 pounds. He can handle this person." I had a huge dog. So I gave the guy a knife and said, "Hey, man, do me a favor. Just put the knife in the mailbox when you're done, okay? I've had a long night, a long week. I need to get some sleep." So, I got up around four or five o'clock in the afternoon and went outside, and there wasn't one flower left in my yard.

[laughter] Śrī Śrī Rādhā-Dāmodara were very well decorated that day.

There was a carnival in town at the time, and my friends were playing at the grandstand that night. So I went to see them, and on the way to the grandstand you had to walk through the midway, where all the vendors were. And there was this boy coming through, and he came up to me and said, "Hey, remember me?" And I said, "Yeah, I sure do, man." [laughter] So, he asked me, "What do you think of the flowers?" I said, "They're beautiful; where are they?" He said, "They're on the altar." And I said to him, "What is an altar?" I had no idea what was going on. He said, "Here. Let me give you some incense for the flowers." I said, "Hey, man, I gave you the flowers. You don't owe me anything."

Years later, I learned that Tamal Krishna Goswami and Viṣṇujana had been walking in Minot, right where I took a walk every single day. They were walking there and planning their next step. When I told this story to Tamal, he said, "Then I also get credit for you, knowingly or unknowingly." [laughter]

So, they did not steal the flowers; they took permission. That boy actually took permission. And Tamal said, "I think I know who that was." But he never told me the devotee's name.

Anyway, I am feeling that we have something really, really wonderful here in this association, and the value of this Vyāsa-pūjā gathering is that we can come together and move forward in our spiritual lives, individually and collectively. Without each other . . . I think Prabhupāda said, "It is hallucination if you think you can advance without the association of devotees." We are realizing how deeply indebted we are to each other in this society. And I cannot express the depth of the debt that I owe to Tamal Krishna Goswami. We were friends on a very limited level until 1999, when he got sick. And then he became practically the closest friend I ever had in my entire life.

As devotees here have revealed, he was both very straightforward and very openhearted. In other words, he would sometimes enter the arena gently, and sometimes just come in and declare, "This is what we are going to do." When I came to Dallas the first time, he had a whole script of how he was going to get me to stay here with him to help him, and I just let him play it all out, and then I agreed to stay and help him. He wasn't the first devotee I helped like that, but he was the one who made the most significant difference in my life, because of the level of appreciation he had for someone who really helped him and because of how he could reciprocate with that person.

I feel that as he and I worked together during that time when he was ill, I learned more about what it is to be a devotee, and what it means to be a devotee, and why I want to be a devotee. In a family there are always dark moments. Even in my family, as I grew up as a child, there were dark moments, and I am sure everybody here has had that experience in their own biological families. As a spiritual family too we have some dark moments and we have some bright moments, but our relationships have to go beyond that. They definitely have to go beyond that, and we have to see their true value. With Tamal Krishna Goswami, in his association, I learned to appreciate devotees. I learned it because I saw in him a real devotee of Kṛṣṇa, someone who could care more about the Society and the needs of his spiritual master than about his own self. Most of us love ourselves more than we love others. It is a type of artificial love for oneself that is based on popular opinion rather than on a deep, intuitive understanding of who we really are. If we can learn to love and appreciate that person—who we actually are in ourselves—then as devotees of Kṛṣṇa we can actually love and appreciate the people around us. That is part of what it means to be a devotee. And to bring ourselves closer to that understanding is one of the great benefits of devotee association and specifically, as I said, his association.

I remember one time we were together, about two and a half months into what we would call "the ordeal." (We used to have different names for it when he was ill.) He looked at me and said, "Mahārāja, you know, there is something about you that has allowed me to tell you things that I would never tell anyone else in the world." And I said to him, "Mahārāja, there are things that I have given you that I could never give anyone else in the world." From that type of exchange our relationship deepened. And now, when we come together and I see the devotees who gather for these Vyāsa-pūjās, it is just a deeply emotional time for me, because of the separation I feel from that type of relationship. It is very easy to give up superficial relationships—very, very easy—but this deeper type of relationship is extremely difficult to give up, because it is so deeply spiritually purifying.

Our purification in spiritual life on the level of *sādhana-bhakti* comes in a regulated way. And then you develop deep, deep loving relationships, as we saw in what Keśava Bhāratī Mahārāja said today, which brought a tear to the corner of my eye—he said, "Tamal, I just want to tell you that I love you." We need to develop these deep loving relationships. They are not material, but spiritual, based on a higher cause. This is the type of love that we need to develop, and when we do, and when we have it and then it is taken away, then the spiritual advancement we get is like somebody all of a sudden slamming on the gas pedal. You are forced to deal with your inner self and your inner being on a level to which most of us do not even have an inclination to go. But we are forced to do that because things in this world are temporary. Our time is very short, and we have to clear all this stuff out. And I was feeling that these relationships that we have with individuals such as Tamal Krishna Goswami—we have to develop them more and more with each other so that we can actually clear up the mess that we have gotten ourselves into in this material world.

So, Tamal Krishna Goswami—he gave me that. He gave me that sense of worthiness, of self-worth, and not in an artificial sense that whatever is wrong does not need to be corrected, but in a way that allows us to appreciate ourselves for who we are and then move forward.

I will give an example. I was taking lunch with Mahārāja at the table one day and something went wrong in the service, and as usual, I didn't notice it. There are a whole lot of things I don't notice. Thank you, Kṛṣṇa! [laughter] So, he was just chastising the server so much. Just chastising, chastising. Finally I said, "Mahārāja, you know, it is so heavy. How can you just . . . I mean, I know you love this person. How can you be so heavy? Maybe I'm not qualified to be a *guru* or teacher, because I could never do that." He looked at me and said, "You just be whoever you are, and I will be whoever I am." Now, that's funny, isn't it? But when you take a look at it, you will understand that it is cutting edge. To understand who you are is the first essential point for making progress. If we take time to identify who we are, what our faults are, what our goodness is, and then take Kṛṣṇa and what Kṛṣṇa has given us, take the *guru* and what he has given us, and utilize all that to go to the place where we want to go, to the lotus feet of *guru* and Kṛṣṇa, then "You just be who you are and I will be who I am" makes perfect sense. It makes very deep sense, because if we don't do that we will never understand.

Today is Tamal Krishna Goswami Mahārāja's appearance day. It is a very, very auspicious day, and we remember him, his life, his legacy within our Society. It is amazing how we can remember these things with so much love and so much affection. When I consider Tamal Krishna Goswami, the thing that I appreciate about him most, and that I am hearing from many of the devotees today, is his unwavering loyalty and his fixed devotion to the service of his spiritual master. It was just so fixed.

He was the loyal, obedient servant of the spiritual master. His chastity to Śrīla Prabhupāda holds great importance for me. I will read just a few words from what I had written: "I saw him as a strong person not limited by a stagnant understanding of Śrīla Prabhupāda's mission, but as a person who could keep the objectives of Śrīla Prabhupāda's purpose intact and at the same time develop and expand our Society beyond its normal limits." It is unique that he was able to do that, to actually remain chaste, remain fixed on the lotus feet of the spiritual master and yet have the boldness and aggressiveness to dare to go where no one has ever gone before—and to get everybody to come with him.

Tamal Krishna Goswami was always looking for the next thing—greater steps, bold steps. If he realized something was right, he would do it. And he often had something up his sleeve, some way of accomplishing what he wanted to get done. When I was with him I was always waiting for him to say, "Okay, now I really want you to do this." But he never did that to me. He would always consider what I needed. We had a slightly different relationship because ours started late and developed in a certain way. But again, he possessed this unique ability to remain chaste to Śrīla Prabhupāda and at the same time take all these steps forward in preaching Kṛṣṇa consciousness. These steps he would take certainly challenged the established parameters of our Society. We all know they challenged ISKCON. Prabhupāda said, "The leader's business is to give people new challenges." New challenges—new frontiers. Kṛṣṇa consciousness is not meant to be stagnant. It is meant to be dynamic, and Tamal Krishna Goswami, in his preaching and in his association with us, had that ability to make the Society, this movement, very dynamic and very alive.

So we look to him for inspiration and guidance in the endeavor that we all should make: to spread this movement. In his boldness and aggressiveness to expand Kṛṣṇa consciousness, he had to tolerate the difficulties that come from that type of effort. Because you get flak. You get flak from inside; you get flak from outside. You will get it from everywhere. But yet, when Tamal Krishna Goswami got hold of an idea—when he knew something was right—he was willing to fight to the end. And that is why we find ourselves here today, feeling so loyal to this person, because of his loyalty to his spiritual master.

I look at Tamal Krishna Goswami as we honor him today. I spent the morning reflecting on my relationship with him and the influence he had on me as a person, and I can only thank him sincerely, from the deepest part of my heart that I can enter into, for the association that he gave me. He deeply understood my needs, which many times included his. He included me in his needs, and I included him in mine, and this developed a deep loving relationship that I feel will never be broken. In one sense we feel the separation. But at the same time, we feel that relationship deeply alive and vibrant even today. I just pray that over time that relationship and that connection will not be forgotten.

Tamal Krishna Goswami was the person whom we could approach for anything and everything. I can honestly say that our relationship allowed a type of complete openness in which I didn't have to think to myself, "Is this person going to prejudge me, or is he going to actually hear me and understand my needs now and where I need to go from here?" I didn't have to fear exposure to elements in our Society that would be detrimental to my spiritual growth. I had that faith in him, the assurance that if I give my heart to this person, whatever I give to him I can give with complete confidence. If he feels that it needs to be exposed, he will expose it, and if he doesn't, he will keep it to himself and personally be my medical assistant, my spiritual medical man.

He used to call me Coach. I was his coach, and Lore, his

mother, calls me Coach to this day. Feeling this type of coaching and this association, and having this type of relationship with somebody, in which you can open up, helps to guide a devotee and to shape him into the type of qualified servant that Śrīla Prabhupāda would want each of us to become. As many devotees were saying, when Tamal Krishna Goswami was taking the *brahmacārīs* from the temples, he actually felt that it was for the *brahmacārīs'* wellbeing, for training and for assisting them. I feel that his association really helped to guide individuals and to shape them into being the type of devotees that Śrīla Prabhupāda really wanted us to become. As we listen to the discussions about the serving of *prasāda*, the cooking of *prasāda*, the temple room, how he entered into different preaching environments—he helped shape our society into what it is today.

I will end on Tamal Krishna Goswami's position as a leader, one who could make things happen in our Society. What he did for ISKCON should not be underestimated. Just take a look at what everyone has said this morning. Practically speaking, he made me a devotee without even meeting me, just by sending somebody out to bring flowers for Rādhā-Dāmodara. And he took the credit, which is cool. He can have it. "He was one of the most instrumental followers of Śrīla Prabhupāda. He set the stage for many of ISKCON's preaching programs. His loyalty and devotion were recognized by Prabhupāda, and Prabhupāda used him like a sharpened tool to sculpt the mission of Lord Caitanya Mahāprabhu in these Western worlds." He used Tamal Krishna Goswami in this way.

Tamal Krishna Goswami was a real leader. He was a real devotee, and he was a real friend. Tamal Krishna, I love you from the deepest part of my heart.

The Older Brother

A talk by Bhakta Carl Herzig at Tamal Krishna Goswami's Memorial Festival in Carpinteria, California, on June 18, 2006.

Hare Kṛṣṇa. Please allow me to offer you each my most humble obeisances.

My relationship with Tamal Krishna began in 1956. He was, besides my parents, the very first person I met in my life. Yesterday, in speaking about him, His Holiness Giriraj Swami used a key word: relationships. That is so much what he was and still is all about. When he was with you, he made you feel that you were for him at that moment the most important person—almost the only person—in the world. He was so personal and had so many loving relationships.

Each of us knew him a little differently, even by different names—Śrīla Gurudeva, Goswami Mahārāja, Tamal Krishna Mahārāja, Tamal Krishna, Tamal. The first one I knew was my brother, Tommy. Right from my birth he was the most loving brother in the world. I wasn't just a little brother; I was his baby. He was not quite ten years old, but he embraced me fully and entirely, took possession of me to the point of wanting to take physical care of me, even change my diapers. Soon after I was born, he collected together his childhood toys and announced, "I'm not a child anymore; these are his," and gave all the toys to me. A child's toys—especially those personal ones, like his stuffed animals—can mean a lot to the child, but he wanted to hand them over. It was a coming of age for him, and a sacrifice, but one that he offered with love. He was declaring that now I was the child, and these became the stuffed animals—an elephant, a giraffe, two monkeys (one with a broken nose)—that I loved throughout my childhood. People have spoken of the many sacrifices that Tamal Krishna made for others. So this is just one example, from early in his life.

He often took me on walks—first me in a stroller, later me churning my legs to keep up with what seemed to me at the time his almost impossibly long and swift stride as we went to play in the park. There he'd push me on the swings or wait for me with open arms at the bottom of the slide. Sometimes we'd stop for ice cream on the way home—all the things a little boy would do with his older brother. Mostly I remember tiny moments, snapshots: rolling a ball across the room, him holding me up to reach the water fountain at the zoo, running across a field as we tried to keep a kite up in the air.

From the beginning, from the first day I can remember, he was my hero; I idolized him. Our father was already in his fifties when I was born, so Tommy was both an elder brother and father figure, doing a lot of fatherly things, like teaching me how to pass a football, shoot a basketball, throw a baseball—how to break in a baseball glove, rubbing it with oil and pounding a ball into it again and again for hours, wrapping it around the ball and tying it with string. All the little details. We'd play catch in the park by the Hudson River. Years later, after he'd left New York, I wrote in a poem:

> How many rains
> on your home in Bombay
> since those winds that came east
> off the Hudson and blew sweat
> from our hair as we ran?

We grew up in the middle of New York City, so we did all the things boys growing up in the City would do, and he taught me how to survive—how to walk, how to hold myself—because you had to walk the street with a certain attitude. Nobody would mess with you if you walked right. He was always teaching me—not just looking out for me, but teaching me to look out for myself.

I thought of this years later, in December of 1999, when Tamal Krishna took me walking through Ramaṇa-reti. He loved it there, where there wasn't yet any of the development that is going on in Vṛndāvana and along the *parikramā* path. "This is what it was like with Śrīla Prabhupāda," he said—just the fields and flowers and trees and children running along the dirt paths. And as we walked together, we were both reminded of our times in New York. Strolling down a path in Ramaṇa-reti, it was like when he was teaching me how to walk the streets of Manhattan—"Take a stick for the monkeys and if the monkeys stare at you, don't stare back but let them know that you know they are there and that you can deal with them." One day he had his stick and there were children playing with a ball on the path, just bouncing the ball from one to the other. And just like when he'd taught me to play stickball, he took his stick, his cane, and turned it around so he was holding the bottom, with the handle up, and he swung it like a bat. He had the little Vraja-vāsī children pitching to him, and he was swinging away with his cane! He often commented that he was still a New York kid, a Manhattan kid, and that's what it felt like.

We never fought—not a single disagreement. And he was never heavy with me, never even raised his voice—never anything but kind words. I think that's rare for siblings, for a brother, even nine years the elder, to be so consistently sweet and supportive in every way.

This was still true years later, when we got back together. I saw how heavy he could be, but he never was with me; I never experienced his hot side. There were many times when I witnessed him distributing his "mercy," but I also could see that this was just another feature of his love and care for devotees, especially disciples. At one point I even began to feel a little jealous; I wanted to relish some of the famous "sauce" that everyone else was getting. I wasn't desperate enough to intentionally do anything to invoke it, but I sort of hoped that someday it would come.

Well, one afternoon I got a call in my university office, and it was Tamal Krishna. His book *Reason and Belief* had just come out, and there was something there—some of my editing work—that wasn't clear. So he called and said—he sounded really upset—"What is this? What were you thinking? How could you do this?" He must have gone on for fifteen or twenty minutes. What he didn't know was that on my end, I was smiling from ear to ear; I was really relishing it. Finally, I was getting the sauce too! When I got off the phone, I was so happy. Then, just a few minutes later, the phone rang again. It was Sārvabhauma Prabhu, who was serving Tamal Krishna in Cambridge. "Carl," he said, "Śrīla Gurudeva asked me to call you. He just wanted you to know that he's sorry if he was heavy with you and that he really appreciates your nice service." But I was thinking "Oh, no!" [laughter] "I barely had a few minutes to enjoy it, and it was snatched away!"

There were other times when I saw him question his effect on others. He might be speaking with a disciple, or dictating a letter, correcting them really strongly. Then the devotee would leave the room or he would finish the letter, and he would ask, "Do you think I was too heavy?" I don't know how many people saw this—how he felt after giving them the sauce. In some ways, I think, his fulfilling the role of the heavy *guru* was sometimes an austerity for him. Yes, he had a strong nature, but he also had the softest heart in the world, which came out especially in the later years, during the period after he and I got back together. And whenever he got heavy with someone, I think it took a little bit out of him. He would wonder if he had given someone more than they could stand—if it would hurt them more than it would help them.

Anyway, back to the mid-sixties—Tommy was living on the

Lower East Side. He would hang out in Washington Square Park playing his flute. He was a really good flute player. In fact, whatever he did, he tried to do perfectly. He'd work really hard at it, put all his energy into it. But then if he couldn't do it really well, he'd get frustrated and move on to something else.

He was also living a kind of hippie lifestyle. I thought that was great. He had curly brown hair that he wore long and out, frizzy—it was really out there. When he came to visit he'd brush it down. But one time he came with it out, and our father got really upset—he thought Tommy wasn't being respectful. And it turned into one of those fights that went on for hours; there'd be a lull and then it would pick up again.

I was still young—maybe nine or ten—and with all the arguing, I was very upset. I wasn't used to them fighting, or even raising their voices to one another. So I just ran back into my room in tears and climbed into bed. After a while, Tommy came back and sat next to me on my bed, stroking my head and assuring me that everything would be all right. "Let's go out," he said. "Let's go have some ice cream or something to eat." (In the heat of the argument, everyone had forgotten about dinner.) But I felt really torn. He was saying, "Let's go out together," but there were my parents in the other room. I felt like I was being asked to choose between him and them, and I couldn't; I wasn't ready. So I didn't go. The argument died down and went away, of course, but over the years I sometimes thought about the incident, even wondering how my life might have been different if I had gone with him that night.

When I first went to visit Tamal in Dallas in the mid-nineties, we went over so many different memories from our lives together and our time apart. I had brought pictures from our childhood, and the whole week was really intense. We had a house to ourselves, across from the temple, and there were many painful emotions coming out. We both had a lot of remorse and sorrow for time together lost. It was the only time I ever saw him cry uncontrollably—he just couldn't stop.

Tamal had forgotten all about that incident of the argument; actually, he remembered very little from those years. He had left everything behind when he became a devotee—not just me, but his whole life. "I can't remember any of it," he lamented. "You have to remember for me." He felt bad for me that he couldn't remember, but I think he was also mourning the loss of such a big part of his life. "I gave it all up. I sacrificed it all for Prabhupāda." It wasn't that he regretted his decision, but he saw how much he, and all the devotees, had had to give up in those days.

The week was also very healing for us. I was finally able to say, "I'm sorry I didn't go with you that night." It was such a big relief. "I never should have asked you," he replied. "It was too much to put on you at that age." And he told me, "I'm so sorry I wasn't a better brother for you, that I left you when you needed me, and couldn't be with you through those years." "I never felt that way," I said, and it was true. "I never felt like you left me. I always loved you." Then he said, "Now I want to do whatever I can to make up for that and be a good brother." It was like now he'd come back again to help take care of me but this time I was ready to go with him. I told him that he was the best brother in the world and that I loved him and knew he loved me, that he'd given me the best gift he could ever give. As Giriraj Swami stated earlier, there is nothing greater than a gift from a Vaiṣṇava. And what greater gift can an older brother give to his younger brother than Kṛṣṇa consciousness, with deep love?

So anyway, soon after that night when I didn't go with him, Tommy left New York and went out west. He would stay in touch with me by mail. Then he was no longer Tommy, just Tom. And I was no longer Carly, just Carl. He sent me postcards from Mexico. He was super intelligent and always very creative—especially playing flute, but also drawing and making pottery. So for a while he went to Mexico and studied pottery-making and would write me from there. Then he wrote from Morning Star—simple postcards: "Dear Carl, How are you? I am living in a tree. I hope you are well. Love, Tom." [laughter] This was now the late sixties and I was maybe twelve or so, and I was just in heaven. "My brother lives in a tree!" What could be better? I was a little hippie and thought, You've really made it in life if you're living in a tree! That was it—the best. I was so proud. Whatever he did, I felt proud. He could have said, "I'm walking down the street," and I would have responded, "My brother is walking down the street—wow!" But I thought *that*—living in a tree—was really cool.

Then sometime later he wrote from San Francisco: "Dear Carl, I just met devotees. I'm chanting Hare Krishna. I hope you are well. Love, Tamal Krishna." First Tommy, then Tom, now Tamal Krishna. I thought, "What is this?" And again I thought, "Wow—that's great!" I had no idea what it meant, but I loved it. And of course anything he did, that's what I wanted to do. I don't think I knew about devotees or anything, or even what "chanting" meant—or "Hare Krishna." But I went to Brentano's bookstore on Eighth Street in Greenwich Village and found the lavender *Bhagavad-gītā As It Is*. I'm not sure how I made that connection. And that summer—it must have been 1968—I was assisting a pottery teacher in a family camp in rural Pennsylvania, and every day, I would climb up into an apple tree and read the *Gītā*. It didn't occur to me until now that he'd been living in a tree and then I climbed into a tree, kind of as a way of being with him. And then in the fall—again, I don't know how I found out about it; maybe the address was in the *Gītā*—I would take the train down into Brooklyn—it was a long way, almost two hours—and go to the Henry Street temple on a few Sundays, to sing and dance and eat *prasāda*, which was really, really sweet (literally!).

That was his only preaching to me—very simple: "I'm

chanting Hare Krishna. Love, Tamal Krishna." But it had a real effect on me; he inspired me so much. I wasn't able to keep up going to the temple for long (I was only thirteen), but I can still remember like yesterday that when you walked up the six or seven steps of the brownstone, the temple building, the first thing was that they would apply *tilaka* on your forehead, right as you walked in the door. In 1999, in Vṛndāvana, I met Daivī-śakti Mātājī and learned that it was she who had had that service, who had applied *tilaka* on my forehead thirty years before. And even now it is like I can still feel her finger on my forehead. Some moments stay with you for a long time.

Everything in the movement being what it was back then, I didn't hear from Tamal for the next nine years. I thought he was on some really cool adventure out in the world. I didn't realize that he sort of had to stay out of touch, that I was *māyā*! But I never felt any resentment or felt abandoned. I always knew he was out there somewhere.

In 1978, after our father died, we spent a day together in the Fifty-fifth Street temple, but after that we didn't see each other again for another nine years. We exchanged some letters over that time, and in 1989, after he found out through another devotee that my wife and I (with our first child) had been attending programs in Santa Barbara, he wrote to ask about our interest. In my reply I expressed to him how much he had inspired me through the years, and how much we had appreciated his books and taped lectures. We were becoming more involved in Kṛṣṇa consciousness, I told him, and more committed in our devotional practice.

"I was extremely pleased," he responded by post, "even deeply moved, to read the contents of your letter. There is no limit to Kṛṣṇa's wonder. I had no idea that my actions, words, and writings would so influence your life. I am very indebted to Śrīla Prabhupāda for making me a devotee and thereby allowing me to fulfill the obligation of an older brother. When we were very young, I used to play with you and keep you entertained. There was natural love and affection between us. But now I feel a great hankering to extend that love and affection in the real, spiritual sense. . . . In you I find the one family relation with whom I can genuinely share Kṛṣṇa consciousness. . . .

"Now I can understand that we must have been related from a previous birth, and thus Kṛṣṇa has placed us in such a close family relationship. Now we must utilize this to advance spiritually. In the *Caitanya-caritāmṛta* as well as *Śrīmad-Bhāgavatam*, you will be able to read of many wonderful examples of brothers engaged together in the service of Kṛṣṇa. The five Pāṇḍava brothers immediately come to mind and, of course, the three brothers Śrī Rūpa, Śrī Sanātana, and Śrī Anupama, the dearmost disciples of Lord Caitanya. These are the most exalted of personalities before whom we are nothing but specks of dust. Yet I pray that we both may follow in their footsteps and prove a credit to Śrīla Prabhupāda." It was, to say the least, a beautiful—and overwhelming—letter.

Later that year my family and I were in New York for a visit. We were staying nearby the Brooklyn temple and thought to go have *darśana* of the Deities. When we walked into the temple lobby, we asked the first devotee we saw, "Excuse me. Do you know anything about a devotee, Tamal Krishna Goswami—where he might be?" The devotee got a kind of funny look on his face. Then he said, "Um, yeah. He's right upstairs." We were really surprised; we had no idea he'd be there, or even that he was in the country. "May I say who's asking?" "His brother." Then the devotee (it turned out to be Kaustubha Prabhu) got an even funnier look. "Hold on," he said, "I'll let him know you're here." And he left for a few minutes. When he returned, he said, "Come back in an hour."

So we came back. I hadn't seen Tamal Krishna for about eleven years, and this would be the first time that he and Stella would meet. When we were all in his room together, he and I hugged, but he didn't quite know what to do. It was a beautiful but awkward moment. He didn't quite know how to be a brother just yet. I think he wanted very much to be that, and he had expressed very loving brotherly feelings in his letters, but it was as if, in person, he'd forgotten how.

We didn't meet again for another four years. By then, my family and I had moved to Iowa. One day I got a call from our dear friend Sarvātmā Prabhu, the first devotee Stella had met. "There's someone here who'd like to talk to you," he said. "Call me back." So I was wondering, "Who could be there—who wants to talk to me? And why do I have to call if they want to talk to me?" [laughter] But I called, and it was Tamal Krishna. We hadn't even spoken since '89. And that was it. We talked and talked—for five hours straight. Every hour or so, Stella would bring me some water, just to keep me alive.

"I want to get back together," he said, "but it can't just be frivolous. We have to be engaged together in service." I thought of what he had written in his long letter—that we must use our relationship for devotional service. "I started a novel based on my experiences in China," he said, "and I'd like you to take it up and finish it. This can be something we can work on together. I'll send you the manuscript." That was the beginning of a different kind of relationship for us. We were able to reclaim our brotherly love by serving together in Kṛṣṇa consciousness.

Then, just a few months later, he called and said that there'd been a change. He'd decided to return to college, to SMU, with the goal of bringing Śrīla Prabhupāda and Vaiṣṇava philosophy to the field of academia. "This will be good for us, too," he said. "I'm entering your world and I'm going to need your help. Put down the novel; I have something else for you. I want to make a book of my essays, and I'd like you to edit and introduce them." So for his next couple of books he engaged me in editing. I'd actually never done any; I was an English professor but I wasn't trained as an editor. And he threw me right into the deep water.

It wasn't just that he had faith in me; he knew that in this way I could make some progress. He would give me each book and say, "Here's a rough draft. Let me know when it's done, ready to go to the publisher." When in his essays he referenced practically any other work—academic or devotional—I had to go and read the work, to learn about the subject matter. As he later told me he'd expected, I had to learn a lot "on the job."

That first book, I had so many questions. So I called him up: "What about this point?" or "What do you mean to say here?" "I can't stop to answer each question," he said. "I don't have the time. Make a list of your questions, and then we'll have one long talk and I'll answer them all." So I made a list and called him. He answered the first question, then the second, and maybe the third. Then he asked, "How many questions do you have?" "About thirty." "Too many. Narrow them down to the ten or twelve most important ones and call back. Answer the others yourself." So I narrowed them down and called again. He answered the first and maybe the second, then said, "I can't do this. Just you decide what's best and go with that." That was our working relationship. He would put his trust in me, and I would try to live up to it. I knew that his books were really important to him, so I wanted to keep doing better. That was one of his great qualities—that he inspired people to want to do their best, and then got them to exceed what they thought were their limitations.

And he always had a plan. It might have taken (or may still take) us years to realize it, but he always saw the big picture, the larger context. Now I can see that he was training me. And I am extremely grateful for that experience—for working with him and helping with his books, and especially for the training to serve his godbrothers after his departure, such as assisting His Holiness Giriraj Swami, and for the incredible loving association that my family and I have gotten from Mahārāja and other of Goswami's godbrothers. All our hope comes from serving them and working together in service to Śrīla Prabhupāda.

One of my sweetest memories of Tamal Krishna was from December 1999. My family and I were in India for six months, and we were in Vṛndāvana for Christmas. Now, Christmas was very important for our children—they were 7, 9, and 12—and Tamal Krishna knew how much it meant to them and how they were giving a lot up that year, especially not receiving gifts. So on Christmas Eve he got together various gifts for them. I heard afterwards that on the way over he was saying, "Do you think Irene will like this? Do you think Jam will like that? Is this okay for Liana?" He was so concerned that they should like his gifts. So, he put them all in a sack and he slung the sack over his back, and he came to our flat in MVT and knocked on the door. "Who could it be?" we exclaimed to our kids. "Ho! Ho! Ho!" we heard from the door. [laughter] And there was Uncle Tamal—that's how they called him, which he liked. He didn't have a beard or long hair, but he came in and played Santa Claus. As soon as he sat down, Irene, the youngest, who always loved to hug him, and whom he loved to hug, ran over and jumped on his lap. And after her, each of the others. "Have you been a good girl this year?" "Have you been a good boy?" He was the best Santa they ever had, and he had presents for everyone. And it was a very, very wonderful Christmas.

I think of him every day. I miss him so much.

Following Goswami Mahārāja

A talk at Tamal Krishna Goswami's Memorial Festival in Carpinteria, California, on June 18, 2006.

Today is a most auspicious occasion, with so many wonderful devotees who are attached to Śrīla Tamal Krishna Goswami gathered here to hear about him, speak about him, and remember him—to learn about him and learn from him.

Yesterday—it seems so long ago—but yesterday, for different reasons, I was really struggling, and in the end I went to the beach. Eventually I got some time alone to chant, which I really needed. And after the first sixteen rounds I started to feel more like myself. As I was thinking about what had happened and what I have to do, I thought of different dear friends who understand me—different aspects of me—in different ways, and help me in different ways. But I was thinking, "Still, there is really no one who understands all of me." And then I thought of Kṛṣṇa: "Oh, yes, that is what Śrīla Prabhupāda always said—'Kṛṣṇa is our best friend. He knows everything about us. He is closer to us than our jugular vein.'" That was one thing Prabhupāda said that I heard when I first joined. "Yes, I should just confide in Kṛṣṇa and depend on Him. Then I will never be disappointed. I will always get the right guidance, and I will be satisfied."

Then I took a step back and thought of Tamal Krishna Goswami. I considered, "Actually, of all the people I have known, he understood me the most completely, in the most different aspects and on the most different levels. There is no one who understands me like he did." And that is *guru*. The *guru* is the external manifestation of the Supersoul, and the Supersoul understands the living entity most intimately and most completely. So, we miss that association. But still, it is a challenge for us now to develop our relationship with Kṛṣṇa more and take more shelter of the devotees—the assembly of devotees—and maybe even express to them more about ourselves so they can understand us better and help us more. And my conclusion from the whole experience was that Tamal Krishna Goswami knew exactly what he wanted and needed and that he arranged for it—and that is something we need to learn.

Listening to the different devotees speak, I had so many memories and realizations. Nṛsiṁhānanda Prabhu mentioned that Tamal Krishna Goswami could be—as was said of Caitanya Mahāprabhu—as hard as a thunderbolt and as soft as a rose. And Bhakta Carl described how he wanted to experience that other side, the "sauce," and felt that those who had were more fortunate. There were many instances when I got the sauce, and I deserved it, but there was one in particular when I felt elated. I didn't always feel elated. In fact, this time stands out because I *did* feel elated.

It was in November of 1977, the last weeks of Śrīla Prabhupāda's manifest presence on earth, and Prabhupāda wanted to form the Bhaktivedanta Swami Charity Trust, to create good relations among the Gauḍīya Vaiṣṇavas, especially the followers of Śrīla Bhaktisiddhānta Sarasvatī Ṭhākura. He wanted to invest some money in the trust so that the trust could finance the completion of different projects in Gauḍa-maṇḍala-bhūmi, and he specifically mentioned some of his godbrothers' projects that they were unable to complete on their own. I was based in Bombay, where I dealt with a lot of Śrīla Prabhupāda's financial and legal affairs. So when I was in Vṛndāvana he sent me with his friend Bhagatji, who was a local devotee, an experienced *vānaprastha*, to Mathurā to register the new trust.

So we went. It was very hot, and the whole situation was very difficult. After hours and hours, we finally returned with the registered document. I brought it to Śrīla Prabhupāda's house and left it there, and then I went to take rest, because I was exhausted. I had a very small room in the Vṛndāvana temple guesthouse. I felt completely drained and wanted to forget the whole experience of dealing with the Indian lawyers and courts and rickshaw drivers and the heat and everything else. So I was lying on my bed, and after about ten minutes I was startled by a loud banging on my door. I thought, "Who could be banging like that?" And there was only one person it could be. [laughter]

So I opened the door, and there was His Holiness Tamal Krishna Goswami. He was furious. He came in and said, "You have made such a blunder! Śrīla Prabhupāda is furious. You have registered the 'Bhaktivedanta Charitable Trust.' That is not the name of the trust. It is the 'Bhaktivedanta Swami Charity Trust.' There could be so many Bhaktivedantas, but there is only one Bhaktivedanta Swami. You blew it." "So, what do I have to do?" I asked. "You have to go to Mathurā tomorrow and redo the whole thing—right."

Apart from feeling chastened by the correction and apprehensive about the next trip into Mathurā, I felt elated. Why? Well, Tamal Krishna Goswami and I were very close. We had become very close friends over the years. His interest was so closely aligned with Śrīla Prabhupāda's that I just tried to be in harmony with the two of them. In my mind my relationship with him and my service to Śrīla Prabhupāda went together. But this incident made it absolutely clear that the center of our relationship was Śrīla Prabhupāda and that when it came to Prabhupāda's service, Goswami Mahārāja would not compromise. He wouldn't be nice to me in a mundane way, for the sake of a mundane friendship, at the expense of Śrīla Prabhupāda's service. And that made me so happy—that our relationship was spiritual. It was based only on Prabhupāda's service. If I made a mistake that was detrimental to Prabhupāda's service, he would let me know in no uncertain terms—and that made me very happy. I had known it, but this incident confirmed it.

Another thing that struck me about Goswami Mahārāja was, in a word, how qualified he was. And hearing different devotees speak about him has expanded my conception of just how qualified he was—his wide range of competence and expertise—and what being qualified actually means. I know that I can never do a fraction of what he could do, but hearing the talks and thinking about how extraordinary he was, I realized that although I can't do anything like what he did, I can learn from him how to give myself fully to the service of the spiritual master and the devotees, which he did. I may not be able to . . . not "may not"—I cannot help them the way he could. I don't have the same capability. But what I can do is learn the spirit of giving myself to the devotees as he did, giving myself to the mission of the spiritual master as he did, even though my personal contribution will be very limited and insignificant compared with his—and realize that we are who we are. I was reminded of an instruction that I received, or felt I received, from our godbrother Sridhar Swami. He said, "Just be yourself and make your contribution." So that is all we can do, and that will please Goswami Mahārāja and Śrīla Prabhupāda.

I always long for the day when I will be back with Śrīla Prabhupāda, and when that fortunate opportunity does come again, I am sure someone else whom we all know will also be there with him. Going back to Śrīla Prabhupāda means Śrīla Prabhupāda with his associates, with his most confidential servants, which includes Tamal Krishna Goswami. Our relationships are eternal. When Śrīla Prabhupāda and Tamal Krishna Goswami were personally present, I always felt that I had a direct relationship with Śrīla Prabhupāda but that at the same time my relationship with Śrīla Prabhupāda was also through Tamal Krishna Goswami. In fact, Goswami Mahārāja helped many devotees approach

Śrīla Prabhupāda. He helped me approach Śrīla Prabhupāda. He helped me to understand Śrīla Prabhupāda. He helped me to understand how to better serve Śrīla Prabhupāda and please Śrīla Prabhupāda. And that will continue. That relationship will continue, and that is encouraging.

Our dear godbrother Bhūrijana Prabhu is an intellectual and an independent, so sometimes he feels a little restless with some of the ways of the institution. Śrīla Prabhupāda had written, "We will have another ISKCON in the spiritual sky," and after Goswami Mahārāja left, Bhūrijana Prabhu commented to me, " 'Another ISKCON in the spiritual world'—with Goswami Mahārāja there, that prospect has suddenly become a little more attractive." [laughter] So, that is the essence of ISKCON: Prabhupāda and Prabhupāda's mission, Prabhupāda's service. And Tamal Krishna Goswami was the most wonderful extension of Śrīla Prabhupāda's mood of love and care, for the devotees and for the world.

Tamal Krishna Goswami was the main executor of Śrīla Prabhupāda's desires—certainly one of the main executors. In the field of practical activity, I would say he was the main one. He embodied Prabhupāda's love and compassion and strictness and fidelity, and he also expanded Prabhupāda's mission in very practical, dynamic, innovative ways. His Holiness Ṛtadhvaja Swami often remarks that there are devotees who can be strict followers but not so creative or imaginative or ingenious and that there are those who can be creative and imaginative and ingenious but not so faithful or strict, but that Tamal Krishna Goswami internally was completely surrendered to Śrīla Prabhupāda and adherent to his core principles but at the same time, like Prabhupāda, was very innovative and imaginative and creative in terms of reaching out to people and offering Kṛṣṇa consciousness to them in ways they could appreciate and accept. It is a great blessing that we had him in our lives, because, like

Śrīla Prabhupāda, he was an extension of Kṛṣṇa in the material world. He was an extension of Śrīla Prabhupāda that we could know intimately and interact with, and he would reciprocate with us and make Kṛṣṇa consciousness more real and practical and approachable—more feasible.

I had so many experiences with Goswami Mahārāja in so many different contexts, there is hardly anything I do now that I haven't already done in some form or another with him, and so I can remember him often. And he was always ahead of me. Shortly after he had his surgery, I had mine. So, he was able to tell me what it meant to undergo surgery and then to recover from it—in detail. And in that context he commented, "I have always stayed a few steps ahead of you."

Ṛtadhvaja Swami: There is that picture of you and him carrying the Deities.

Giriraj Swami: Mahārāja is referring to a well-known picture, a favorite of both Goswami Mahārāja's and mine. He liked it so much that he made copies and gave them to his friends and disciples. It was on Rādhāṣṭamī in Vṛndāvana. As Gauḍīya Vaiṣṇavas—and especially at that time, with what we were studying and learning in Vṛndāvana—we gave more importance to Śrīmatī Rādhārāṇī, to the service of Śrīmatī Rādhārāṇī, and we liked to see Kṛṣṇa in the mood of chasing after Rādhārāṇī. We didn't want Rādhārāṇī chasing after Kṛṣṇa; we wanted Kṛṣṇa chasing after Rādhārāṇī. Of course, Kṛṣṇa is the Supreme Personality of Godhead. Anyway, as it happened, the temple *pūjārīs* had brought small brass deities of Rādhā and Kṛṣṇa into the courtyard and placed them on a swing. There were various talks and cultural presentations related to Rādhāṣṭamī, and afterwards Goswami Mahārāja and I were to carry the deities back to the altar. I don't know how I lucked out, but I got Rādhārāṇī and he got Kṛṣṇa. And I was a little bit ahead, which was just the way he wanted it, and then someone clicked that photo of the two of us, with me a little ahead, carrying Śrīmatī Rādhā-rāṇī. But otherwise, on a more earthly plane, he was always ahead of me, and he was always eager to share with me his experiences and the knowledge he had gained, so that it would be easier for me to follow along after him.

Here is an example of how all these memories can come to mind in different situations: It became a tradition here that on Rādhāṣṭamī we would have a boat festival and take our Deities Gāndharvikā-Giridhārī for a ride on Lake Casitas in Ojai. Now we have learned better—we have the picnic at Mother Urvaśī's house—but that year we had it in a park. And after being out on the boat for three hours, I needed to use the men's room, which, it turned out, was quite far away. Internally, I was really hoping I could get there in time, while at the same time trying to look very dignified and proper. But really I was just hoping I could get there in time. First we had to find an opening in the fence, just to get through, and then we found that the men's and ladies' rooms were way at the other end of the park. Finally I somehow managed to get there, and then I found it was locked, apparently because it was after dark. So it was a crisis. And I didn't know what to do. But there was only one thing to do: head for the bushes. As it was, somehow I was already feeling deep separation from Goswami Mahārāja, and going in the bushes heightened it even more, because it reminded me of all the times on *parikramā* when we would go to the bushes together and try to look very dignified and be inconspicuous about it. That was part of the whole *rasa* of going on *parikramā*. We were so close to each other that one wouldn't go without the other.

So many memories. It is sad that he is not with us now—definitely sad—but we get solace in this association and in these discussions, and in the fact that he was there for us. Now he is there for the whole movement. So many devotees have dreams about him. He is still active, very active. We miss him, but he does manifest his presence. And we have each other. And I think he is very pleased that we have come together today. That was one of the main things he showed at the end—of course, *kīrtana*, hours and hours of *kīrtana*, but also just being together. *Kīrtana* is the best way to be together, and his *kīrtanas* were uniting everyone. And I think that one of the most significant consequences of his departure was how the whole ISKCON family was united as never before. Everyone who had been in Māyāpur, and those who came just after he left, were united in glorifying him. This is an example of how sometimes a Vaiṣṇava does more in separation than in his personal presence, although we miss it. But what he did in his departure by bringing everyone together—and not only bringing them together, which itself was an achievement, but bringing them together to glorify a Vaiṣṇava, which is so important for us to learn to do and to do more often—was unique. And today's event is yet another example; he has brought us all together to appreciate a Vaiṣṇava. We don't all know each other, but he has given us an occasion to come together and remember him and glorify him and in the process rededicate ourselves to Śrīla Prabhupāda and his mission and strengthen our affectionate attachment for each other in Śrīla Prabhupāda's family.

Sridhar Swami

The Heart of ISKCON

A letter written for Sridhar Swami's Vyāsa-pūjā celebration in Mumbai on September 6, 2002.

My dear devotees and friends,

His Holiness Sridhar Swami is my life and soul.

Recently I happened to visit a store in Ojai, California. There on the wall was an original piece of art, a large red heart coming up from a black-and-white-check background. The black and white checks looked exactly like the floor of the Kṛṣṇa-Balarāma temple in Vṛndāvana. And the painting symbolized to me Sridhar Swami's role in and message to ISKCON: *Bhakti* is a process of the heart, a condition of the heart. We need heart. Once, Sridhar Swami told me that ISKCON lacked heart and would never succeed until it had heart. So if we take the checkered backdrop as ISKCON, the heart represents Sridhar Swami, who has put heart into ISKCON. And if we take the checks as the practice of *bhakti* in the temples, such *bhakti* should give rise to a heart full of love and care and humor—as he embodies. He speaks and acts from the heart. And he has touched the hearts of many others, including me.

His Holiness Sridhar Swami has also encouraged me to act and speak from the heart. And since I have tried to follow his instructions I have felt and done better, and when I actually do follow, other people around me also benefit. Thus Sridhar Swami is my *śikṣā-guru* and is in fact worthy of being a *śikṣā-guru* for anyone and all.

So you all are blessed to have the shelter and guidance and love of His Holiness Sridhar Swami.

Sridhar Swami also represents to me the ideal servant of *guru* and Kṛṣṇa. He depends solely on their mercy, and without personal consideration he travels around the world to serve and associate with devotees—simply depending on Śrīla Prabhupāda and Śrī Gaurāṅga Mahāprabhu and Lord Nṛsiṁhadeva. And because of his unfailing trust in them, they never fail in their care for him. Thus he has defied all medical predictions, and served and served and preached and preached without care for personal gain or loss. And thus he embodies the statement of Śrīla Prabhupāda in *Śrīmad-Bhāgavatam*:

"Sometimes a representative of the Lord engaged in preaching work meets various so-called difficulties. But such difficulties are very gladly suffered by the devotee in preaching, because in such activities, although apparently very severe, the devotees of the Lord feel transcendental pleasure because the Lord is satisfied. . . . [Such] pure devotees take up the order of the spiritual master as the sustenance of life. They do not mind what becomes of the future of their lives." (*SB* 2.8.6 purport)

On this occasion I place my head at the lotus feet of His Holiness Sridhar Swami Mahārāja and pray for his mercy, to follow his example. And I embrace him—heart to heart—and pray for his continued friendship and love.

Thank you very much. Hare Kṛṣṇa.

Yours in service to Śrīla Prabhupāda and his beloved servant Sridhar Swami,
Giriraj Swami

Memories of Sridhar Swami

Talks given one and two days after Mahārāja's departure, on March 14 and 15, 2004, in Laguna Beach and Los Angeles.

We have gathered on a most auspicious day, the appearance day of Śrīvāsa Ṭhākura, one of the members of the Pañca-tattva. He lived in Navadvīpa-dhāma in Māyāpur, near the residence of Jagannātha Miśra and Śacīdevī, where Śrī Caitanya Mahāprabhu appeared. Later, when Lord Caitanya began the *saṅkīrtana* movement in Navadvīpa-dhāma, He and His other most confidential associates would meet at Śrīvāsa-aṅgana, the home of Śrīvāsa Ṭhākura, and have *kīrtana* throughout the night. The *kīrtanas* at Śrīvāsa-aṅgana were most ecstatic, and only the most intimate devotees of Śrī Caitanya Mahāprabhu were allowed to enter. In fact, the nocturnal *kīrtanas* at Śrīvāsa-aṅgana in *gaura-līlā* are compared to the *rāsa* dance in *kṛṣṇa-līlā*.

In his identity in *kṛṣṇa-līlā*, Śrīvāsa Paṇḍita is Nārada Muni, the great preacher who travels throughout the universe chanting the holy names of Kṛṣṇa and enlightening the fallen souls in Kṛṣṇa consciousness. So it is most auspicious that His Holiness Sridhar Swami Mahārāja has left on Śrīvāsa Ṭhākura's appearance day—this most auspicious day—in Śrī Māyāpur-dhāma—that most auspicious place.

We now have a special opportunity and responsibility to honor and glorify His Holiness Sridhar Swami Mahārāja.

My own association with His Holiness Sridhar Swami goes back to Bombay, over thirty years ago. Śrīla Prabhupāda had requested disciples from America to come to India to help him there, and in particular with his three main projects—Bombay, Māyāpur, and Vṛndāvana. From 1972, His Holiness Sridhar

Swami Mahārāja served Śrīla Prabhupāda in India, mainly in Bombay.

When we got permission from the municipality to build on Hare Krishna Land in Juhu, Bombay, Śrīla Prabhupāda wanted Sridhar Mahārāja to take charge of the construction materials. Sridhar Mahārāja had a hefty build, like a football player, so Śrīla Prabhupāda thought he would be appropriate to keep track of the construction material and make sure none of it was stolen. But Sridhar Mahārāja (then a *brahmacārī*) said that he didn't want to look after the construction material; he wanted to preach. I was the temple president in Bombay, so I was going back and forth between Śrīla Prabhupāda and Sridhar Mahārāja. Śrīla Prabhupāda again said he should look after the construction materials, so I went back to deliver the message to him, but Sridhar Mahārāja insisted, "I want to preach!"

Mahārāja had never really preached much in India before then, and we didn't know how well he could preach to the aristocratic Indian gentlemen we were mainly approaching at that time. But he was so sincere in his desire to preach that he became one of the best preachers in India, and one of the best preachers in the world. This story illustrates Mahārāja's sincere desire to preach, and his strong determination to serve Śrīla Prabhupāda and the mission even in ways that may not have been easy for him.

In India, Śrīla Prabhupāda had introduced the life membership program. And he actually based the society's progress there on the membership program. He said that making someone a life member was almost as good as making him into a devotee. He also said that he introduced the life membership program as a way to distribute his books, because if someone became a life member by paying a certain subscription, he would get a set of Śrīla Prabhupāda's books and a subscription to *Back to Godhead* magazine.

Eventually, Sridhar Swami led one of the life membership teams in Bombay. I was the membership director, and the other leaders of teams were Sridhar Swami, Lokanath Swami, Jagat-puruṣa Prabhu, and Haridāsa Prabhu (who since then has become a producer of Kṛṣṇa conscious television programs). Those were our main teams. In the early 1980s, Sridhar Mahārāja became the Juhu temple president, and so he increasingly joined me in cultivating the most important people in Bombay. And between 1984 and 1990, when I was unable to return to India because of visa problems, Sridhar Mahārāja deepened his relationship with many of our most important members, and they really came to love him deeply.

Later, in about 1991, Sridhar Mahārāja began BHISMA, a fund-raising-by-mail program in Juhu. Many devotees criticized the proposed program, saying it would never work. To prepare the letters and post them would cost more than two lakhs rupees (Rs. 2,00,000/-), and where was the guarantee that we would ever get the money back? Yet in spite of all the negativity, Mahārāja took the risk. (Śrīla Prabhupāda had said, "To preach means to take risks.") So Sridhar Mahārāja took the risk, and the experiment proved to be successful. The first effort itself made money, and subsequent mailings proved even more profitable. Soon, Mahārāja received invitations from centers in India and abroad to help them organize fund-raising-by-mail campaigns, and the campaigns proved to be successful everywhere. They became one of the most reliable sources of income many temples had. Even today, the BHISMA office started by Sridhar Mahārāja raises funds for the Juhu temple by mail.

More recently, Sridhar Mahārāja started the Vedic Academy of Spiritual Technology (VAST). This pioneering program uses the latest multi-media methods to teach the corporate sector stress management and time management—all in relation to Kṛṣṇa consciousness. Mahārāja always tried to find innovative ways to present Kṛṣṇa consciousness. He studied experts in various fields and applied what he learned to Kṛṣṇa consciousness.

Many of my most vivid memories of Mahārāja, and of his good influence on me and on others, are from the last few years. You may know that in 1977, some months before he left this world, Śrīla Prabhupāda named eleven disciples to initiate devotees on his behalf while he was still here. Then, after he left, the same disciples continued to initiate. Later, slowly, a few more were given that responsibility, beginning with three others. Sridhar Mahārāja was not one of the first to initiate, or even one of the early ones to be added later. The attitude of the movement then was quite restrictive. So at one stage, he joked that he wanted only three disciples—one to cook, one to do his laundry, and one to collect for him.

Eventually, Sridhar Mahārāja was given the responsibility to initiate disciples, and he took his duty very seriously. He was very sincere. Mahārāja initiated one of his earliest disciples, a devotee from Croatia, in his first initiation ceremony at Juhu. Mahārāja named him "Māyāpur dāsa" and instructed him to be a servant of Māyāpur. Even up to the end, Mahārāja was very sincere in his duties to his disciples and in his care and affection for them. He really cared for them, and he loved them very much. At the same time, he cared for devotees and people in general, and I think this is one of his most remarkable traits: his almost universal care for others. He really was like an ocean of love.

In Kārtika of 1999, Sridhar Mahārāja and I met in Vṛndāvana. One morning we went to the Bhaktivedanta Ashram at Govardhana, where I was to meet His Holiness Indradyumna Swami and choose a Govardhana *śilā* to worship. Indradyumna Mahārāja placed two *śilās* next to each other on his shelf and asked, "Who do these look like?" They looked like Rādhā and Kṛṣṇa, and so I accepted them. Then Indradyumna

Swami gave me his deity of Gopīśvara Mahādeva, and he gave Sridhar Mahārāja *śilās* of Lord Nṛsiṁhadeva and Varāhadeva. Earlier, Indradyumna Swami had told Sridhar Mahārāja, "I will have something for you when you come to Govardhana." Sridhar Swami was a great devotee of Lord Nṛsiṁhadeva.

The next day, Indradyumna Swami took Sridhar Mahārāja and me to Loi Bazar in downtown Vṛndāvana to get paraphernalia for our worship. We spent most of the day in various shops, looking for just the right items for the deities' service and bargaining with the merchants. Finally, we became satisfied that we had done the best we could for our worshipable Lords—and besides, we all were hungry—and so we returned to the Kṛṣṇa-Balarāma Mandira.

During the same stay in Vṛndāvana, Sridhar Mahārāja and I did Govardhana *parikramā* together, followed by a group of devotees. We had wonderful *kṛṣṇa-kathā* all around Govardhana Hill. Although we both were ill, we did the full *parikramā* barefoot in the hot sun, and only afterward did we take *prasāda* at the Bhaktivedanta Ashram.

Within a month, we both were in the hospital—he in a coma, with encephalopathy from hepatitis C, and me on the verge of a heart attack, about to have cardiac bypass surgery. Later, Mahārāja praised the power of that *parikramā*—that it put us both in the hospital so quickly. He told me, "The only reason I went all the way around was to keep up with you." I replied, "But, Mahārāja, the only reason I went all the way around was to keep up with you!" Such was our relationship, and such is the mercy of Giri Govardhana.

Anyway, two years earlier, Sridhar Mahārāja had been diagnosed with hepatitis C and cirrhosis of the liver, a severe condition that is usually, in the course of time, fatal. After Kārtika, Mahārāja's condition deteriorated, and some liquid, called ascites, accumulated in his abdominal cavity—nearly twenty or twenty-five liters of fluid, which caused massive swelling in his legs as well. So he returned to Bombay for tests and treatment.

In Bombay, Mahārāja was admitted in the Bhaktivedanta Hospital at Mira Road, which is run and staffed mainly by devotees. There, Mahārāja had a further reversal, and he went into a coma. Soon, His Holiness Tamal Krishna Goswami and some of Goswami Mahārāja's close friends—Giridhari Swami and Keśava Bhāratī Mahārāja—came from Vṛndāvana to Bombay to meet Sridhar Mahārāja in the hospital. Mahārāja was so grateful to them for coming all the way from Vṛndāvana just to be with him, and their visit had a very deep effect on him. From then on, one of the main themes in his life was how much he appreciated his godbrothers, how much he wanted their association. He would say, "My godbrothers are my life," and he felt, as a humble Vaiṣṇava, dependent on them. Even at the end, when he was in Canada, just before he left for Māyāpur, he was asking different godbrothers, "Please help me. Help me to chant the holy name." He was very, very humble.

Eventually, Sridhar Mahārāja was discharged from the hospital, but his condition remained delicate. Many devotees suggested that he return to Vṛndāvana and spend his last days there, hearing and chanting about Kṛṣṇa. Again, he was so sincere that he accepted the advice of his godbrothers and well-wishers. But soon he felt, "This is not me, just to sit and chant and hear in Vṛndāvana." Again he came to the same point: "I want to preach." So, Mahārāja stayed in Haridāsa Prabhu's vacant flat at Mira Road, and he would meet devotees and friends—and preach.

In April of 2000 Mahārāja was again admitted into the Bhaktivedanta Hospital in an early stage of hepatic coma. Later, he had difficulty breathing and actually felt that he might leave his body then. But he recovered from the crisis, and soon he got the idea that he would like to travel again. And he was adamant.

To travel then, from the medical point of view, was a doubtful decision, but Mahārāja was determined. His first stop was to be Carpinteria, where I have a small ashram. He wanted to visit, to spend some time with me, and to rest and recuperate. Thus, in May of 2000, he and his very faithful and wonderful servant, Māyāpur dāsa, somehow got on a plane and reached Los Angeles. From the Los Angeles airport they came straight by car to Carpinteria, but by the time he reached the ashram, he was in a terrible condition. We were shocked. Already he had been terribly sick, but then he had caught the flu before leaving Bombay—although the symptoms hadn't manifested until he had reached Hong Kong. Some devotees said that he shouldn't have traveled at all—that he was too sick—and that the disease was affecting his discrimination. But in retrospect, I see his traveling in spite of his illness as his love and his desire to serve and preach. And sometimes I take it that he risked his life just to come and visit me.

So he came, and we spent some time together. He was on a very strict diet that he didn't much like, and he would cheat a little now and then. One night I went out to a preaching program. Although he wasn't well enough to come, he encouraged me to go. So we left him in the care of Māyāpur dāsa and Kuntīdevī dāsī, who could cook in case he needed anything. After I left, he decided that he wanted to indulge himself a little; he asked for veggie burgers and French fries, which were not at all on his diet. Kuntī dutifully prepared the veggie burgers and chips, and Māyāpur reluctantly served them. Mahārāja ate them, and he was in very jolly spirits.

In Bombay we had two highly aristocratic life members, very affluent yet very devoted—Mr. Brijratan Mohatta and Mr. M. P. Maheshwari. Every Sunday, they and their wives would come to Juhu. Out of their deep affection for Mahārāja, these two gentlemen began to call him "the jolly swami" because, well, he was always so jolly. The name stuck, and a few years ago, Mahārāja's brother Stuart actually wrote an article about him called "The Jolly Swami." It was a nice article and was published in a magazine in Canada. Recently, this nickname became even more popular—and deservedly so—because Mahārāja remained so jolly even up to the time of death.

So, happily enjoying Kuntīdevī's tasty burgers and chips, "the jolly swami" was in a very jolly mood indeed. The next morning, however, he wasn't quite so jolly—or at least he didn't manifest his mood. In fact, he wouldn't get up. We thought, "He must be exhausted." Time passed, and still he wouldn't get up. We waited, tried again, waited, and tried again. Finally, we realized he was in a coma, so we rushed him to the hospital, to the emergency room. He was eventually put in the intensive care unit. (Later, Mahārāja would joke, "I want to come to Carpinteria and have some more of Kuntī's 'coma burgers'!")

Physiologically, there was a certain course to be run, and the doctors were confident that he would come out of the coma. It just had to be treated in the proper way and the condition would reverse itself.

Again, in the hospital, Sridhar Mahārāja's great affection and care became evident. Because of the liver's malfunction, it wasn't able to take out the toxins—that was the basic problem. And eventually the toxins go to the brain and cause encephalopathy. If the toxins in the brain reach a certain level, the patient goes into a coma. Then the process of coming out of the coma and toxic influence is gradual. In a way, you could say that at first Mahārāja was sort of delirious. But the beauty of his delirium was that his goodness came out freely: He just wanted everyone to chant. He wanted everyone to become Kṛṣṇa conscious—the doctors, the nurses, the nurses' assistants, the room cleaners. He really just wanted everyone to become Kṛṣṇa conscious.

And then, too, he would think of his brothers in Canada. He really wanted them, Malcolm and Stuart, to become devotees. He would talk to us about them, not completely coherently, but with great love and care. And he would talk with them, as well as with his mother and sister (who were also in Canada), on the phone. He saw some spark in them that he wanted to fan. He really wanted them to become devotees.

When the crisis began, we informed his family. His sister Fiona was just wonderful—so helpful and responsible. And eventually his brother Malcolm came down and stayed with Mahārāja and us for a while. Also, Hridayānanda Mahārāja visited Mahārāja in the hospital. And again, Sridhar Mahārāja was so appreciative. The two of them joked a lot, and soon Sridhar Mahārāja was discharged and came back to our ashram. Despite his trying medical condition, he really was "the jolly swami," so friendly to the nurses and staff and everyone.

(After some days, the bill from the hospital came—for almost $30,000. Mahārāja studied it carefully. Finally, he concluded: "I want my money. They can take back my consciousness!")

From then on, despite his hepatitis, he would travel a lot, sort of like Prabhupāda—more or less six months in India, based in Bombay, and six months traveling. He would visit London and Croatia and Slovenia, and he would always attend the New York Ratha-yātrā. He made a point always to go to the New York Ratha-yātrā. And he would regularly visit Alachua, Los Angeles, Vancouver, and even Brazil. He had many disciples in Croatia and Slovenia. Many of the young people there became initiated by him.

In September of 2001, His Holiness Sridhar Swami, accompanied by Nṛsiṁhānanda Prabhu of ITV, came to Carpinteria for my Vyāsa-pūjā. There he said: "For me, in my stage of life, if I have learned even one little lesson, it is *dāsa-dāsānudāsaḥ*.

Cultivate service to the Vaiṣṇavas and you will get everything. We need a family in which we can love and trust each other and not fear. We have to preach to so many materialistic people. Their very aura is permeated with lust and greed and anger, and there is a possibility of getting infected. But if we can come back to a community of friends, of brothers and sisters, where we love each other and care—not superficially saying something, but really caring deep down inside that this person is suffering and care, even materially—we will be protected. Prabhupāda cried when he saw people suffering materially in the material world. So what to speak of exalted Vaiṣṇava devotees—we should care for them and love them. This is our family."

January 14, 2003, marked the twenty-fifth anniversary of the grand opening of the Juhu temple, and Sridhar Mahārāja took the lead in arranging the silver jubilee celebrations. He wanted every devotee who had ever served in Juhu, especially in the time leading up to the grand opening—which was basically when Śrīla Prabhupāda was personally present—he wanted every one of them to come. The Juhu temple had a modest budget to help devotees with their airfares, but eventually another very nice devotee in Bombay, Kṛṣṇacandra Prabhu (Hrishikesh Mafatlal), gave several lakhs of rupees to pay for devotees' tickets. Any Prabhupāda disciple who had served in Bombay, Sridhar Swami tracked down. He phoned and personally requested him or her to come and then offered free tickets as required.

So many came, and the reports of that event were extraordinary. People couldn't believe it. Everyone there felt that Śrīla Prabhupāda had manifested himself again. Even His Holiness Śacīnandana Swami, who hadn't served in Bombay earlier but who happened to be there for the celebrations, said that he felt Śrīla Prabhupāda's presence descend in a very tangible way. And everyone gave the credit to Sridhar Swami. He deserved the credit because he got so many devotees to come, and he made wonderful arrangements for them—with help, of course, from devotees from Chowpatty and Juhu. And when it was time for the devotees to give their remembrances of the early days of serving Śrīla Prabhupāda in Bombay, he wouldn't allow the *gurus* and *sannyāsīs* to speak. He said, "We hear them all the time; we want to hear others." Of course, they also spoke, but mainly he wanted to give others the chance to speak. He really was *paṇḍitāḥ sama-darśinaḥ*; he really saw everyone equally. He truly saw the soul, and he appreciated everyone. He appreciated everyone's good, and he wanted to encourage everyone.

Anyway, it was a wonderful event. Once, I phoned, just to be part of the celebrations, and the receptionist in the guest-house in Juhu picked up the phone. I asked for Mahārāja, but he didn't happen to be right there, and it was going to take time to find him. They were going to look for him. In the meantime I asked, "Who else is there?" Just then, Jagat-puruṣa Prabhu was walking by. I said, "Okay, I'll speak to him." Jagat-puruṣa was in high ecstasy. *He* wasn't speaking; the ecstasy within him was moving him to speak. And he said that he had not experienced such bliss in Kṛṣṇa consciousness since the time he was actually in Bombay serving Śrīla Prabhupāda. He just went on and on, emphasizing that it was the most memorable occasion of his life, and I think everyone felt pretty much the same way, because they felt Śrīla Prabhupāda's presence. What more do any of us want? For us, the highest perfection is to be with Śrīla Prabhupāda, and Sridhar Swami, I feel, was instrumental in creating that situation in which Śrīla Prabhupāda was pleased to manifest himself in such a vivid and personal way.

After a few days of recuperating from that major effort, Mahārāja wanted to travel again, so he came to Los Angeles. That time his schedule didn't allow him to come to Carpinteria. Also, I think he was a little upset because I hadn't come for the celebrations in Juhu, so he didn't want to come to me. I went to him, and he was wonderful—as usual. After Los Angeles he went to Vancouver. While he was there, I began to consider that I had offended him because I hadn't gone for the celebrations in Juhu. I don't think I could have gone, but at the same time I was concerned that I had offended him. So I phoned him in Vancouver to apologize and explain why I couldn't come, even though he (and many others) had so much wanted me to participate. I asked him to forgive me. He was very gracious. He was sorry I hadn't come, and he did want to understand why I hadn't. But he said I hadn't committed any offense or anything.

So, we would frequently talk on the phone, and we would meet whenever he came to Los Angeles. Then, last November, he phoned from Bombay and told me he was planning to go to Vancouver in April for four to six months. I replied, "I will definitely come and spend time with you there." Soon thereafter, however, I got an e-mail from him saying that he had been diagnosed in Bombay with liver cancer and that he was going to Vancouver immediately to see if he could get a liver transplant, which was his "only hope."

He flew to Vancouver. The first day he went for tests, they found three places where cancer had affected his liver, which prima facie made him eligible for the transplant. But they still had to do more tests. When they did the next tests, however, they found more cancer—and because the cancer had spread beyond the limit allowed for transplants, his "only hope" was dashed. He was ineligible for the transplant because the cancer had spread so much. So it seemed like he was soon to leave his body.

I was very distressed. I phoned him, but he wasn't answering on his landline. I then got him on his cell phone. I asked, "Where are you?" He answered, "I'm shopping." He seemed so jolly—like always. But then he confirmed my worst fears: "The doctor says that I could go at any time. Phone me back later. We have to talk."

After that, we would speak every day, usually twice a day. And we had wonderful talks. The question arose whether he should go to Māyāpur—and when. He decided he *would* go to Māyāpur, and eventually, in consultation with his godbrothers, he concluded that he should go as soon as possible.

He had three desires, as he told me: "I just want to survive until I reach Māyāpur. Then, if possible, I want to live to see the Pañca-tattva installed. And then, if possible, I want to live until Gaura-pūrṇimā. And then—whatever." (He meant, of course, "And then—whatever Kṛṣṇa wants.")

With these three desires in his heart, although no one knew how much travel his weakened body could bear, Sridhar Mahārāja flew to London. There Indradyumna Swami joined him. (Mahārāja's sister, Fiona, had informed Indradyumna Swami of the doctor's pronouncement: If Sridhar undertook the journey, he probably wouldn't make it. And she added, "If that happens, I want someone to be there with him.") So Indradyumna Swami flew to England to accompany Mahārāja onward towards Māyāpur, and he was very apprehensive.

In London, devotees had rented a room for Mahārāja in a hotel near the airport. He was so sick and weak that he could hardly walk. The devotees just had to get him from the airport to the nearest place possible—as soon as possible.

Because the news had spread that Mahārāja was going to Māyāpur to leave his body, many of his disciples from Europe—mainly from Croatia and Slovenia—came to London to meet him. They were crying because they knew they would never see him again. He told them, "You can cry when I go. You can cry for a few days, but then you have to get back into your service, and then you have to be happy."

Mahārāja wanted to reciprocate with the disciples who had come to be with him. He said, "The king is good for the people, and the people are good for the king. I never had my own family, but when I had disciples, I was able to benefit tremendously. I felt emotions I thought I never would. I just don't think it will stop. When we love one another, we are together. Of course, when I leave, we can't play football [soccer] together. But I can come along in the form of a picture." It was so bittersweet. Mahārāja was so sweet and so humorous. Yet his disciples were feeling, "We will never see Guru Mahārāja again. We're going to take his picture with us when we play football."

Then he told his disciples, "When I leave, we can be together in more significant ways." He said that love in separation is actually stronger. And we do experience that when we are with people we love, we may take them for granted. But when they are gone, we realize how valuable their association was and how much we loved and still love them. And the feelings become more intense than when we were with them.

There were some disciples who didn't have second initiation, so Mahārāja decided he would initiate them. But because of his disease, his brain didn't always function properly. Toxins went to his brain, and then, too, he had to take a derivative of opium to kill the pain, as prescribed by the doctor. Anyway, he decided, "Okay, I'll give second initiation—but all together, all four at once." He began reciting the Gāyatrī *mantra* for them, "*Oṁ bhūr* . . ."—but then he couldn't remember the next word. He asked Indradyumna Swami, "What comes next?" Indradyumna Swami pronounced the word, and Mahārāja repeated it to his disciples. When Mahārāja couldn't remember the next word either, he told Indradyumna Swami, "Look, why don't you just say each word, and then I'll repeat it, and the disciples will hear it from me." So they got through the first two lines. Then Indradyumna Swami, who himself was exhausted from his long flight from South Africa, couldn't remember the next word. So Sridhar Mahārāja asked, "Are there any *brāhmaṇas* in the house who know the next word?" Then one *brāhmaṇa* told the word to

Indradyumna Swami, Indradyumna Swami repeated it to Sridhar Swami, and Sridhar Swami repeated it to the disciples.

Sridhar Mahārāja remarked, "*Harer nāma harer nāma harer nāmaiva kevalam.* We don't need this Gāyatrī *mantra. Hari-nāma* is enough." Then he started quoting:

harer nāma harer nāma
harer nāmaiva kevalam
kalau nāsty eva nāsty eva
nāsty eva gatir anyathā

["In this age of quarrel and hypocrisy the only means of deliverance is the chanting of the holy names of the Lord. There is no other way. There is no other way. There is no other way." (*BnP* 38.126)]

kṛṣṇa-varṇaṁ tviṣākṛṣṇaṁ
sāṅgopāṅgāstra-pārṣadam
yajñaiḥ saṅkīrtana-prāyair
yajanti hi su-medhasaḥ

["In the Age of Kali, intelligent persons perform congregational chanting to worship the incarnation of Godhead who constantly sings the name of Kṛṣṇa. Although His complexion is not blackish, He is Kṛṣṇa Himself. He is accompanied by His associates, servants, weapons, and confidential companions." (*SB* 11.5.32)]

kaler doṣa-nidhe rājan
asti hy eko mahān guṇaḥ
kīrtanād eva kṛṣṇasya
mukta-saṅgaḥ paraṁ vrajet

["My dear King, although Kali-yuga is an ocean of faults, there is still one good quality about this age: Simply by chanting the Hare Kṛṣṇa *mahā-mantra*, one can become free from material bondage and be promoted to the transcendental kingdom." (*SB* 12.3.51)]

He quoted all these verses in glorification of the holy name. Indradyumna Swami exclaimed, "Mahārāja, you are perfectly quoting all these verses about the holy name, but you can't remember the Gāyatrī *mantra*?!" Sridhar Swami explained, "The Gāyatrī *mantra* is just meant to assist us in chanting the holy name. The real thing is chanting the holy name. The Gāyatrī *mantra* just supports it—helps us to become purified—so we can chant the holy name."

You may have heard how Mahārāja arrived in Calcutta. Jayapatākā Mahārāja had sent his van to pick him up, and Sridhar Swami lay unmoving in Jayapatākā Mahārāja's bed in the van all the way from the airport to Māyāpur. In Māyāpur, thousands of devotees came out to receive him with *kīrtana*—sometimes roaring and sometimes soft and sweet.

Now, because Mahārāja's diseased liver wasn't processing different materials in the body, his body again filled with liquid and became bloated. In Canada, as well as in India, doctors would remove five to seven liters of liquid from him at a time. That was part of his discomfort. Anyway, after the installation of the Pañca-tattva, he had a physical setback, maybe because of the exertion and excitement in the ceremony. The situation looked grave, and in the evening he asked for devotees to come and do *kīrtana* in his room. He didn't know what would happen, and it looked like he was going to leave. Mahārāja's servant, Māyāpur dāsa, informed the devotees. So devotees came. Senior devotees and disciples alike gathered in Mahārāja's room, ready for the worst. As Mahārāja lay silently on his bed, they performed *kīrtana*, most of them crying, seeing that the end was near. Somehow a devotee managed to call a doctor, who entered the room and came to Mahārāja's bedside. The doctor was serious and grave, and he began to feel around Mahārāja's body as Mahārāja lay motionless on his bed, his eyes closed. Mahārāja's abdomen was completely bloated from the accumulated liquid. The doctor put his hands on Mahārāja's abdomen, squeezing it gently to assess the situation. Then Mahārāja slowly opened his eyes, looked in the direction of the doctor, and said, "It's a boy."

Everybody cracked up. Mahārāja was so funny, even in the most dire of circumstances. The devotees were going mad; they didn't know whether to laugh or cry. The situation was so critical, yet Mahārāja was so funny. Anyway, Mahārāja told me that story on the phone—I think he rather liked it.

So, *jīvo vā maro vā*: a devotee can live or die. Both are the same. Certainly that was true of Sridhar Swami: He could live or die, because if he lived he would serve Kṛṣṇa here, and if he died he would serve Kṛṣṇa in the next life. For Sridhar Swami, life and death were the same (*jīvo vā maro vā*). Thus, he was truly fearless and jolly. He really had no fear of death. Although he wanted to stay so he could preach, he wasn't afraid of death. He knew he would continue to serve Śrīla Prabhupāda in the next life.

A few days before Gaura-pūrṇimā, Indradyumna Swami came to say farewell to Mahārāja. At Mahārāja's room he met Māyāpur dāsa, who told him, "Mahārāja is in the shower." From inside, Sridhar Swami overheard the talk and shouted out, "Indie! Is that you, Indie?" He used to call Indradyumna Swami "Indie," short for Indiana Jones, because Indradyumna Mahārāja is such an adventurous preacher. (Later Indradyumna Swami remarked what a wonderful experience this was: When someone really loves you and is proud of you, he shows you off to his friends. In this way, Sridhar Mahārāja would show off Indradyumna Swami to people who came to his room. He would say, "This is our Indiana Jones, but he is the real thing! This one is the real thing!")

So, Sridhar Mahārāja called out, "Indie! Is that you out there?"

"Yes, Mahārāja."

"Come on in!"

"But Mahārāja, you are in the shower."

"So what? Come on in."

He went in, and there was Mahārāja with nothing to cover him but the air (and water from the shower). Sridhar Mahārāja said, "Don't worry about it. We are not these bodies!"

Indradyumna Swami was choked up, because he was feeling he would never see Mahārāja again. This was it—saying good-bye. So he said, "Mahārāja, I have come to say good-bye." Mahārāja said, "Don't say good-bye." Indradyumna Swami replied, "I may never see you again in this life." Sridhar Swami responded, "Don't you know that old song?" And he sang: "Happy trails to you, until we meet again." And that was it.

So I think that is a good conclusion, especially for Indradyumna Swami: "happy trails"—because his trails take him all over the world. Yet all of us, in our own ways, have our own trails and paths in devotional service, and Sridhar Swami wishes that they be happy—until we meet again.

I wanted to phone Mahārāja every day, but the way it worked out with the time difference and all the difficulties in just getting through to Māyāpur, it averaged about every third day that I would speak to him. The last time I spoke to him, two days before he left, he was having a very good day. The previous day had been a bad one, but the night before, they had given him some additional medication. So when I spoke to him that last time, he was having a very good day, and we had one of the best talks I have ever had with anyone in my entire life. We spoke mainly about the Māyāpur project and Śrīla Prabhupāda's mission. It's really something that I'll cherish for my whole life—the experience of it and the lessons it contained.

That was Thursday, March 11. The next day, Friday, we installed beautiful brass deities of Gaura-Nitāi in our Carpinteria ashram. They had come from Vṛndāvana, originally commissioned by Mother Kīrtidā for Tamal Krishna Goswami. I felt that Their coming was also part of Sridhar Swami's mercy, because he so fervently desired that the glories of the Pañca-tattva be spread and that we build the great temple for Them in Māyāpur. So, two representatives of the Pañca-tattva had come, and I felt that Their arrival was his desire.

On Thursday I had told Mahārāja, "I don't know if I will be able to phone you again before then, but the deities have come and we will install them Friday evening, and by your mercy we'll try to serve Them and Their *dhāma*." And now, whenever I look at Their beautiful forms and Their appealing faces, I feel that we have to do something for Them—we have to build Their wonderful temple, as Sridhar Swami always reminded me.

I think this may be Mahārāja's main contribution in recent years, at least to me in my service: He impressed upon me—and upon our entire movement—the importance of the Māyāpur project, of the "wonderful temple" (*adbhuta mandira*) that Nityānanda Prabhu had desired for the service of Caitanya Mahāprabhu, and that Bhaktivinoda Ṭhākura had envisioned. (One day, when Śrīla Bhaktivinoda Ṭhākura was chanting *japa* on the balcony of his house in Godruma-dvīpa, he looked across the Jalāṅgī River to Māyāpur, and he had a vision of a transcendental city with a magnificent temple rising like a mountain in its midst.) Mahārāja's whole life was dedicated to Śrīla Prabhupāda, and I think he felt that this was one of Śrīla Prabhupāda's main desires left to be fulfilled. And he felt that *we* had to do it—and that we *had* to do it; it would benefit the whole society, and the whole world. He would quote Ambarīṣa Prabhu: "This will be the tide that will make all the boats rise." So, although Sridhar Mahārāja left so many wonderful legacies for us in terms of his personal qualities and activities, I think one legacy that may serve to unite the movement and fulfill one of Śrīla Prabhupāda's main desires is his inspiration to push on the construction of the great temple in Māyāpur.

When I was a new devotee, maybe less than two years in

the movement, I approached Śrīla Prabhupāda one day while he was getting his massage on the veranda of the Calcutta temple. "Śrīla Prabhupāda," I said, "I have been thinking about what pleases you most." Śrīla Prabhupāda was so pure he took every word into his heart. He replied, "Yes." I said, "The two things that seem to please you the most are distributing your books and building the big temple in Māyāpur." Śrīla Prabhupāda smiled with great appreciation and said, "Thank you very much."

So, those were Śrīla Prabhupāda's two main strategies for spreading Kṛṣṇa consciousness, and Sridhar Swami helped him in both. In his early days, Sridhar Swami was instrumental in developing book distribution in North America. And in his later years, he was very involved with the Māyāpur project, planning and raising funds for the great temple. And by Mahārāja's mercy, on Gaura-pūrṇimā, standing in front of the Pañca-tattva deities in Laguna Beach, I got the inspiration: "Now it's time for Māyāpur. Sridhar Swami understood that long ago. Now it's time for you [me] to join the effort, too." And that was important for me in other ways as well—to let go of the past: "Forgive and forget. Now let's all work together for Māyāpur, for Sridhar Swami, for Śrīla Prabhupāda, to build the wonderful temple."

When I asked Sridhar Swami how I could help, he requested me to speak about my experiences of Śrīla Prabhupāda related to Māyāpur. So, in 1973, when Śrīla Prabhupāda came to Calcutta from England, he was very excited and enthusiastic about Māyāpur. Tamal Krishna Goswami had gotten the first land, we had observed the first Gaura-pūrṇimā festival there, and now Śrīla Prabhupāda had come with the plans for the first building. There was a detailed discussion, but at the end Śrīla Prabhupāda said, "If you build this temple, then Śrīla Bhaktivinoda Ṭhākura will personally come and take you all back to Godhead."

Now I think, "That might be my only hope, so I'd better get to work. We'd better build the Māyāpur project, because I don't know how else I will ever get back to Godhead."

His Holiness Sridhar Swami has given me a lifetime of work in service to Śrīla Prabhupāda. Although *jīvo vā maro vā*, to live or die is the same for a devotee—and certainly that was true of Mahārāja—my own feelings are mixed. I think, "Now he has left so much service for me, given me so many instructions." (I think the same about Tamal Krishna Goswami.) "So I must stay and execute his mission." Even though part of me misses them terribly and wants to be with them, mainly I think, "They left me so many instructions. I have so much service to do for them here."

Of course, how long we have to do what they have asked, what they would want, all depends on Kṛṣṇa. Therefore, whatever time we do have left we should use in the best possible way—in Kṛṣṇa consciousness.

* * *

EPILOGUE

Three days after Sridhar Mahārāja left, while on my daily walk, in Santa Barbara, I suddenly began to feel blissful, and I felt Mahārāja's presence. Then I felt that he gave me two instructions. The first was "I am still here. Be happy." And the second was "Just be yourself. Each one of us has his own contribution to make, so just be yourself and make *your* contribution." And then he left.

After he left, I considered what had happened. Clearly, his two instructions were meant not only for me. They were meant for everyone. And his instructions covered all points. Especially his last statement had said it all: "Just be yourself and make *your* contribution."

Thank you, Mahārāja. We love you.

The Blessings of the Spiritual Master

A letter to Sridhar Swami on the occasion of his samādhi *dedication in Māyāpur on March 6, 2005.*

brahma-bhūtaḥ prasannātmā
na śocati na kāṅkṣati
samaḥ sarveṣu bhūteṣu
mad-bhaktiṁ labhate parām

"One who is thus transcendentally situated at once realizes the Supreme Brahman and becomes fully joyful. He never laments or desires to have anything. He is equally disposed toward every living entity. In that state he attains pure devotional service unto Me."

—*Bhagavad-gītā* 18.54

My dear brother Sridhar Swami Mahārāja,

I feel so much separation today. What can I say? Now Mrs. Singhal, Śrīla Prabhupāda's beloved daughter and our affectionate mother, has also left us here. Somehow her departure has served to awaken my feelings of separation from you, from His Holiness Tamal Krishna Goswami, and ultimately from our Śrīla Prabhupāda.

We all shared so much together, especially the struggles at Hare Krishna Land—to get the land, to build the temple, to use the facilities as Śrīla Prabhupāda would have wanted, according to his standards and priorities and mood.

We relished those struggles, because in them we came close to Śrīla Prabhupāda, and close to each other. We came close, in fact, to pure love. And we knew that in the end Śrīla Prabhupāda and Śrī Śrī Rādhā-Rāsabihārī would be pleased, however successful we might or might not have been by external standards, by our effort to serve them—by their grace.

As Sāndīpani Muni told his disciples Kṛṣṇa and Sudāmā: "My dear boys, it is very wonderful that you have suffered so much trouble for me. Everyone likes to take care of his body as the first consideration, but you are so good and faithful to your *guru* that without caring for bodily comforts you have taken so much trouble for me. I am glad to see that bona fide students like you will undergo any kind of trouble for the satisfaction of the spiritual master. That is the way for a bona fide disciple to become free from his debt to the spiritual master. It is the duty of the disciple to dedicate his life to the service of the spiritual master. My dear best of the twice-born, I am greatly pleased by your acts, and I bless you: May all your desires and ambitions be fulfilled." (*Kṛṣṇa*, Chapter 80)

And as Lord Kṛṣṇa told His old friend Sudāmā: "If a man is sufficiently educated in student life under the guidance of a proper teacher, his life becomes successful in the future. He can very easily cross over the ocean of nescience, and he is not subject to the influence of the illusory energy. . . . As the Supersoul of the living entities, I sit in everyone's heart and observe everyone's activity in every stage and order of life. Regardless of which stage one is in, when I see that one is engaged seriously and sincerely in discharging the duties ordered by the spiritual master and is thus dedicating his life to the service of the spiritual master, that person becomes most dear to Me. . . . Both of us can realize that without the blessings of the spiritual master no one can be happy. By the mercy of the spiritual master and by his blessings, one can achieve peace and prosperity and be able to fulfill the mission of human life." (*Kṛṣṇa*, Chapter 80)

Our dear godbrother Bhūrijana Prabhu recently quoted a statement by one of Śrīla Prabhupāda's godbrothers. That godbrother, at an advanced age, was walking, with some difficulty, on his veranda, chanting softly. And under his breath he muttered, "Eleven years with Śrīla Prabhupāda [Bhaktisiddhānta Sarasvatī]; forty years without him."

Even advanced souls feel separation—what to speak of us. I so much depended on your guidance and encouragement and friendship. Where will I find them now? Even till the end I would look forward to phoning you and talking with you. In your humility you called me your *śikṣā-guru* and asked for my guidance. But you were the one who was instructing me—and the whole movement—how to serve our spiritual master with all energy and resources, and how to encourage each other with love and good humor.

As a teacher you were heavy. "*Guru* means heavy." Yet you were like an angel. "Angels fly, not because they know how, but because they take themselves lightly." You took Śrīla Prabhupāda and his mission most seriously. But you took your own bodily pains and pleasures lightly. And so you could easily give of yourself to others and be our guardian angel in service to Śrīla Prabhupāda.

I wish I could just fly to you now, fly into your loving embrace. But I fear I do not have the strength. I am too strongly tied to the body and the world.

But I do have one hope: your mercy, in the form of your love, your care, your example, your instructions, and the strength and inspiration we get from them to continue to serve Śrīla Prabhupāda and ISKCON to the end, whenever that may be.

You wished His Holiness Indradyumna Swami "Happy trails." I wish mine could be happy too. And they will be, as long as they lead to you, in eternal service to Śrīla Prabhupāda, Śrī Pañca-tattva, and Śrī Śrī Rādhā-Śyāmasundara.

Today is the grand opening of your *samādhi-mandira*. It is beautiful, just like your heart, befitting the king that you were—king of Śrīla Prabhupāda's staunch, surrendered, stubborn servants. May you and your *samādhi* give shelter to all who come to you.

On this auspicious occasion I, among many, pray to you:

Please bless me and keep me under your shelter. Teach me to serve as you did, without duplicity, with heart and soul. And teach me to laugh as you did, even in the face of death, convinced that "there is no utility in negativity" and that in the end "the joke is on me."

Your eternal servant,
Giriraj Swami

Serving Śrīla Prabhupāda's Servant

From talks by Māyāpur dāsa on May 1, 2004, and July 14, 2007, in Carpinteria, California.

Giriraj Swami: My association with Māyāpur dāsa goes back to Bombay. He was His Holiness Sridhar Swami Mahārāja's main servant, and he had a lot of association with Mahārāja, up until the end.

Māyāpur dāsa: I would like to thank His Holiness Giriraj Swami Mahārāja for inviting me and making it possible for me to come here. I started associating with devotees in 1993, and in 1995 I joined full time and moved into the temple in Cakovec, Croatia. I met many advanced Vaiṣṇavas in Europe that year—Harikeśa Prabhu, Kṛṣṇa-kṣetra Prabhu, Śacīnandana Swami. I was looking for a *guru*.

The main thing that inspired me to come to Kṛṣṇa consciousness was Śrīla Prabhupāda—his life, his biography, his example mostly. I saw videos and read books about him. Of course, I read the *Bhagavad-gītā* and *Śrīmad-Bhāgavatam*, but his example was what I was looking for in my life, because in my environment I saw that people were speaking in one way and acting in another way in terms of religion and their duties. So, here I could see that it is possible to follow the highest standard of love of God and follow whatever God asks us to do. So in 1995 I started praying to Śrīla Prabhupāda, "Please help me to connect to your *paramparā*, to your teachings. I want to become a follower of your follower, of a bona fide spiritual master who is your representative." There are different spiritual masters, and different qualities attract us to surrender to them, but I didn't really feel the inspiration to surrender fully to any of them, although they all were inspiring, all very scholarly and preaching to their utmost capacity, and I had no doubt that they were pure devotees.

That year there was a summer camp in Slovenia. I read the program—the seminars that were to be given and the names of the Vaiṣṇavas who were to give them—and there was one name that was new to me. Very few devotees in my zone knew who the person was. It was His Holiness Sridhar Swami, and the seminar was "Seven Habits of Highly Effective Vaiṣṇavas." When I came to the camp, almost all the devotees who were to give seminars had already arrived and the seminars were already going on. But on the second day a car came, and a very effulgent person was in it. I could not see his face properly from a distance, but I felt inspired from within. For the first time I bowed down fully. It just happened, and it was something strange for me; it was very unusual for me to bow down fully. And at that moment Sridhar Swami came out of the car. So it was a very interesting, strange experience for me. I didn't understand it.

We met at the camp seminar, and what attracted me the most was his attachment to Śrīla Prabhupāda—whatever he would say, he would quote Śrīla Prabhupāda or give an example from his life, from his teachings—and his extreme honesty about himself. There was no pretense. He was extremely honest about his devotional life—very simple. Whatever he thought, he would say. There was no duplicity. Sometimes someone might not accept or like something he said, but I could see that whatever he said was coming from his extreme openness. He was not a cheater. Whatever he practiced and however he practiced, he was honest about it.

Another thing that struck me about him was that he was a very jolly person, very humorous, but at the same time very serious and dedicated to Śrīla Prabhupāda's mission. His humor had a function. It was not just humor for the sake of humor. It served to enliven devotees and present sometimes very heavy points in a nice package. That was his style.

At that time I had my first *darśana* with Sridhar Swami. I just asked for some basic spiritual instructions for my life—what I should follow, what I should do. He stressed *sādhana*. At that time in Croatia, *saṅkīrtana* was the main focus, not *sādhana*. He said that for me as a new devotee it was most important to follow *sādhana* in the temple. Although others may not have been following so strictly, for me it was very important. So, I started following his instructions, and I became more attached to him.

I wrote him a letter then, saying that I wanted to go to India. At that time I was working as a courier. I would give half of the money to the temple, and half I would save for my trip to India. I thought, "Let me go to India. Prabhupāda wrote so much about India. These teachings are coming from India, so let me see how this process is practiced at its roots, at its source." I thought, "If I go now, I'll carry those impressions from India for the rest of my life and be inspired." So he replied to me, "You know, I don't want to interfere with local management, but it will be good for you." At that time two devotees had asked me to join Bhakti Vikāsa Swami's *saṅkīrtana* party in Gujarat. They were going by bus from city to city, village to village, distributing books, doing *hari-nāma-saṅkīrtana*. Sridhar Swami said, "It will be good for you to come to India and serve in the association of Bhakti Vikāsa Swami and other devotees and distribute books." So I decided, "Okay, I'll go." I talked to my authorities. Ultimately I joined up with a few devotees who were collecting for their tickets to India. I had already collected the money for my ticket, so I was just going along with them.

We were in Rome, in Italy. It was the biggest adventure of

my life. We had a car, and we would sleep on the beach at night, wake up, and whatever we would collect from *saṅkīrtana* we would use to buy some food. We would meet people, and sometimes they would invite us to come and sleep at their houses. We would cook for them and ourselves, and we would preach. For me as a new devotee, it was a real experience of how Kṛṣṇa really takes care if you sincerely try to preach.

Italy is a very nice, very interesting country. I went out distributing incense every day in Vaiṣṇava clothes, and I didn't have a single bad experience of people criticizing or in any way being disturbed by me. After we had collected the money, somehow one devotee decided to stay. The other devotee had already left, so I was going to have to go to India alone. Now I was wondering, "I am going to India—how is it going to work? I've read so much about India and seen documentaries. It's a wild country. When I get there, how will I get to Vṛndāvana?" I was supposed to meet devotees in Vṛndāvana and my flight was to Delhi, so I was in big anxiety.

The whole time I was in the airport and while I was boarding the plane, I was in this anxiety—what's going to happen? I got a seat next to a nun. So I thought, "Okay, this is a sign of Kṛṣṇa, a sign of God. This is a spiritual lady. She is going, so it must be a sign from God. Okay, Kṛṣṇa is taking care." And I just chanted as we waited for the time of departure. It was maybe five minutes before the flight was to leave, but the seat on my other side was still empty. Then I saw a devotee coming, and he came and sat right next to me. He was a Prabhupāda disciple, Supta-vigraha Prabhu. He said, "Oh, Hare Kṛṣṇa. I am going to Vṛndāvana." Then I saw, "Okay, this process must be working."

So, I went to Vṛndāvana. I didn't expect to see Sridhar Swami at that time, because there was no plan as such. I didn't know where he was. The last time he had written to me was when he wrote that it would be good if I came to India. Anyway,

I was going to my service in Gujarat at the end of Kārtika. Then, maybe two days before we were to go, a devotee came to my room. He said, "I can see how Kṛṣṇa is taking care of you. So you have to promise me to take care of me in my spiritual life." Then he said, "Your spiritual master has come; you should go and see him."

I hadn't asked Sridhar Swami to accept me as a disciple or anything, but I felt that he was my spiritual master, my link to Śrīla Prabhupāda, my link to the *paramparā*. So I just went to him and met him. He was very happy that I had come. At that time he gave me some clothes to wash. The next day, I asked him if he would accept me as his disciple, and he said something like, "Well, there are so many devotees more qualified than I am. I am a very simple devotee. I do not know what you expect. You should think about it, and if you really want, I will accept you as my disciple." I took it that he accepted me.

Then I went to my service in Gujarat, and in January—on the tenth of January, to be exact—I got a phone call in Ahmedabad; Sridhar Swami was calling me to come to Bombay. Actually, that morning I had a dream that I was in an airport, waiting for someone. I had come to the airport in a small blue car, a Maruti, and was waiting for someone to arrive. Then, after I woke up that morning, I got the message that Sridhar Swami was calling me to come to Bombay. So I went to Bombay. He was coming from London. I came in the same blue car—everything was exactly the same as in the dream. Then he came. At that time he was being assisted by Vikram Prabhu—a *gurukulī* from the Vṛndāvana *gurukula*. I think Vikram wanted to do some other service, so Guru Mahārāja asked me if I wanted to stay and serve him. From that time I stayed. That's how I first came to his service.

Before I became a devotee I was into astrology. In 1990 an astrologer told me, "Oh, you will go into some spiritual movement, and when you are 24 [in 1996] you will receive a very great benediction"—something like that. I was always wondering what it would be. So, in 1996 I was lucky to receive initiation, and Śrīla Giriraj Mahārāja was there to bless me. It was on the occasion of Guru Mahārāja's Vyāsa-pūjā. I felt privileged that I received initiation alone. I felt—and still feel—very unqualified. There were maybe four or five of Śrīla Prabhupāda's disciples, *sannyāsīs*, at the occasion. Guru Mahārāja always stressed that I should always take blessings from his godbrothers, in the same way as I would ask blessings from him. He would always tell me, "As much as you should honor me, you should always honor my godbrothers." I specifically remember once in Māyāpur when I came with a garland and he was with a *gṛhastha* godbrother. As I was approaching him, he saw that I wanted to give him a garland and asked, "You have two garlands?" I said, "No." He said, "Then go away." And then later he explained to me, "Whenever I am with my godbrothers, if you want to give me a garland, there should be garlands for them as well." He always wanted his godbrothers honored the same way we honored him.

Serving the spiritual master is all-auspicious and brings us closer to Kṛṣṇa. By the mercy of *guru* one gets Kṛṣṇa, and, as Giriraj Mahārāja has explained, serving the Vaiṣṇavas can be even more important than serving Kṛṣṇa Himself. But serving the spiritual master is not always very pleasurable for the senses. We can sometimes bring ourselves to the limits of our understanding, to the limits of our potential, and the spiritual master is there to push us beyond those limits. And even when we are not successful we can always draw out some realization that can make us successful in the long run.

Once, in the year 2000, when my spiritual master was in the hospital in Bombay, many Vaiṣṇavas were coming through and visiting him. So, His Grace Gopīparāṇadhana Prabhu and his family came to visit and enliven Guru Mahārāja by reading from the works of the Vaiṣṇava *ācāryas*. Every day, Gopīparāṇadhana Prabhu, who I would say is an exalted Vaiṣṇava and one of the top scholars in our society, would come and read a couple of verses from *śāstra*, along with the commentaries of the Vaiṣṇava *ācāryas*. First he would recite translations of Viśvanātha Cakravartī Ṭhākura and Baladeva Vidyābhūṣaṇa; of the original Śrīdhara Svāmī, the commentator on *Śrīmad-Bhāgavatam*; and of Śrīla Jīva Gosvāmī. He would just translate the Sanskrit on the spot. Then he would read Śrīla Prabhupāda's translations and purports.

It was amazing to see how Śrīla Prabhupāda's purports contained the essence of all the commentaries of these previous *ācāryas*. Some details were not covered completely, but the essence of each and every commentary was there in Śrīla Prabhupāda's purports. It was just amazing to see. When you hear, "Śrīla Prabhupāda gave everything in his books," it is not just saying, "Okay, we got something from Śrīla Prabhupāda, so for us he is everything." He is, but he also literally gave everything, the essence of all the commentaries on Vaiṣṇava *siddhānta*.

The day when Gopīparāṇadhana Prabhu and his family were to leave and go back to Vṛndāvana was a big rush. As you know from the ashram here in Carpinteria, it is not always easy to serve when there are guests and daily duties and many details to take care of. It was that kind of time; many Vaiṣṇavas were coming through. I was up day and night and a little worn out—very tired, at the edge of my limit. About one and a half hours before they were to leave on the train to Vṛndāvana, Guru Mahārāja said to me, "Māyāpur, why don't you go to Juhu and get some *prasāda* for Gopīparāṇadhana Prabhu and his family. Just take the car and come back."

It was three-thirty or four o'clock in the afternoon. Those who know Bombay know that this is the time of the main traffic jam—rush hour. Even getting on a train is a lottery. I was thinking, "One and a half hours to go there and back and then take Gopīparāṇadhana Prabhu to the train station?" So I said, "Guru Mahārāja, I'm sorry; it is not possible." He just looked at me and said, "Can you please go." I said, "I am sorry. I don't think . . . Why should I go if it is not possible?" During that period, he smashed me many times, but at that moment he just had a disappointed look on his face and asked another devotee, another servant, to go. "Adbhuta," he said, "can you please go to Juhu. Just go to Juhu and get the lunch and come back."

My godbrother Adbhuta Hari was a humble devotee. So he went. When he didn't make it back in time I might have said, "See, I told you. I was right. I knew this was going to happen." But after Adbhuta Hari left, shortly before Gopīparāṇadhana and his family were to leave for the train, I realized how it could have worked. Adbhuta was supposed to come back and give them the packed lunch where we were, and then they were to leave by taxi for the train station. But I saw that if he had gone to Juhu and from there gone directly to the station and met them there, he could have made it in time and delivered the *prasāda*. So it *had* been possible. But instead of seeing this when Guru Mahārāja had asked, instead of saying, "Yes, it is possible," I hadn't believed it.

For me, this was a very beneficial experience. I realized that because of my limited vision and lack of faith, I hadn't performed the service successfully. So I got a realization: Don't doubt the instruction of your spiritual master or take it for granted, because it is not by chance that he is giving it. Even though my godbrother Adbhuta hadn't made it in time, Guru Mahārāja was very pleased with his attitude, because he had gone. He had followed the spiritual master's instruction.

Since then, whenever I get an instruction, I don't think, "Impossible." I look for a solution. Some mistakes stay in your mind, and then you try to derive what you can from realization. At the very least, someone else can benefit from my mistake. And I think that by a different approach now, I can somehow do some *prāyaścitta*, atonement, for my stupid approach then. So, this was one experience—not a very glorious one—but auspicious anyway because I had this realization.

Another time when my *guru mahārāja* tried to push me out of my comfort zone was in Brazil, when we went to see a well-known healer. The healer lived in a small village. We met people from all over the world there—from the United States, Australia, and Europe—who were looking for this healer to help them with their health problems. We stayed in the village, in one of the many small, simple inns called *pousadas*. To me they looked like the *dharmaśālās* of India, very cheap places—not very sophisticated or well built. But somehow it was a place to stay overnight and eat. Many groups were coming from the US. And they offered a variety of food for breakfast and lunch, and every day there was meat. They also had vegetables, but it was all cooked in the same pots. So there was a problem.

We arranged that I could cook for Guru Mahārāja in the kitchen. But the cooking was not a very pleasant experience. When I cooked the *prasāda* I would get the smoke from all the other things being cooked in the kitchen. Anyway, I would cook there and offer the food in our room, to our *śālagrāma-śilās*. Finally we made a joke. I would come to Guru Mahārāja and say, "Okay, Guru Mahārāja, it is time to dishonor *pousada*." [laughter] You couldn't really call it *prasāda*, because there was so much smoke from the other food, but I think Kṛṣṇa somehow accepted it. It was mainly *kicharī* or pasta—something simple—because I only had one fire to work on while the others were cooking.

One day we came to honor *prasāda*, or dishonor *pousada*, in the main room where all the others were eating. There was a new group that had come from the United States, with different kinds of people—from places like New York and California—many into New Age lifestyles and different alternative types of healing. Some had come out of curiosity, some out of their genuine need to be healed. As soon as I entered, one person caught my eye. In ISKCON, we have a variety of people from all over the world. But you can often recognize another person from your own country. You know the facial expressions; you know the way they act. So immediately I knew, "That person is from Croatia." And immediately I also got the feeling, "He is an immigrant, a nationalist, and a hardcore Christian." I thought, "Should I go and see him? I really don't want to meet him at all, because I know what his approach is going to be." So I just kept quiet, and we had *prasāda*.

As we were leaving, I said, "Guru Mahārāja . . ." I wanted to boast that I could see who was from where, so I said, "That person there, he is probably from Croatia. I didn't hear a word he said, but I just know he is from there. He is probably an immigrant." Guru Mahārāja said, "Why don't you go and see him." I said, "Forget it. Never. He is going to blast me immediately." A day passed, and Guru Mahārāja said, "No, just go and see him, and you know . . ." But I was so attached. I didn't want to have unpleasant feelings from talking with this person.

So, one day as I was washing the pots after lunch, I saw Guru Mahārāja talking to this person and pointing me out. I heard him say, "You know him? He is from Croatia." This guy was cordial, but as soon as Guru Mahārāja said that, his face changed and he said, "What the hell is he doing in Hare Krishna?" [laughter] So I said to myself, "Oh, no! Here it comes."

The next day, the man approached me and said, "I heard you are from Croatia." I said, "Yes." "Well, I was thinking you are such a nice boy. You are handsome. You can have a nice family and continue the Croatian dynasty. But here you are.

You are a monk, and you are serving this sect. How did they . . . We have to get you out. What happened? How did they brainwash you?" He took a very aggressive approach.

As time passed, he actually mellowed out. The whole group he came with was going to different places and doing shaman worship, worshiping the spirits of nature—worshiping this spirit, that spirit. So he got really frustrated, because all of them were going and he didn't want to go. He said, "Why are they going to see all these things? I thought they were God conscious." And then we opened this conversation and I tried to present the Vedic viewpoint. "Yes, there is one God. There is ultimately only one God, and there is no need to worship His energies separately." And slowly he opened up, and he said that he was reading some other books. He was really into reading different kinds of religious literature. It turned out that he was a very nice and pious person.

One of the reasons why I hadn't wanted to meet the man is that I always cringe when I see a nationalistic type of person, because in Croatia nationalism brought out so many animal instincts—killing people not because they were of other faiths but just because they were of other nations. People treated each other like animals—worse than animals, actually. I can't stand being close to that kind of mentality.

But finally the man said, "I left Croatia in the 1960s. I couldn't live there, because of all the communists; they couldn't stand our nationalism. When the war started, I even helped some people from the other side." Serbs and Croats are actually like one people, he realized, just a little different. They have this love-hate relationship. So he actually helped some people from the "other side" settle in America when they were seeking asylum.

He just opened up, and he even began to help Guru Mahārāja and me. Every day he would bring water for Guru

Mahārāja, even though he kept his distance and didn't want to get too involved. He was in some way afraid, but he became very friendly, very favorable. He said, "Whenever you come to New York, please call me." It turned out that he worked for the American government somewhere in New York.

The experience showed me that by the mercy of the spiritual master, if you try to surrender to what he wants you to do, you can get so much benefit—even if at first it is not very pleasurable for the senses, or not conceivable by the mind. And it is not that there is only one spiritual master; there are many. There is one *dīkṣā-guru*, initiating spiritual master, but there can be many *śikṣā-gurus*. It was really one of the experiences that stuck in my mind, that showed that we should go beyond our limitations, especially if we are trying to please a Vaiṣṇava.

I will relate one other experience, a short one, to conclude this topic. When I joined the movement and was staying in the temple, I always thought that I needed to get the personal association of a spiritual master, because I knew that if I didn't get that, my ego would never be purified. I can say to someone, "Yes, I hear you," or, "I understand," and still keep my own idea, but with the spiritual master, when you serve for a long period of time, you can't remain hidden. The impurities and attachments you cling to cannot remain hidden. So I knew I would have to expose myself for a long time. I don't say this is a universal rule, but it was true for me. And serving the instructions of the spiritual master is a higher platform of service than just serving him personally.

So, my first *Bhāgavatam* class was, again, not a very pleasurable experience. I had served Guru Mahārāja for four or five years, and during that time I was just hiding, clinging to his dhoti. Whenever someone would ask me, "Prabhu, can you please give *Bhāgavatam* class?" I would say, "I really don't have time. I am engaged in service the whole day. Guru Mahārāja is here. Why don't you ask him?" But Guru Mahārāja would say, "Yes, one day you give. I will give five days; you give one day." It was my worst fear. As you know, for many people, speaking in front of an audience is the biggest fear.

So I never really dared to speak in front of others. Then one day, in Vancouver—Guru Mahārāja was giving classes every day—one morning after *maṅgala-ārati*, they just announced my name to give the *Bhāgavatam* class. I was thinking, "Nobody asked me anything." I went to the temple president, and he said, "Well, your *guru mahārāja* actually wrote your name." I was forced to speak. And then, of course, there was panic. First look for the verse. Look for the materials, what I was going to say. It was like a red alert. I was going to be exposed, and I was going to fail. My mind was telling me, "You are going to be there, and you are going to get stuck, and everyone is going to laugh at you."

Anyway, I prepared a few basic points, and it came out fine. At first there were about ten devotees—not so many—and then I expected that Guru Mahārāja would be merciful and not come for the class. I thought, "He usually works in the morning." And then he came. And then another *sannyāsī* came. And I was thinking, "Okay, wonderful—big-time failure." But somehow or other, it went well. I got through it, and again the same realization came. Surrender is not easy, but you just have to try to go along with it. You get liberated from some of your fears, from some conditioning in the mind.

I wanted to share these experiences because they very much helped me in my Kṛṣṇa consciousness, and it is an everyday struggle—for all of us. But I often remember my spiritual master and his gentle ways, and sometimes not-so-gentle ways. But they were all very effective, and they were all ways by which he actually showed me love. He just wanted me to progress. He didn't want me to go into a cocoon and stay there for the rest of my life. I think that the purpose of the spiritual master, or of any teacher, is to bring the best out of everyone. Knowledge is good, but as I heard many times from Guru Mahārāja, knowledge alone is not power. Power is the application of knowledge. And that's what he pushed me to do—to apply my knowledge. I have always wanted to stay in the background, to not expose myself, and not be engaged in preaching, but because I know that he would be pleased, somehow I try to do my best to fulfill his orders.

There was not a day, not an hour, when Guru Mahārāja was not thinking of pleasing Śrīla Prabhupāda. In his last days one of his former lady disciples wanted to come and see him. She had taken reinitiation from an elderly *sannyāsī* in another institution, but it's not about that. She is a very sincere *mātājī*, but somewhat, I would say, troubled. She never was happy. She always had some problem, and that was how she left. She had started to criticize Guru Mahārāja and left, and later she took reinitiation in another institution. So, she wanted to come and see him, and she wanted to serve him, because she knew that he was going to leave the planet very soon. I was kind of against it, because I didn't want anything to disturb him in his last days, and I knew her very well from the time when she and I had been serving Guru Mahārāja in Bombay.

So, after two or three days, the problems started, and Guru Mahārāja invited her to talk. He told her that if she wanted to serve him she should just do humble service, not interfere with other devotees, not try to preach anything else to other devotees, not try to start any controversy among other devotees. But unfortunately she could not control herself, and devotees started complaining. Basically she tried to canvass devotees and preach for her present *guru*. So Guru Mahārāja called her and told her, "I think it's best for you to go. I gave you the chance. I thought that you came here with a sincere desire to serve me, but I see that it's not like that. I think you should leave for your country now. If you still want to serve me, you can serve me from a distance. That's good. It's not going to cause any trouble." Then this *mātājī* said, "Please, I have come here to deliver a blessing from a *sādhu*, from my spiritual master. You should accept it, because when I was coming here he asked me, 'Why are you going there? He is against me.' And I told him, 'No, no, no, he is not against you.' And he said, 'Okay, if he is not against me, then tell him that I sent my blessings.' " So she said to Guru Mahārāja, "Please now accept his blessings."

Guru Mahārāja said, "You know, I really appreciate it, but all the blessings I need I get from Śrīla Prabhupāda. I really don't require—I mean, everything I know in my life, everything I have, is Śrīla Prabhupāda. I am aware that your spiritual master is a *sādhu*, a venerable Vaiṣṇava, but he is not Śrīla Prabhupāda." And then she just went wild. She said, "Are you afraid of him?" And that made Guru Mahārāja upset. He said, "Afraid of him? I am afraid of him as much as I am afraid of George Bush. I know George Bush is there. I know what he is doing and I know he exists, but I don't have any connection with him. I don't hate him, I don't love him, but he is there. Śrīla Prabhupāda is everything that I know, that I really need in my spiritual life. You should really just go now."

Basically, she was trying to pull a kind of trick. If he had said, "I accept," then she would have gone to all the disciples and said, "Oh, before he left, your spiritual master accepted the blessings of this *sādhu*, so you should also accept." But Guru Mahārāja was smart. He knew what was going on. His chastity and integrity were some of the qualities that attracted me. And it was inspiring to see these qualities throughout his spiritual life.

Then there was his attachment to his godbrothers. I remember in 1999 when Śrīla Giriraj Swami and Śrīla Sridhar Swami went for Govardhana *parikramā*. That was the most ecstatic

Govardhana *parikramā* I have ever been on. I don't know if there will ever be another one like that. But later Guru Mahārāja would also say, "Right after that, Giriraj Mahārāja went to a hospital for heart surgery and I went into a coma in Bombay, in Bhaktivedanta Hospital." [laughter]

Even then, it was also a very ecstatic time, because so many of his godbrothers came to see him and spend time with him and have *kīrtanas*. I could see how much he valued their association, how much he loved them, and how much attachment he had for his godbrothers. That was also a great blessing—to serve all the Vaiṣṇavas. And that was the greatest blessing he gave to his disciples after his passing—the association of all his godbrothers. He would always stress that.

A month before my *guru mahārāja* left this world, during his first conversation with me after he got the news that he had an advanced stage of cancer and was not going to stay with us much longer, he called me in and said, "Māyāpur, you know Tamal Krishna Mahārāja, and you know his disciples. Mahārāja would take care to personally train them very strictly, so all of them are very well trained. You can always recognize Tamal Krishna Mahārāja's disciples by how together they are. Everything is pukka, first-class. You can recognize them anywhere you go. I want you and all my disciples to become humble, to be known as humble and gentle servants of the Vaiṣṇavas." He always stressed these points, and he said, "I want my disciples to stay in Prabhupāda's family and serve all my godbrothers, just like you have served me. If you serve my godbrothers, I will be happy. I will be pleased." So there is no doubt what he wanted us to do.

There is a *śloka* that Prabhupāda used to quote: *bhajana kara sādhana kara mūrti jānle haya*—"Whatever *sādhana* and *bhajana* you do during your life will be tested at the time of death." I could see that whatever Guru Mahārāja had, he gave to

Śrīla Prabhupāda, to Śrīla Prabhupāda's institution, to the devotees. He was very easily approachable. It didn't matter whether it was a low-rank or high-rank devotee. Guru Mahārāja was very easy to approach, and he would give spiritual advice, or even simply his friendship, to make that devotee attached to Śrīla Prabhupāda.

So, it was a very emotional time for him when he arrived in Māyāpur and saw the reception that his godbrothers had arranged for him. As we were coming, Bhakti Charu Swami was calling every twenty minutes and asking, "So, where are you now?" After two or three times, Guru Mahārāja understood what was going on. He was almost crying. He said, "I just want to slip in somewhere on the side. I don't want any big reception." But he was very happy when he arrived. Each and every godbrother came to his window. When he came from Vancouver I thought he was not going to stay with us for long, because he was very exhausted. He was all pale. He had gone twice to the emergency ward for the fluid to be taken out of his stomach, and the second time they did it, they poked some other organ, so there was some internal bleeding and his belly was purple. So I really didn't know what to expect. It was not certain how long he would stay, but I didn't want to think he was going, because he wanted to stay for the installation of the Pañca-tattva—that was for sure—because, also, his godbrothers had decided that he would be among the few GBCs who would personally take part in the installation.

There I saw the most wonderful exchanges between him and his godbrothers. The most enlivening part of the day was in the evenings when Hari-śauri Prabhu came and read from his *Transcendental Diary*. Guru Mahārāja would pay attention, remember, and comment about whatever was happening. The reading was from the upcoming volume of the *Diary*. There were many things dealing with India in it. And so the days passed.

The installation of the Pañca-tattva was really wonderful and gorgeous, the biggest festival I have ever seen. I don't know if something like that will ever happen again—maybe when the big temple opens.

Guru Mahārāja would spend the whole day in bed, and he would maybe sit for his lunch or go outside to chant in the morning or to take bath in the Gaṅgā. He was very weak, but he was ready for the installation, for the *abhiṣekas*. It was incredible to see—it was always incredible to witness his willpower. Whatever he wanted to do, he would just overcome his bodily needs and bodily pain. He would never speak about how much it hurt him, or if there was any pain. When he was in serious pain, he just would not talk much. That morning he just stood up and went for the *abhiṣeka*, and he was doing it for about an hour. Many devotees said that they were very inspired when they saw him. The *kalaśas* were made of pure silver, and each one was probably about five to six kilos, plus the liquid inside. He just kept lifting them up, for one or maybe one and a half hours.

It was a very touching experience to see him there. He was behind Lord Nityānanda. When they asked him where he wanted to be—maybe he wanted to bathe everyone—he said, "No, I want to bathe Lord Nityānanda. I want to do the *abhiṣeka* of Lord Nityānanda." So he was crying for about ten minutes. He was behind and touched the body of Lord Nityānanda, and he was crying. I had never seen him like that before. Really, he was a very open-hearted, great-hearted, compassionate person. He would empathize with everyone, whatever they would feel or suffer, but I never saw him crying very much, except sometimes when he would talk about Prabhupāda. I could feel that he was feeling he was going to go. In the last days he was feeling so much gratitude just for being there and receiving the mercy of all the Vaiṣṇavas and of Śrīla Prabhupāda. He became very open. Normally he would hide his emotions, but he didn't cover anything anymore. Those moments were really something for me to treasure, to see an example of how a Vaiṣṇava departs from this world—what is his mood, what is his consciousness. His biggest fear was that he wouldn't be able to stay conscious, because 95 percent of people with his disease go into a coma. He was afraid of that and said, "I really don't want to go into a coma." He wanted to leave in clear consciousness. Kṛṣṇa fulfilled all his desires. He wanted to come to see the installation. He wanted to stay until Gaura-pūrṇimā. Someone approached him and said, "So, Mahārāja, you are leaving—maybe Gaura-pūrṇimā would be . . ." Mahārāja interrupted, "I don't want to make this Sridhar Swami's festival. It's not Sridhar Swami's festival—it's the Gaura-pūrṇimā festival." That showed that he actually wanted to leave when not many devotees were there. He didn't want to make a big thing of it. He felt very humbled because there was so much attention on him. And the next auspicious day, he left—Kṛṣṇa just took him.

In the evening, he was in a lot of pain, and as doctors were observing his condition, they prescribed certain painkillers. Some painkillers were very heavy, like morphine, but the doctors were afraid that if he took those he might go into a coma. So they prescribed some not-so-strong ones. He said, "The pain is not going away." The pain was all over his body. Then later, after a few hours, they prescribed another one, which was heavier. But it didn't take any pain away. Finally they gave the heaviest. He was still in completely clear consciousness, but he said, "I guess it's time to go." He called me at around 3:30 a.m. He said, "Māyāpur, now it's time for *kīrtana*. I need *kīrtana* now more than ever." I asked him, "So, Guru Mahārāja, how are you feeling?" He answered with a grin, "Never felt better in my life." He was so exhausted. He was in so much pain. But he kept his humor till the last breath. He would always joke, "When I pass away, the last joke will be on me. I am going to go away laughing."

So, we had *kīrtana* from around 3:35. At around six o'clock he wanted to go to the bathroom. When he came out, he couldn't walk anymore. His body collapsed, but his consciousness was still present. He didn't fall—we caught him and took him out of the bathroom, and his hand got caught against the door. He said, "Stop! You are going to break my hand." So we could see that his consciousness was completely clear and that he was completely aware of everything that was happening, but he was exhausted from not sleeping all night, being in pain all night.

That was maybe ten, fifteen minutes before he left. The *kīrtana* was going on from around three-thirty until the moment he left his body. When the situation became critical, the doctor checked Guru Mahārāja's bodily symptoms and said, "He is leaving." We put a large photo of Śrīla Prabhupāda in front of him, and he focused intently on that. Maybe half an hour before that, Paṅkajāṅghri Prabhu had come and brought the *tulasī* from Lord Nṛsiṁhadeva's lotus feet, and I was periodically giving him Gaṅgā water. Guru Mahārāja was sipping Gaṅgā water for the last two hours while we were having *kīrtana*. At about ten past six in the morning, looking at Śrīla Prabhupāda's photo, he left. I could see that leaving in such a way was something that any Vaiṣṇava would desire. It was perfect. His consciousness was perfectly clear. He was fully Kṛṣṇa conscious, Prabhupāda conscious, as he had always been. So wherever he has gone, he is with his spiritual master again.

So, I'll stop here. Are there any questions or comments?

Sarvātmā dāsa: Last night I dreamed that I was traveling in a place that looked a lot like old England. I was with Sridhar Swami and Brahmatīrtha Prabhu. We traveled for a while, changing trains. I didn't know exactly that Sridhar Swami was about to depart, that these were actually his last days. Then we went to a town. We wanted to take rest, because we were very tired from the trip. So Brahmatīrtha arranged for us to stay in an expensive hotel. The next day we started traveling again.

Sridhar Swami was very jolly all the time, cracking jokes. He was very funny and Kṛṣṇa conscious. Finally, he decided that he was going to leave his body at Brahmatīrtha's house. So when we arrived there, Brahmatīrtha set up a large bed for him. He was sitting up in bed, just being himself. (He was fond of saying, "Be yourself and give your contribution to the movement.") That was his mood. He wanted everybody to see that this was not a counterfeit Sridhar Swami, that this was the real Sridhar Swami, as he had always been. Then I woke up.

MĀYĀPUR DĀSA: Thank you. I remember when you told us about your other dream, the day Guru Mahārāja left. I loved it—about carrying him in *samādhi*. In the dream, Sridhar Swami was smiling while being carried to the *samādhi*. The day after Guru Mahārāja's body was actually placed in his *samādhi* one *mātājī* said that her daughter had had a dream that Mahārāja was in the *samādhi* pit. She was standing in front of him, and he suddenly opened his eyes and smiled—typical—like a joke. He was always like that.

While you were talking, I felt inspired to tell one other pastime that took place when we were in Brazil. There was a healer there who worked with subtle entities, subtle energies. So we went there a few times, and it seemed that it helped Guru Mahārāja at first, but the last few times, Mahārāja said, "There is no significant improvement." It seemed that this healer was becoming so popular that it went to his head a little bit, and he was losing some of his powers.

The healer really liked the devotees, and every time we went there, he would call Mahārāja to give a five-minute speech in front of everyone. Then he would call his helpers. He was supposedly working with invisible entities. The entities would take over and then work through his physical body. Some of those entities were former surgeons, so he didn't need an x-ray to see what was happening inside the body.

Because he could see the subtle body, he could see subtly

what was wrong with a certain part of your body, and he would operate. So, once, there was a whole scene there. His helpers—volunteers who were there at his disposal to control the crowd, to help translate to foreigners, or to sit and meditate—were all into subtle beings. Subtle things were happening, but the other people—not his assistants, but the people who came to get healed—did not understand what was happening. Sometimes it looked a bit like a show, something extraordinary, but externally you couldn't really tell what was happening, or what was extraordinary about it. Most of the people were speculating about what was actually happening.

In order to be treated by this healer, people would line up and everyone would have "*darśana.*" The healer would then see them personally for 20–30 seconds and say, "Okay, you come for operation tomorrow" or "You take this medicine." So, one of those days, Guru Mahārāja came before him and the healer said, "Okay, please stay here." Then he called all his helpers. We had been there a few times over a few months and I had never seen this happen, although he would sometimes call some of his helpers and they would all gather and hold hands, like a medium session. So, he called everyone there, and they all gathered around Guru Mahārāja to see what was happening. Then the healer took a towel, and a rose from a vase. The healer put the rose in Guru Mahārāja's hand, and then put the towel around his hand, and then he brought all his helpers to listen to what he was saying to Mahārāja. He said, "This ritual is 1,800 years old. Do you remember what it is?" Guru Mahārāja was watching, and everyone was just waiting. There was pin-drop silence. Then Mahārāja said, "Sorry, I don't remember." The healer asked, "Can you tell us what you were in your past life?" Guru Mahārāja said with a sigh, "I was a worm in stool." [laughter] The biggest joke was that these translators, because they were Portuguese, were asking—they did not understand—"Stool? What is stool?"

Mahārāja was just dead serious. I laughed to myself, as I did not want them to understand that it was such a comical situation.

The healer looked very disappointed that Guru Mahārāja was not into their game.

He said, "All right, everyone go now."

A little later, Guru Mahārāja went and apologized. He said, "I am sorry, but I really don't remember what I was in my past life. I really don't. I am sorry that it was disappointing for you. I am simply a servant of my spiritual master." The healer said, "It's okay. I know. It's okay."

The whole scene was hilarious—"I was a worm in stool."

So, even in the most intense situations, he would crack jokes, and he would always tell his disciples, "Don't take yourself so seriously. You know, laugh in life. Relax. Don't take yourself so seriously. Kṛṣṇa has the best sense of humor, and the joke is on us." When there would be some reverse with his health, he would say, "Kṛṣṇa must be laughing now." His famous words were "There is no utility in negativity." He would say that to every disciple who came with lots of problems. He would paraphrase Śrīla Prabhupāda's "Chant Hare Kṛṣṇa and be happy" and say, "Chant Hare Kṛṣṇa and have no worries and just be happy. Relax. Nothing is as serious as you think it is." This does not mean that he did not take the devotees or the process of devotional service seriously. He was serious, but at the same time he was a jolly person.

Bhakti Tirtha Swami

Preaching and Compassion

A talk at Bhakti Tirtha Swami's disappearance festival on June 15, 2009, in Dallas.

Today we are observing the divine disappearance day of Śrī Śrīmad Bhakti Tirtha Swami Mahārāja. He left this world on this date on the Vedic calendar—or actually yesterday—four years ago, in 2005. We shall read one verse from *Śrīmad-Bhāgavatam* about the disappearance of the spiritual master and then discuss more specifically about His Holiness Bhakti Tirtha Swami Mahārāja.

We read from *Śrīmad-Bhāgavatam*, Canto Four, Chapter Twenty-eight: "Purañjana Becomes a Woman in the Next Life."

TEXT 48

uttiṣṭhottiṣṭha rājarṣe
imām udadhi-mekhalām
dasyubhyaḥ kṣatra-bandhubhyo
bibhyatīṁ pātum arhasi

TRANSLATION

O best of kings, please get up! Get up! Just see this world surrounded by water and infested with rogues and so-called kings. This world is very much afraid, and it is your duty to protect her.

PURPORT by Śrīla Prabhupāda

Whenever an *ācārya* comes, following the superior orders of the Supreme Personality of Godhead or His representative, he establishes the principles of religion, as enunciated in the *Bhagavad-gītā*. Religion means abiding by the orders of the

Supreme Personality of Godhead. Religious principles begin from the time one surrenders to the Supreme Personality of Godhead. It is the *ācārya's* duty to spread a bona fide religious system and induce everyone to bow down before the Supreme Lord. One executes the religious principles by rendering devotional service, specifically the nine items like hearing, chanting, and remembering. Unfortunately, when the *ācārya* disappears, rogues and nondevotees take advantage and immediately begin to introduce unauthorized principles in the name of so-called *svāmīs*, *yogīs*, philanthropists, welfare workers, and so on. Actually, human life is meant for executing the orders of the Supreme Lord, and this is stated in the *Bhagavad-gītā* (9.34):

man-manā bhava mad-bhakto
mad-yājī māṁ namaskuru
mām evaiṣyasi yuktvaivam
ātmānaṁ mat-parāyaṇaḥ

"Engage your mind always in thinking of Me and become My devotee. Offer obeisances and worship Me. Being completely absorbed in Me, surely you will come to Me."

The main business of human society is to think of the Supreme Personality of Godhead at all times, to become His devotees, to worship the Supreme Lord, and to bow down before Him. The *ācārya*, the authorized representative of the Supreme Lord, establishes these principles, but when he disappears, things once again become disordered. The perfect disciples of the *ācārya* try to relieve the situation by sincerely following the instructions of the spiritual master. At the present moment practically the entire world is afraid of rogues and nondevotees; therefore this Kṛṣṇa consciousness movement is started to save the world from irreligious principles. Everyone should cooperate with this movement in order to bring about actual peace and happiness in the world.

COMMENT by Giriraj Swami

This section of *Śrīmad-Bhāgavatam* describes a king and his devoted wife, who have entered the forest as *vānaprasthas* to perform austerities and realize God. At a certain stage, the king leaves his body, and feeling great anxiety in his absence, his widow begins to cry piteously. Śrīla Prabhupāda, following the previous *ācāryas*, explains in the purport that figuratively, the queen is the disciple of the king, or spiritual master.

So, here the widow is praying for her husband to get up and protect the world from rogues and so-called kings. Of course, because he actually has left his body, he will not return, at least not in the same form in which she had known him. But still, the principle of being protected by the instructions of the *ācārya* continues even after his disappearance, and the essence of those instructions is that one should surrender to the Supreme Personality of Godhead, Kṛṣṇa, and become His devotee, always think of Him (*man-manā*), worship Him (*mad-yājī*), and bow down to Him (*māṁ namaskuru*).

It is interesting that in the purport Śrīla Prabhupāda states, "It is the *ācārya's* duty to spread a bona fide religious system and induce everyone to bow down before the Supreme Lord." Not only does the *ācārya* present the system, but it is also his duty to induce people to actually follow. Thus the *ācārya* thinks of ways and means by which he can induce people to surrender unto the Supreme Lord.

One example that is prominent in our line is that of Lord Caitanya. He was a teacher in Navadvīpa, but His own students misunderstood Him and criticized Him. So He thought, "As long as they disrespect Me, as long as they criticize Me, they will not be able to be delivered." And, as described in *Śrī Caitanya-caritāmṛta*, the Lord, after full consideration, accepted the *sannyāsa* order of life, because followers of Vedic culture in every *varṇa* and *āśrama* respect a *sannyāsī*.

Śrīla Prabhupāda explains that an *ācārya* must think of the ways and means by which he can spread Kṛṣṇa consciousness, that preaching methods are not stereotyped. His Holiness Bhakti Tirtha Swami, following in the same line, also considered how to induce people to surrender to the Supreme Personality of Godhead, Kṛṣṇa. Like every *ācārya*, in doing so he preserved the basic principles of Kṛṣṇa consciousness, but he adjusted the presentation to attract people and induce people to actually take up the process of Kṛṣṇa consciousness.

When I first heard of some of Bhakti Tirtha Swami's preaching, specifically to members of the black community, I was a little surprised, because I'd never heard anyone preach like that. Śrīla Prabhupāda, at least superficially, never preached like that. So I wondered what was going on. But then I had the opportunity, together with His Holiness Tamal Krishna Goswami, to visit Mahārāja's institution in Washington DC—the Institute for Applied Spiritual Technology (IFAST)—and we met some of the devotees who had come to Kṛṣṇa consciousness by his preaching. I was very impressed by them—extremely impressed. They were very intelligent, sincere, competent, and respectful. They were just wonderful. It was so nice to be there with them. After attending the morning program and seeing the devotees there, seeing the organization, we had breakfast and later lunch with His Holiness Bhakti Tirtha Swami, and he explained some of his unique approach. He told us that he had people chanting sixteen rounds and following the four principles, engaging in the service of Kṛṣṇa and the worship of Kṛṣṇa, for months, if not years, before they knew that such a thing as the Hare Kṛṣṇa movement even existed. So I thought, "Wow! How did he do that? How does he do that?"

Śrīla Prabhupāda himself made many innovations, and some of his godbrothers criticized him. They thought he wasn't following strictly or that he was deviating; they had certain misconceptions about Śrīla Prabhupāda. But Śrīla Prabhupāda would say, *phalena paricīyate*: you have to judge by the result. And we could see the results of Bhakti Tirtha Swami's preaching at IFAST: the number of people who had joined, the caliber of the people, and the way in which they had been trained and engaged. It was striking.

In 1985 the Śrī Śrī Rādhā-Rādhānātha Temple of Understanding in Durban, South Africa, opened. It is a beautiful temple that in a way reflects Bhakti Tirtha Swami's—and Śrīla Prabhupāda's—mood of preaching, in that it contains some of the basic elements of a Vedic temple, with domes and other features, but at the same time is constructed with unusual materials in an innovative design. The basic traditional elements are there, but the whole complex combines traditional temple architecture with a modern design and modern materials.

When the temple was built, South Africa was under the regime of apartheid. It had its categories: whites, "coloreds," Indians (or Asians), and then blacks—in that order of gradation—but, as Śrīla Prabhupāda said at the first Bombay *paṇḍāl*, "We are the real United Nations." We wanted to show that we—and it is a fact, not a staged production—that we had Europeans and Indians and Africans all living together in harmony and serving together with Kṛṣṇa as the center.

The construction of the temple was a major achievement, and very prominent people from these three main ethnic categories came for the opening ceremonies. We had the mayor of Durban, who was white. The apartheid regime had allowed a degree of self-government to the Indians, and they had their own legislative assembly and judicial system and police force and managed their own affairs in relation to public welfare and utilities. (Of course, the military was in the hands of the whites.) So, we had the head of the Indian legislative assembly. And we had Chief Buthelezi, the head of the KwaZulu government and a most prominent leader of the Zulus, the largest tribe in South Africa. And we also wanted to have an outstanding black preacher from ISKCON. We had black devotees in South Africa, but not of that caliber, so we invited His Holiness Bhakti Tirtha Swami.

I was deputed to receive Mahārāja when he arrived. He came wearing a Nehru jacket and an ornate African cap—not the usual traditional *sannyāsa* dress—and he was very effulgent, very bright, very friendly. And he spoke very powerfully at the *paṇḍāl*. It was a huge gathering; maybe twenty thousand people came—very impressive.

Mahārāja and I had some quite intimate personal talks during that visit. Somehow I felt I could really trust him and open up to him. And he was extraordinarily perceptive. He had a keen sense of what was going on. At the time, there was an issue in ISKCON about more devotees accepting the responsibility of initiating disciples. And it was coming up about me, but I didn't feel qualified; I didn't want to do it. Somehow my reluctance came up in my talks with Bhakti Tirtha Swami. I really don't know how he found out these things. I think he got them from talking to people—even though he had been there for only a few days. So, I explained to him what I considered to be my disqualifications, and he pointed out that the thing about me is that I really care about the devotees and that the most important thing for a devotee is to feel that his or her *guru* really cares about him or her and isn't just concerned with getting service out of them. So he thought that was an important qualification. Then I said, "Well, what about accepting the sinful reactions of the disciples?" And he replied, "Yes, that is something to be concerned about, but you are mainly preaching to Indians who come from pious backgrounds, so I don't think that should be such an issue for you."

In subsequent years, Bhakti Tirtha Swami and I would meet

in Māyāpur during the annual GBC meetings, and we had many interesting discussions. During one, we were talking about how some devotees race ahead to reach the goal and then stumble and fall, whereas others don't go so quickly but advance more gradually, and don't fall down. Mahārāja gave the example of climbing up a pole. He said, "When you climb up a pole, you are going straight up. You are going straight to the top, and you can succeed if you have the strength. But the difficulty is that if you lose your grip, you fall all the way down." Then he gave a different example—of a winding staircase that goes around the pole. It is a much slower and more gradual process, but at least with the staircase, taking one step at a time—maybe not big steps—you are going up and not coming back down. Even if you are not going very quickly, at least you are making progress. So, it is not that one approach is better than another in any absolute sense. One is faster, but you have to have the strength, and there is a greater risk; the other is more gradual, but it requires less strength, and it is more certain.

Bhakti Tirtha Swami's Purpose

A talk at Mahārāja's disappearance festival on June 16, 2009, in Dallas.

Today we will continue our discussion of His Holiness Bhakti Tirtha Swami. Although I intend to focus on his last year, I will begin by mentioning some factors in his earlier history that contributed to the way he executed his service in his last year with us.

Mahārāja was born and grew up in an inner-city ghetto. At the time, there was—there still is, but it was much worse then—a lot of racial prejudice and mistreatment of minorities in America, and in particular of black people. Furthermore, he had a speech defect. He would stutter when he spoke, and people also ridiculed him for that.

Mahārāja's father left home, or wasn't fully responsible, when Mahārāja was still quite young, and so Mahārāja's mother was the main person in his early life. She was a very pious lady. Even toward the end, she demonstrated her spirituality in her appreciation for her son.

At Mahārāja's first Vyāsa-pūjā observance after he left, when his *samādhi* at Māyāpur was dedicated, one of the speakers was His Holiness Devamrita Swami. Perhaps the main theme of Devamrita Swami's talk was how Bhakti Tirtha Swami had exemplified the principle of *yukta-vairāgya*, a most important principle in devotional service.

anāsaktasya viṣayān
  yathārham upayuñjataḥ
nirbandhaḥ kṛṣṇa-sambandhe
  yuktaṁ vairāgyam ucyate

"Things should be accepted for the Lord's service, not for one's personal sense gratification. If one accepts something without attachment and accepts it because it is related to Kṛṣṇa, one's renunciation is called *yukta-vairāgya*." (*Brs* 1.2.255) Without attachment for material sense objects (*anāsaktasya viṣayān*), one who engages things appropriately (*yathārham upayuñjataḥ*) in relationship with Kṛṣṇa (*nirbandhaḥ kṛṣṇa-sambandhe*) is situated in proper renunciation (*yuktaṁ vairāgyam ucyate*). Devamrita Swami made the point that Mahārāja had used experiences from his youth, along with ideas he had developed, in Kṛṣṇa's service, in Kṛṣṇa consciousness.

Despite being born in a situation full of disadvantages and obstacles and difficulties, Bhakti Tirtha Swami still became a success, even before he came to Kṛṣṇa consciousness. For instance, he was elected president of his class at Princeton University, which was really extraordinary. It would be a great achievement for anyone, at any time, but for a black person to be elected president of his class at that time at such a prestigious university was a tremendous achievement.

Mahārāja became a fierce fighter for the principle that anyone from any background should be given a chance, and believed that everyone should have an equal opportunity to achieve success in life. And he applied the same principle in Kṛṣṇa consciousness—that everyone, regardless of their background or condition, should have the opportunity to become Kṛṣṇa conscious. Of course, that was also Śrīla Prabhupāda's mood from the very beginning.

Devamrita Swami related Mahārāja's affection for his mother, and his appreciation for all she did for him and the whole family, to his appreciation for all the mothers, the ladies, in ISKCON—that they should be respected and appreciated as mothers and also be encouraged to realize their full potential in Kṛṣṇa consciousness.

Then Devamrita Swami brought up the point that Bhakti Tirtha Swami had always been eager to get publicity. Whenever there was a camera, Mahārāja was in front of it. A conditioned soul seeing Mahārāja with mundane vision could take it that he was egoistic—that he wanted publicity, attention, fame—but the fact is that he really wanted to bring people to Kṛṣṇa consciousness. He understood that if he was a known and respected figure to whom people would be attracted—fame is one of the six opulences that are attractive to people—he could use that to bring people to Kṛṣṇa.

Mahārāja did extraordinary service as a book distributor during Śrīla Prabhupāda's presence, especially with the library party. When he went behind the Iron Curtain, he distributed huge numbers of full sets of Śrīla Prabhupāda's books. Śrīla Prabhupāda was extremely pleased with his service and bestowed extraordinary blessings on him. At one stage he said, "Thank you very much. Your life is perfect."

Then, in 1977, when Bhakti Tirtha Swami went to Māyāpur for the Gaura-pūrṇimā festival and Śrīla Prabhupāda was there, something happened that radically altered his view of devotional service. In Māyāpur he came to learn that the members of his book distribution party had met and were all considering resigning because they found that working with him was too intense. Mahārāja would get up at one in the morning, chant all his rounds, and read Śrīla Prabhupāda's books; he had a very strong morning program. He wouldn't take *prasāda*, and when the university libraries opened for the day, at eight or nine in the morning, he would be there, waiting; he didn't want even one moment to be lost from distributing Śrīla Prabhupāda's books. And he wouldn't take *prasāda* until nighttime, until the last library's doors had closed, often as late as ten o'clock. He felt that if he took *prasāda*, it would take up time that he could use to distribute Śrīla Prabhupāda's books. But the other members of the party couldn't all handle the intensity; it was just too much for them. So they had met and considered resigning from the library party.

When Mahārāja heard this, he was very hurt, and he rethought his whole mood of devotional service. He realized that just distributing the largest number of books and getting the greatest encouragement from the spiritual master wasn't everything. "If all the members of the party are so disturbed," he considered, "how could Śrīla Prabhupāda be pleased?" He had the realization that, as Śrīla Prabhupāda himself had said, it was not enough just to be the servant of the spiritual master; one also had to be the servant of the other servants of the spiritual master. And from then on, serving the devotees, caring for the devotees, became one of his most prominent concerns. And that concern was very much manifest in his final year.

In his last Vyāsa-pūjā offering to Śrīla Prabhupāda, Bhakti Tirtha Swami prayed to His Divine Grace to do whatever was necessary to him—to his body or mind—to purify him, and at the same time to enable him to better help the devotees and serve Śrīla Prabhupāda's mission. He was in the mood of Vāsudeva Datta, the great devotee of Lord Caitanya who prayed to the Lord, "Please let all the sinful reactions of all the living entities in the entire universe come upon me so that they can be liberated."

Actually, being relieved from sinful reactions and taking to Kṛṣṇa consciousness are related. In the *Bhagavad-gītā* Kṛṣṇa says,

yeṣāṁ tv anta-gataṁ pāpaṁ
janānāṁ puṇya-karmaṇām
te dvandva-moha-nirmuktā
bhajante māṁ dṛḍha-vratāḥ

"Persons who have acted piously in previous lives and in this life and whose sinful actions are completely eradicated, are freed from the dualities of delusion, and they engage themselves in My service with determination." (*Bg* 7.28) Those who are free from sin, whose sinful reactions have been eradicated, can take to devotional service. That is why at the time of initiation the spiritual master accepts the sinful reactions of the disciple, so that the disciple can understand what devotional service is and proceed in Kṛṣṇa consciousness. It includes being relieved of the miseries of sinful reactions, but the real idea is to be purified so that one can properly understand and execute devotional service.

So, Bhakti Tirtha Swami prayed in his offering to Śrīla Prabhupāda, in the same mood as Vāsudeva Datta, "I want to help the devotees. They are suffering . . ." He could see clearly that everyone was suffering—people outside the movement and people inside the movement. He saw within the movement, for example, that so many couples were becoming divorced, that so many of the younger generation, who had been raised in Kṛṣṇa consciousness and perhaps educated in Kṛṣṇa consciousness, had lost faith in Kṛṣṇa consciousness, that so many were angry and resentful—and depressed.

In Mahārāja's last months, a number of former *gurukula* students and other devotees—all very upset with ISKCON—came to meet with Mahārāja. They were so hurt and angry that for years they had never gone to an ISKCON temple or attended an ISKCON program. They couldn't face that atmosphere, which reminded them of all their pain and hurt and abuse. He repeatedly encouraged them to come and see him, and a number came—not only *gurukulīs*, but also older devotees who had experienced things that had led them to become angry and resentful. He chanted with them and spoke with them, and their hearts melted. They were crying. They would go up to him, offer prostrated obeisances, and then go back and sit down, listen some more, then go up again, offer prostrated obeisances, and go back and sit and listen some more.

His Holiness Radhanath Swami was with Bhakti Tirtha Swami during that period. Mahārāja had told him, "I want to die in your arms. Please stay with me." So Radhanath Swami stayed with Mahārāja for his last seven weeks. And he knew many of the people who came to see Mahārāja, and he had also tried to help them overcome their anger and resentment, but in his estimation he had never been successful. Now, as they came out of Mahārāja's room, they said, "This has been the most extraordinary experience of our lives. Our lives are changed forever. Nothing like this has ever happened to us."

Afterward, Radhanath Swami said to Bhakti Tirtha Swami, "What you did was extraordinary; the effect you had on these devotees was unprecedented. I've seen you for many years, and you've always been an empowered preacher, but I've never seen anything like this. How did you do it?" Bhakti Tirtha Swami replied, "I don't know how I did it. I don't think I am the one who did it. I did not know what to do or say. Something happened through me."

In his Vyāsa-pūjā offering to Śrīla Prabhupāda, Mahārāja had prayed that Prabhupāda use him, that Kṛṣṇa use him, in any way possible—do anything to him or for him, whatever it took, to simultaneously bring him to a higher level of purity and effect a more significant change in the lives of the devotees in ISKCON. He had expected that he would have to leave his body, but he didn't think it would come so soon. He had thought it would come in the following year. But Śrīla Prabhupāda responded to his prayer very quickly, and Mahārāja discovered that he had cancer.

His mood was not that he wanted to leave his body but that he was ready for whatever it would take for him to help the devotees more, to serve the mission better, whether it meant staying in the body or leaving.

Naturally, devotees wanted him to stay. We all wanted him

to stay, and he undertook various courses of treatment. He didn't want anyone to feel that he hadn't tried his best to get cured. At times he appeared to be getting better, but ultimately his condition deteriorated. The cancer spread and became more and more painful. Yet he felt that he was doing more during his illness, effecting more significant change, than he had done when he had been traveling, leading *kīrtana*, dancing, giving classes, and meeting with devotees. Some of our godsisters related to me that in Washington DC he had told them that he felt that when he had been engaged in those activities he hadn't had as much of a lasting effect. Devotees would be ecstatic when he was there, but he wasn't sure how much of an effect his visits had after he left. He felt that now, during his illness, he was doing much more than he had ever done before.

So many people were phoning and opening their hearts to him, revealing their minds and taking his counsel, taking shelter of him. When he had been active, when he had been a GBC, some devotees had harbored reservations because he was a leader in ISKCON. They didn't know whether if they told him something confidential—confided in him about their weaknesses or difficulties—it could negatively affect their service, their reputations, their positions. They were not necessarily concerned for their own sakes, but for them to serve effectively, they needed devotees to have faith in them. But when Bhakti Tirtha Swami became so sick and wasn't traveling, wasn't performing his regular duties as a GBC, wasn't even in the mood to act on that managerial level, they began to feel that they could open up to him without fear of any institutional repercussions. And he felt that he was able to help so many more people than he had when he had been more physically fit and active.

One godsister, Rukmiṇī dāsī, also visited him at the Institute house in Silver Spring. Mahārāja's caregiver Vraja-līlā dāsī insisted that she go up to his room to see him. Rukmiṇī was a bit angry at Mahārāja for making that prayer. She was thinking that he was one of the most progressive voices on the GBC and that it would be a great loss for the devotees and the mission to be without his voice advocating devotee care, imploring us to honor all Vaiṣṇavas. "How is this prayer going to help anyone?" she wondered, and she expressed that to him. But he was emphatic: "No, no, it's already working." He told her that so many devotees who had lost faith, had lost their connection with devotees or the society, were approaching him on the phone or by e-mail and were receiving help and solace, were reviving their desire to chant, or serve, or associate again with the devotees.

Bhakti Tirtha Swami manifested a real potency for healing—healing hearts, mending broken hearts, healing relationships, mending broken relationships—and it was something that we could feel. I am sure it was felt throughout the movement, but it was something that we felt tangibly all the way across the country, in Los Angeles, during the Prabhupāda Festival at the end of May. Everyone's consciousness was elevated by his mercy and potency, and we could feel it. And it was reflected especially in the way devotees were relating to each other and responding to each other.

I wasn't the only one to feel it. One morning, outside the temple, perhaps during the breakfast break, I happened to meet two devotees, Yudhiṣṭhira and Bhakta Avatāra. I didn't know them very well, but Yudhiṣṭhira had assisted Bhakti Tirtha Swami when he was trying various treatments in Mexico and Southern California, and later visited him in Gita Nagari. And they too were appreciating how Bhakti Tirtha Swami was raising the consciousness of all the devotees in ISKCON. Amoghalīlā Prabhu joined us, and he also felt the same thing. He told stories from the Bay area of devotees who had held anger or grudges, and how things were all getting worked out. These incidences of healing were very powerful, and they continued, even intensified, after Mahārāja left.

Shortly after the Prabhupāda Festival, a godsister named Caitanya dāsī phoned me to interview me for the Friends of the BBT newsletter, and somehow the subject of Bhakti Tirtha Swami came up. Caitanya dāsī commented on what a tremendous influence he had had on her life, even though they had really met only twice. One time, he was visiting some devotees in North Carolina and she had been invited to join them. Early in the morning Mahārāja was chanting his rounds in their temple room. She was also chanting there, and she could feel how deeply he was going into his chanting. She felt that he was in Vṛndāvana and that he was somehow in touch with Rūpa Gosvāmī. And by Mahārāja's mercy, she also felt like she was in Vṛndāvana.

After chanting some rounds, he was ready to go for his morning walk. She had never gotten to go with Śrīla Prabhupāda on one of his morning walks—or if she had, she had been so far behind the group of devotees with him that she hadn't been able to hear the discussion or really participate. So, she asked Mahārāja if she could go with him, and he said, "Yes." She felt from the way he answered that he was not in the bodily concept at all; he was just seeing her as a spirit soul.

On the walk, she told him about what she had experienced while he was chanting, and he replied, "You can also have the same experience if you chant with the same intensity. Anyone can." She took that as an important instruction.

The only other time she had really had Mahārāja's association was in Alachua during a seminar he was conducting on depression. In the course of the seminar, he mentioned that an important factor in depression was loneliness and the sense of feeling alone. And for twenty minutes he guided the participants in a visualization, a meditation on Kṛṣṇa in the heart. He described Kṛṣṇa extremely vividly and in great detail—His locks of curling hair and His reddish eyes, His beauty and His mercy. And this most beautiful person, Mahārāja said, this most wonderful and most loving person, is right there with you in your heart; you can access Him at any time. So where is the question of being alone? You have the most beautiful, wonderful, caring, loving friend—your best friend—right in your heart. She said that after the twenty minutes, when the devotees opened their eyes, they saw every single devotee in the room was crying—out of relief, release of emotion, and happiness that Kṛṣṇa was there in their hearts, really there, and that He was available to them, and for them.

After Bhakti Tirtha Swami left his body, Caitanya dāsī, like others, felt great separation. She hadn't anticipated how much separation she would feel. Everyone was expecting his departure; at the end they knew it could be any day. But still, she felt so much separation. She was just crying and crying and feeling a great sense of loss. And it went on for some days. In the midst of that, when she came to the most desperate state, he manifested himself to her, and he reminded her of the instruction he had given her in North Carolina: "If you go deep into the chanting and into the mood of devotion, you can experience Vṛndāvana wherever you are." And that had a profound effect on her. For years she had been thinking, "Oh, I just want to go to Vṛndāvana, retire from all other activities and just go to Vṛndāvana, but I have children. Until I finish my duties to my children, I can't go." And that was a very clear message: "You can experience Vṛndāvana wherever you are if you go deep into the chanting and the mood of Vṛndāvana."

Every Sunday, Mahārāja would speak in the temple room at Gita Nagari, and it was tremendous. The lectures would be uploaded on the Internet, and I would watch them from California. They were so powerful. The intensity of emotion, the clarity of thought—it was very profound. He was really affecting people's hearts.

Many devotees, godbrothers and godsisters, who had gone to New Vrindaban for the Festival of Inspiration in May 2005 really wanted to see Bhakti Tirtha Swami, and they knew that he came out on Sundays to speak. So they left early Sunday morning for Gita Nagari to see and pay their respects to Bhakti Tirtha Swami, perhaps for the last time.

That Sunday, Mahārāja was too sick to go to the temple, but the devotees set up a place for him in the garden and then carried him down from his room. His body was so delicate and sensitive, and he was experiencing so much pain, that they had to carry him extremely carefully, because any movement could cause even more intense pain. He couldn't speak very loud. He began by singing, and he was crying; all the devotees were crying. Sometimes it was hard for him to speak. And then at a certain stage he stopped. He just couldn't continue. So the devotees took him back. And then the other devotees thought, "We should just talk about Bhakti Tirtha Swami." Mahārāja was too weak to sit up and remain with them, but they later learned that he had been listening from his bed, lying down hearing all the affectionate words that were being spoken about him.

Rukmiṇī told me that she was especially moved by the words of a *sannyāsī* godbrother, Candraśekhara Swami, who said, "As we are witnessing the last days of the glorious life of Bhakti Tirtha Swami, we are all weeping over the impending loss of such a great personality." He said that through this experience he was getting some understanding of how the stone heart actually melts. It is like when water seeps into the sediment in rocks and stones and then, as the temperature rises and falls, freezes and thaws, causing the stone to break into smaller and smaller pieces, from rocks to small pebbles and from small pebbles to sand, which can then mix with the earth, and then seeds can enter and sprout and grow. In the same way, our tears at this time of the impending loss of such a great and beloved godbrother are cracking our stone hearts. And now the *bhakti* creeper can truly take root and sprout deeply within us. As Rukmiṇī noted, *bhakti* is a softening of the heart. And this they all experienced that day as they honored Mahārāja.

Rukmiṇī added that after all the devotees spoke about Bhakti Tirtha Swami under the tree, the godbrothers and godsisters were invited into his house to take *prasāda*. After *prasāda*, they went into his room, and each approached him individually to bid him farewell and to offer his or her prayers. Many of them felt that when he spoke to them, it was as if Śrīla Prabhupāda were speaking through him. Mahārāja said different things to each devotee, exactly what each needed to hear, to be inspired, to be corrected, to be validated in his or her service. Satyarāja Prabhu came away shaking his head in amazement. When Rukmiṇī asked him, "What did he say?" Satyarāja just replied, "I know what he was saying. He knows, and I know"—something that intimate and personal. To Anuttama Prabhu he said, "Continue the work you're doing. You're building bridges. It's very important. Continue." Rukmiṇī said that at that time it seemed as though the line, the division, between this world and the world beyond this world was blurred. He was so close to entering that realm, that reality—and we were being encouraged to enter that reality.

Amoghalīlā told us a story in Carpinteria that he had heard then at Gita Nagari from a devotee named Nārada Muni from New Vrindaban. After Bhakti Tirtha Swami had done his service with the library party, after Śrīla Prabhupāda had left, he went to New York, and he was going to people's homes and distributing full sets of Śrīla Prabhupāda's books. What he was doing was unprecedented—imagine just going to some stranger's home and getting the person to buy a full set of Śrīla Prabhupāda's books. In New Vrindaban Kīrtanānanda Swami was getting reports about Mahārāja's activities, so he said to one of the devotees there, Nārada Muni, "I want you to go to New York and find out how he does it, so we can also do it."

So, Nārada Muni went to see Mahārāja, and Mahārāja said, "Yes, I'll tell you how I do it. You can even come with me and see how." It is not like he was thinking, "Oh, I have a secret. I am not going to let anyone know so I can be number one and no one can get close to me." What he did, he told Nārada Muni, was research various organizations that dealt with UFOs, unidentified flying objects, which some people thought were spaceships carrying aliens from other planets. He would get the names and addresses of people who were into UFOs, and then he would pay each a visit.

Dressed in suit and tie, wearing a wig, and carrying a briefcase full of Prabhupāda's books, Mahārāja would visit people in their homes and tell them, "I have these books for you. These are from another world." He'd show them the books—the Sanskrit script, which they'd never seen before, and the pictures of demigods, demons, and the spiritual world. It was obvious that these personalities and places were not from this planet. He would say, "These books are not from this world and they tell about life in other realms." And the people—that particular audience—were often very interested.

Finally, if someone wasn't ready to buy a set of books, Bhakti Tirtha Swami would suddenly whip off his wig and reveal his shaved head. And they would be shocked. They would think, "He has really come from some other planet—I better buy these books!" Mahārāja would do anything and everything to serve Śrīla Prabhupāda and the mission.

One of Mahārāja's disciples, Puruṣa-sūkta Prabhu, has taken up his mood of spiritual care for devotees and formed an institution called Bhagavat Life, which focuses on *japa*, our central practice in Kṛṣṇa consciousness. One topic in *japa* retreats and weekends is one's mood during *japa*, and I asked Puruṣa-sūkta if Bhakti Tirtha Swami had told him anything about his mood when he chanted. Puruṣa-sūkta Prabhu smiled and replied, "My *guru mahārāja* would always like to sit at the lotus feet of Śrīla Prabhupāda and chant. And he said that his meditation while chanting was that he would like Śrīla Prabhupāda's lotus foot to kick him." Of course, I am sure there are many levels to Mahārāja's meditation when he chants, but I thought his answer was apt. Although humorous, it was also genuine, because that was Bhakti Tirtha Swami's mood: "Whatever it takes to wake me up in Kṛṣṇa consciousness—whatever it takes to make me a better instrument—do it."

In his last days, Bhakti Tirtha Swami was in so much physical pain that he could hardly sleep. Even when he did manage to fall asleep, he would soon be awakened by the pain. And he was so weak that he couldn't move himself, even to turn over. But remaining in one position became very painful. So his servants would change his position every hour. Still, sometimes he would chant his rounds in the middle of the night, when he could have at least been lying in bed and resting. One night, His Holiness Radhanath Swami approached Mahārāja and said, "Why are you up at one in the morning chanting *japa*?" Mahārāja answered, "From the day I took my vows of initiation I've chanted at least sixteen rounds every day, and I don't want to stop now." Radhanath Swami said, "But you are in so much pain. Kṛṣṇa will understand. You've done enough." But Mahārāja replied, "No. I've followed this vow every day of my life since my initiation, and I am not going to stop now." "So," Radhanath Swami later said to a group of devotees to whom he was relating the exchange, "what excuse can we have?"

Bhakti Tirtha Swami was so concerned about the care of devotees. I also wanted to pick up that mood, and when I asked him for his advice on how best to serve them, he replied in a letter, with special reference to the hospice project in Vṛndāvana:

"The programs that you are setting up are already guaranteeing a better future for many devotees in ISKCON. Just stay focused to see that this wonderful project is not slowed down or sabotaged."

Then he made a very valuable point, which is that while we engage in projects for the benefit of the devotees we should also go deep in our own spiritual lives. "We need to simultaneously go deeper in our consciousness. Śrīla Bhaktivinoda Ṭhākura always said that offenseless chanting naturally brings forth compassion in a *sādhu* and that compassion should be manifest externally in various ways to protect the creepers of as many devotees as possible, through certain tangible projects. So there must be these two parallel activities going on: our own diving into internal, richer, devotional consciousness, whilst allowing it to be a catalyst to help us to create greater projects and arrangements." He enunciated a valuable principle, and he demonstrated it in his own life. He went very deep in his own spiritual practices, his chanting of the holy name, his reading of scripture, his mood of prayer, and of course, his surrender to *guru*, which is the basis of everything. At the same time, he was so active, so dynamic, so creative in developing programs both to bring new people to Kṛṣṇa consciousness and to help the devotees already on the path of Kṛṣṇa consciousness to overcome the obstacles that keep them from making good progress on the way.

The way Śrīla Prabhupāda finally called for Bhakti Tirtha Swami is quite mysterious and confidential. After trying various treatments in Mexico, Hawaii, and DC, Mahārāja returned to Gita Nagari, where he had a dream in which Tamal Krishna Goswami came to him on Śrīla Prabhupāda's behalf. In the dream, as Mahārāja described it to Radhanath Swami, Tamal Krishna Goswami was weeping and Bhakti Tirtha Swami asked him, "Why?" Tamal Krishna Goswami replied, "Because I know how much my disciples and followers have suffered from separation since I left, and I am thinking of how much your disciples and followers and well-wishers will also suffer. I am crying for all of your followers, but you must come now, because Śrīla Prabhupāda is calling for you, just as he called for me." And he told Bhakti Tirtha Swami that he would come and see him once more.

So Bhakti Tirtha Swami was waiting, and one day several devotees from Dallas came with Tamal Krishna Goswami's personal Deities, little Rādhā-Dāmodara, and set up an altar with Them and sang beautiful *bhajanas*. On the altar Bhakti Tirtha Swami saw a small photo of Tamal Krishna Goswami, and he understood that now Tamal Krishna Goswami had come. And he told Radhanath Swami that Tamal Krishna Goswami had come as promised, in the form of his Deities and his photo.

So, we remember His Holiness Bhakti Tirtha Swami, and we pray to him for his mercy, that we can follow his mood of simultaneously going deep in our spiritual practices, our spiritual consciousness, and extending ourselves in the mood of loving care and compassion to help others. Although at the end he was more focused on the devotees, he was concerned about everyone. Once he said that he gave 60 percent to helping devotees and 40 percent to reaching out to new people. He did both, though at the end he focused more on the devotees—who in turn will reach out to new people.

Having come from an underprivileged background—of course, it is also Vaiṣṇava humility and compassion—Mahārāja didn't want to be privileged. (He noted that sometimes a black person would become successful and live a very high lifestyle while other blacks were suffering in deprivation and poverty.) At the end, devotees took up a collection for his medical treatment, and because he was so loving and caring toward others, and so dear to Prabhupāda and Kṛṣṇa, money poured in. So, he joked, "Well, I know I'll be able to pay off my contribution to the youth fund now. Kṛṣṇa accomplishes many things with one action." But he was really very concerned about what would happen to other devotees in their old age, in their infirmity, in cases of terminal illnesses. So he willed that whatever funds were left after his treatment and ultimate departure and funeral be kept in a fund and distributed to devotees in need. He wanted all devotees to have the benefit of good care in their old age, in illness, and at the end of life.

He is a magnanimous, merciful, compassionate personality, like Śrī Caitanya Mahāprabhu and Nityānanda Prabhu, and our whole line of *ācāryas*, preachers. We do miss him, but at the same time we can feel his presence, especially by following his instructions and taking up his mood of service to Kṛṣṇa, to Caitanya Mahāprabhu, to Śrīla Prabhupāda, to the Vaiṣṇavas, and to the world, to the fallen souls.

We miss Bhakti Tirtha Swami very much.

The Last Year

From interviews with Ekavīra dāsa and Vraja-līlā dāsī, May and July, 2010, in Dallas and Gita Nagari.

Giriraj Swami: How did you meet His Holiness Bhakti Tirtha Swami Mahārāja?

Vraja-līlā dāsī: I was new to Kṛṣṇa consciousness and, encouraged by my boyfriend, had recently moved from New York to the Los Angeles temple, where I was being trained to distribute Śrīla Prabhupāda's books. Bhakti Tirtha Swami visited the temple during that time and coincidentally met my friend, whom he knew from New York. Mahārāja inquired about his activities and invited him to Washington DC to help with his new restaurant project. And he suggested that I come too.

Two days later, I was traveling back across the country, from Los Angeles to Washington DC, only this time it was to meet this swami who needed help with his restaurant project. When we arrived, we were picked up at the bus station by one of Mahārāja's servants and brought to a two-story building in a developing section of the inner city. The restaurant, Govinda's, was on the ground floor in the front, and in the back was a small temple room.

When we entered the temple area, I saw a person dressed in saffron sitting on a low seat. I didn't really look at him; I simply offered my obeisance, raised myself to my knees, lifted my head, looked at him, and said, "Oh, I know you." I felt a childlike excitement. I didn't know how I knew him, or from where, but I felt like I did. Then he said, "Yes, and I know you. And I have been waiting for you." That was late in 1979.

During our talk Bhakti Tirtha Swami asked me, "So, are you two married?" I said, "Well, we are not legally married, but we are together as a couple." He seemed to be disturbed that we were together but not married. I didn't really believe in the institution of marriage then, so I was thinking, "Wait, is he going to tell me to get married?" But he was very serious, and he explained the need for us to be married. That was his first instruction to me: "You must get married." And I knew I would accept his instruction, because I knew he was looking after my best interests.

I was to stay with another lady in a room downstairs, in the rear of the restaurant. The men stayed upstairs. So I wondered, "Where does he stay?" When I asked, he replied, "Well, I have a room over here, in the back."

He apologized profusely for the accommodations, because it was really austere. There wasn't a full shower, so I would have to bathe in the restaurant bathroom, which had three toilets and three sinks. I would have to fill a container with water and pour it over myself, and the water would flow through a drain in the bathroom floor. He explained apologetically that they were trying to make other arrangements but that because there were more men than women, the upstairs was reserved for the men.

A day or two later, I asked the other devotees where Mahārāja was living, and they told me that he slept on a bedroll in the room where they stored the books he received as donations for Africa. He would get up much earlier than the ladies and use the same bathroom.

I could see that this was an austere person, and I was struck by the austerities he was performing. I also understood that he was performing them for someone he loved. I had seen the intensity of the devotion and commitment of the book distributors in Los Angeles, and I knew they were doing it out of love for Śrīla Prabhupāda. And I saw the same thing in him. He had a kind of commitment that I had never seen before, and that I wanted to have. I thought, "I want to learn this from him."

From the moment I met him, I saw that he always was very welcoming—to both devotees and just people off the street. Even if someone came into the restaurant and didn't have money, he would tell the devotees, "Please make sure they get something to eat." He was always concerned about others. That was just his mood.

These were some of the things that made me want to understand more about the love he had for the person who motivated him—Śrīla Prabhupāda—and Mahārāja helped me develop that understanding. Even though in Los Angeles I was being trained to distribute Śrīla Prabhupāda's books, I had never fully understood why we were doing all that we were doing. Mahārāja took the time to explain why we went out to distribute books, why we solicited donations. He spoke to us about Śrīla Prabhupāda's dedication, and we saw that everything he was doing was out of his love for his *guru*; he wanted to please Śrīla Prabhupāda however he could.

One morning at the restaurant Mahārāja came out of the bookroom and called everybody and said, "We need to have a short *iṣṭa-goṣṭhī*." We went into the small temple room, and when we were all sitting together, he said, "Śrīla Prabhupāda came to me in a dream last night, and he showed me all these black faces and he kept pointing to them. So I have to go to Africa." Just like that. We were stunned. I asked, "What do you mean you have to go to Africa?" And he replied, "I just have to go. I have been avoiding this. I knew that Śrīla Prabhupāda wanted me to reach out and connect with the African people, and now I have to go."

Within a few days, he had his passport and was gone. One minute he was there, and the next he was gone. We were all amazed: "Wow! So this is what it means to be surrendered."

Before leaving for Africa, Mahārāja arranged for my boyfriend and me to be initiated, in New Vrindaban, and for me to go to New York to get more training as a book distributor. Then he sent Ekendra Prabhu and me (we were married by then) and another couple to Nigeria, West Africa, where we joined Brahmānanda Swami. And for the next eight years Ekendra and I lived in West Africa, pioneering temples and preaching centers and distributing Śrīla Prabhupāda's books in Nigeria, Ghana, Ivory Coast, Liberia, Sierra Leone, Zambia, and Zimbabwe.

Bhakti Tirtha Swami would come regularly—sometimes two or three times a year—and encourage us in our service. When we had been in Zimbabwe for a short time, Mahārāja came for a visit, and he had an urgent request: "I want you to go to Zambia." We had just started the temple in Zimbabwe—we hadn't quite gotten settled—and we didn't understand. He explained, "We need to preach to the president of Zambia. He is a vegetarian. So we need to get in there."

He was always seeing ahead. He always understood the needs of the country and the people, and the strategy to use to get our message to the leaders. He would have us go into each country and meet people, and then he would develop relationships with them and cultivate those who could help.

So we packed our stuff and drove to Zambia. In Lusaka, with the help of a kind Indian family, we got to know a judge, and when Bhakti Tirtha Swami came he developed the relationship, and the next thing we knew we were meeting with President Kaunda and giving him a set of Śrīla Prabhupāda's books!

As Ekendra and I went from country to country, we realized more and more the depth of Bhakti Tirtha Swami's commitment. He hadn't planned to go to Africa, but Śrīla Prabhupāda had come to him in his dream. And when he told us to go and make the arrangements for him, we were ready, because that is what he had taught us. That is how he did it. He just got that dream, and he was gone. So we thought, "Okay, he wants us to go, so we go." My *guru mahārāja* always taught by example, and that meant a lot to me. I appreciated that a person could be so committed, love someone so much that he would do anything for him. His dedication nourished whatever little desire I had to understand more about Kṛṣṇa consciousness. And even today this is what keeps me going. I remember his faith, his commitment, his loyalty, and his deep love for people. He had deep affection and wanted to help people. When I get confused (which happens sometimes) I remember those things about my *guru mahārāja*, how committed he was to serving Śrīla Prabhupāda through deepening those qualities. He spent a lot of time on self-improvement, self-development, and he would share with us all the work that he did to make himself a better servant of Śrīla Prabhupāda.

One of the things I really appreciate about my *guru mahārāja* is how open he was to feedback and suggestions. Although he was our *guru*, he would ask, "What do you think about this? How do you think this will work? Do you have any suggestions?" He didn't need to consult us. Or he could have done so just as a formality. But we could see that he was consulting us in a genuine way, and he would sometimes act on the things that disciples suggested. It was a quality he had right up until he left his body.

Ekavīra dāsa: That also attracted me—that he accepted feedback and that it was genuine when he asked—but that happened when we became closer. Before that, I was attracted by how he could enter any environment and develop relationships with people from any walk of life and stimulate in them a desire to come closer to God. (At that point he didn't speak about "Kṛṣṇa" in public preaching—just God.)

Giriraj Swami: How did you first meet Bhakti Tirtha Swami?

Ekavīra dāsa: I first heard him on the radio when I was living in Washington DC. Even though on the surface everything was going well in my life—my career was going well, I had many friends and associates, and I had an active social life—I wasn't satisfied. I remember driving back from a trip to Atlanta one time and just crying. It was raining outside, and my tears were flowing like the rainfall. So I prayed: "My dear Lord, I just want to know You. I don't understand why it is so difficult. Please help me know You."

The next day, I went back to work. And during my lunch hour I went to get something from my car, but when I got there I couldn't remember what I had come to get. My memory went blank. But it was time for a radio program I listened to—Reverend Ambrose Lane—so I turned on the car radio. "This is Reverend Ambrose Lane," I heard, "and today I have a very special guest. His name is Swami Krishnapada." And Reverend Lane proceeded to give a detailed description of Swami Krishnapada—Bhakti Tirtha Swami.

In the interview, Reverend Lane asked Bhakti Tirtha Swami about secret societies, and that piqued my interest. "Tell us a little about secret societies," the Reverend prompted. And Bhakti Tirtha Swami replied, "Well, we have been talking about secret societies for the last thirty years. That's nothing new." And then he elaborated. For the first time, I found someone who was aware of what was going on in society but who was then able to take the discussion to another level and present a spiritual perspective.

That evening, Bhakti Tirtha Swami was scheduled to speak at one of the local universities, and I decided to go. The topic was "Demigods and Archangels and Their Position in the New World Order." George Bush Sr. was president then, and he spoke of establishing a "new world order," and Bhakti Tirtha Swami was using the phrase to attract people to his talk.

When I got to the auditorium, it was packed with hundreds of people, and when Bhakti Tirtha Swami came in, everyone stood and applauded. I listened to the lecture, and from that point on I was captivated. Each week, I took someone different to his weekly lecture in the auditorium of Howard University. And I would have them sign up for an audience, or *darśana*, with him, and I would also sign up. And each week, those persons would get called for *darśana* but I wouldn't. After four weeks, I was wondering what was going on. "What is this? Is there some conspiracy here?" Then I thought, "Well, maybe I am just not supposed to meet him." And on Monday evening, when I had actually accepted that I was not meant to speak with him, someone phoned me and invited me for *darśana* the next day.

While waiting to have *darśana*, I met a few of Mahārāja's close associates, including Vraja-līlā, and we had some discussion, and then I had *darśana*. I don't know why, but I had brought a gift for him.

I remember another radio interview, on a Christian program, and the Christian minister, who knew that Bhakti Tirtha Swami had been a child evangelist, asked him, "Why, with your background, are you a Hare Kṛṣṇa?" He responded, "I am no more a Hare Kṛṣṇa than you are. I have no desire to become Christian, Muslim, Hare Kṛṣṇa, or any other temporary designation. I desire to love God, and if I could learn how to love God in the Boy Scouts, I would become a Boy Scout." He said, "It just so happens that this process helps me to learn to love God more than any other process I've encountered. If you can show me another process that can help me develop love for God more, then let's talk about it." In the beginning, the minister had been quite cantankerous, but by the end he had become respectful and receptive. And personally, I wasn't looking for a sectarian religion; I was looking for a higher understanding. So I thought, "Wow! This is quite interesting."

Over time, I became more and more captivated by this person who could go into any environment and connect with people in all walks of life. At the Howard programs, mainly African-American professionals attended, including many professors. Radio talk-show hosts would attend, and they would invite Mahārāja to speak on their shows. And Mahārāja had programs in other places as well, where people were not aware of Śrīla Prabhupāda's teachings—some mainly for white Americans; some specifically for doctors, for attorneys, or for martial arts practitioners; some in churches; and some at the Pentagon. Wherever he went, he showed appreciation for the people he was addressing, and they felt valued and took interest in what he had to say—what he had learned from Śrīla Prabhupāda.

GIRIRAJ SWAMI: Now can you tell us about Bhakti Tirtha Swami's last year?

EKAVĪRA DĀSA: Just before Bhakti Tirtha Swami was diagnosed with melanoma, he was concerned about devotees worldwide not really being happy. It made him sad, going to different places and seeing how devotees were struggling and suffering, and he wondered how Śrīla Prabhupāda would use him to help them become happy in Kṛṣṇa consciousness. He used to talk about that quite often, and it culminated in 2004 when he composed a prayer to Śrīla Prabhupāda as part of his offering for His Divine Grace's Vyāsa-pūjā. "Dear Śrīla Prabhupāda," he wrote. "I would like to ask you, Can you arrange that [your followers'] sufferings come to me so that many can be freed from their anguish and thus joyfully serve you and return to Kṛṣṇa with fewer encumbrances?" He wanted to relieve the devotees of some of their distress so that they could experience Kṛṣṇa consciousness on a deeper level.

That spring, he showed symptoms of having physical difficulties, and we started taking him to the doctor and dentist. In June we went to the New York Ratha-yātrā, and for the first time he didn't dance the entire way. The devotees weren't aware of it, but he was not feeling well. He had to leave early because he was tired and his foot was hurting. He would always push himself to dance and try to encourage the devotees to take shelter of the *kīrtana*, but this time he was really fatigued, and right after the procession he told me, "You should get the car so we can leave. I don't know what's happening, but I am really exhausted." So we went back to Gita Nagari. We were supposed to stay in the New York area longer, but we went right back. Mahārāja didn't even take *prasāda*. He was really grave.

VRAJA-LĪLĀ DĀSĪ: Soon thereafter, I noticed Mahārāja paying more attention to his foot. He had me call his disciple Nimāi Caitanya, a naturopath, to tell him that he was having some throbbing. He always wore socks, so we never saw much, but one time I saw a big growth there. He was to attend the Toronto Ratha-yātrā, but I said, "Guru Mahārāja, I don't think you can go." He was limping when he walked. "This is obviously giving you pain. Maybe going is not the best thing. We can call and let the devotees know." But he wouldn't relent. "No; the devotees have paid my ticket, and they are expecting me. I must go."

EKAVĪRA DĀSA: He participated in the Ratha-yātrā, dancing the entire time and inspiring the devotees. But the devotees serving him phoned that night and said that he couldn't sleep because he was in so much pain and that he was rushing to Detroit the next day and wanted us to come there to pick him up. In Detroit he saw a doctor, who advised him to see a specialist, so we took him back to Washington.

Madhvācārya, one of his early disciples in America and a doctor in Washington, set up an appointment with a podiatrist. He was concerned about the growth on Mahārāja's foot. There had been a dark spot there from Mahārāja's birth, but it had developed into a growth in the 1980s, when Mahārāja had started taking disciples, and become more pronounced in the 1990s. Mahārāja had had the foot examined, but when the doctors performed a biopsy, it hadn't indicated any malignancy, so he didn't think anything of it. They had also said that if they operated on it he could possibly lose some functioning of his foot. But this time the podiatrist said that he needed to have it removed, because it was causing so much pain.

He was scheduled for surgery to remove the tumor, but during the pre-op procedures the doctors determined that they couldn't proceed, because his blood pressure and sugar levels were too high. Over the course of the next week, we addressed his diet, and his blood pressure and glucose level came down into normal ranges, and he had the operation.

Afterward, Bhakti Tirtha Swami and Madhvācārya spoke with the podiatrist. The podiatrist said that he had tried to remove the tumor but that as soon as he had cut it, he saw black cells. "This isn't good," he had thought. He had removed as much as he could and had had the specimen biopsied, and it had come back positive for melanoma. He said that he was referring Mahārāja to an oncologist.

When Bhakti Tirtha Swami came back from the hospital, he asked to see us. Sitting on his bed, he smiled and said, "Well, I'm out of here." "What do you mean?" we asked. He said, "They cut the tumor and found that it was positive for melanoma. I have cancer." At that point Vraja-līlā collapsed and started crying. "Oh, Vraja, Vraja, come on now," he said. "Get it together." So then we just sat and talked about it.

Mahārāja talked about plans to address the cancer, but at the same time he was concerned about the devotees he was reaching out to in different places, like Russia, where he was going to speak to them, and how they would be disappointed if he were unable to come. He had an itinerary, and his trip was scheduled to take place in the following couple of weeks.

VRAJA-LĪLĀ DĀSĪ: We were getting his passport ready. (Ekendra had left ISKCON, and on Guru Mahārāja's advice, I had married Ekavīra Prabhu.)

Ekavīra dāsa: Yes, we had been getting everything ready for him to travel, and he was concerned about how the devotees would respond. But he had to address his health. And yet, he was thinking about the devotees in Russia, how they would be disappointed.

Vraja-līlā dāsī: Then Ekavīra and other disciples—including Dhruva Mahārāja dāsa, from South Africa; Murāri Gupta Prabhu, a retired doctor; and Devarṣi dāsa, a chiropractor—started researching alternative approaches, because Guru Mahārāja didn't want to continue with allopathic treatment. He had already done that, and he wanted to find a different way to address the cancer. Within the next couple of weeks Mahārāja decided on the Hope4Cancer Institute in Mexico, and then we were off—Bhakti Tirtha Swami, Ekavīra Prabhu, and I—to Mexico, to the Hope clinic.

Ekavīra dāsa: At the clinic, Bhakti Tirtha Swami was being treated by Dr. Antonio Jimenez, affectionately called "Dr. Tony," from Colombia.

Vraja-līlā dāsī: Bhakti Tirtha Swami was taking treatments throughout the day until late at night, and at the same time he was preaching to the doctors and nurses, dictating replies to the e-mails he received, and working on *Spiritual Warrior VI*. The Hope Institute had many patients and visitors; busloads of people would come from San Diego. So Mahārāja gave programs for the people who were coming, often speaking on the theme "We are not this body"—that the body will die but that we, the soul, will continue.

Ekavīra dāsa: From Mexico, we went to San Diego for a day and then to Palm Springs for a week or two, so he could continue the protocol from the clinic and then return there so the doctors could examine him and see if he was making progress. It was a very difficult time for Mahārāja, but in each place, despite pain, fever, nausea, and other reactions to his treatment, he insisted on somehow, in some way, preaching to whomever he could.

Once, Yudhiṣṭhira dāsa and Rādhā dāsī, whose mother had arranged the time-share where Bhakti Tirtha Swami and we were staying in Palm Springs, organized a program for Mahārāja at their home. Before the program and even on the way, Bhakti Tirtha Swami had been regurgitating and perspiring, but at the program he simply smiled, spoke, answered questions, and met attendees individually. Because we had arrived late, I wanted to give Yudhiṣṭhira Prabhu a little idea of what had happened. He asked, "Is Mahārāja all right now?" "No," I replied, "he isn't," and I elaborated. Yudhiṣṭhira looked at him and said, "You can't tell." After speaking for two hours, Bhakti Tirtha Swami returned to the condominium, exhausted but happy.

VRAJA-LĪLĀ DĀSĪ: In Hawaii we had similar experiences. He was really ill, in and out of the hospital, but he was always disciplined and focused. Every day, he would go outside for a walk, using his cane and limping. And each day, he would write. That's where he wrote *Die Before Dying*.

He was also disciplined in terms of reaching out. There were a lot of different groups in Hawaii—the Nārāyaṇa Mahārāja group, the Purī Mahārāja group—and they all invited him. And wherever he went, he would bring devotees together. He always considered that they were devotees and that devotees should engage in loving relationships and support each other in their growth in Kṛṣṇa consciousness. So he would go and speak about Śrīla Prabhupāda. He was determined.

Before we left for those programs he would be sick, and when we came back he would be sick, but when he was in the programs he was just so focused, and he always spoke about loving and caring for each other and keeping a spiritual focus, remembering our relationship with the Divine Couple. He never dealt with the different political things that were going on. He just spoke lovingly and used his illness to bring people together. Everywhere we went devotees were so appreciative and reciprocated with him so much. People would want to come and do service for him at the house where we were staying, but although Mahārāja didn't want too many people around, he would still find a way to let them do some service. But he was very reclusive—chanting and writing and working on the dying process. He was really using that time to prepare for his ultimate departure.

GIRIRAJ SWAMI: Why Hawaii?

EKAVĪRA DĀSA: He wanted to continue his treatment, and he wanted to do it in an area more conducive to healing. In November Gita Nagari is very cold, and the cold wouldn't allow him to go outside and get fresh air, which we thought would be conducive for his healing. We wanted him in a warmer, more peaceful climate, or area.

VRAJA-LĪLĀ DĀSĪ: Also, he didn't want to be in a busy devotee community, because he knew that he was in a critical period. There was both an external and an internal aspect to his departure. He knew he needed time alone to deal with certain internal matters, so he encouraged us to find a place where he could do that, where he wouldn't be distracted.

Our *guru mahārāja* was very frugal, and Daśaratha Prabhu had offered us his house in Hawaii.

EKAVĪRA DĀSA: Guru Mahārāja did not want to spend *lakṣmī* unnecessarily. In many cases we had to encourage him, "This is the money being raised for your care, and we need to use it." He said, "Yes, but this is not our *lakṣmī*; therefore we have to use it with discretion."

In Hawaii Bhakti Tirtha Swami went through many challenging periods, and his deep reflections enabled him to write *Die Before Dying*. It seemed that he was being empowered by these personal experiences. He was showing, both through his writings and by example, how to deal with situations that we all have to face in our lives.

Initially Mahārāja had thought that he might overcome the cancer before even going to Hawaii. But in Hawaii he had to accept that he might not overcome it at all. Sometimes he felt sad about not being available for devotees. And sometimes he felt anger. The devotees were in such need, and he was questioning, "Why must I leave now?"

VRAJA-LĪLĀ DĀSĪ: Sometimes it became a little bewildering and confusing to experience our *guru mahārāja* making the transition to acceptance—from hoping to get better to accepting that he was leaving. His Holiness Radhanath Swami was instrumental in helping us reconcile the fact that even though this was our spiritual master he could still be having such a difficult time. Once, he phoned to talk to our *guru mahārāja*—and also to check with us and see how we were doing, and I took the opportunity to share some things with him, beginning with some of the physical things. Then I said, "Mahārāja, it is a little difficult for us right now. Sometimes it is hard." And Radhanath Mahārāja told us, "Just remember that what you are getting a chance to see is his human side. Try to see things from that perspective." Until then, we hadn't framed it in those terms: "Yes, he is our *guru*, but at the same time he is going through this human experience of having to make a transition." That was a big help.

Before we left Washington, both Madhvācārya Prabhu and the oncologist suggested that Guru Mahārāja amputate his leg. But Guru Mahārāja did not want to do that. We had always had it in the back of our minds that things weren't improving because his leg needed to be amputated, but we would have regular conversations with the doctor from Mexico, and he would assure us, "Just keep doing what you are doing." He wanted to avoid amputation, and so did Guru Mahārāja.

So we were trying everything we could—all different kinds of treatments—to avoid amputation. But things were getting worse, and finally we said, "Guru Mahārāja, we have to call Dr. Tony to come; we need to know what is going on."

Soon after, Dr. Tony was en route to Japan, and he arranged to stop in Hawaii. After examining Guru Mahārāja he concluded, "Amputate the leg." It was then that Bhakti Tirtha Swami said, "Okay." He accepted. It took over a month for him to get to that point. And then, "Okay."

Then everything became focused on connecting with devotees. Guru Mahārāja had made a transition and said, "Okay, I may not survive this, so let's get to work." He had us use the computer to reach out to devotees by sending regular reports about his condition.

Ekavīra dāsa: In Hawaii he had some devotees who kept in contact with him. Bhūrijana Prabhu used to write by e-mail, and those exchanges were very important to him. I also remember his interaction with Śivarāma Swami. Guru Mahārāja had asked me to read him Śivarāma Swami's latest book, *Na Pāraye 'Haṁ*, which I would do every day. And Śivarāma Swami phoned him a couple of times while we were there. One day I was reading the book to him, and after about an hour he became very meditative. He said, "This book is absolutely amazing. Throughout my years of serving Śrīla Prabhupāda, I never had much association with Śivarāma Swami, but now I am getting his association through his book, and I really appreciate that."

Now Bhakti Tirtha Swami's mood had shifted to one of calm determination. But at the same time, the tumor was growing, and he was extremely weak. He had been in the hospital, and when we brought him home he couldn't even stand up; I had to carry him. Then, that evening, he had a crisis. He was really weak, and his eyes were glazed. There was a slight click in his voice, and his breathing was rapid and sometimes strained.

Sometimes he was out of breath, and he said that he had never felt so weak. His physical symptoms were such that we thought he would leave his body. He said, "Vraja-līlā, get a pen and paper. I need to give you instructions. I may leave tonight, so I want you to write these things down." And then he gave us what he called his "last instructions"—what he wanted done in case he left his body while we were in Hawaii. In the middle of dictating his last will to us, however, he stopped and said, "You all should take rest. I am not going to leave tonight."

VRAJA-LĪLĀ DĀSĪ: The next day, Guru Mahārāja explained what had taken place later that night. He said that he had been on the verge of leaving his body but had considered what would happen if Ekavīra came up and found him dead—whether Ekavīra would be able to deal with it. So he had prayed to be granted some more time, and his prayer was accepted.

We had already arranged for devotees to send tickets for Guru Mahārāja's flight back to Maryland, where he could be with his other disciples. And we began to pack everything and get ready to go.

EKAVĪRA DĀSA: Before we left, however, a sympathetic nurse came and looked at Mahārāja and told us, "They may not let him on the flight, because he is so weak and looks unwell." So we told Mahārāja, and he said, "Really?" Then he sat up in the bed and said, "Bring me some *prasāda*. Vraja-līlā can cook something." So she prepared something for him, and two hours later he was giving us directions on what to pack and what not to pack. We thought, "Oh boy, he's back!" It was as if he were a new man.

We flew out late that night. The devotees had bought Mahārāja a first-class ticket so that he would have more room, but in the airplane he found that there wasn't any way he could elevate his foot. Vraja-līlā and I were in the back in economy class. Mahārāja had an attendant call me forward, and when I got there he said, "Ask the man next to you if he wants to trade seats with me. He can come up to first class, and I will go back in economy class." I said, "Really?" He said, "Yes, I don't want to sit here." I said, "What about your foot?" And he replied, "I can put my foot on top of you."

So I went to the back and approached the person seated next to me: "My teacher would like to know if you'd like to trade seats with him. You can go up to first class, and he'll come back here." He said, "Are you kidding? No problem, I'll be glad to." So they switched seats, and Mahārāja had me take the center seat and threw his leg across my lap. And so I rode from Hawaii to DC seated between Mahārāja and Vraja-līlā, with Mahārāja's foot on my lap.

VRAJA-LĪLĀ DĀSĪ: And our *guru mahārāja* slept.

EKAVĪRA DĀSA: It was the first time in days that he actually slept. We were most grateful.

In Hawaii Bhakti Tirtha Swami had said to me, "I know this service is very difficult. But there aren't many disciples who can handle it." And then he had said, "But I want to let you know that it may get even more difficult." And I had replied, "Thank you for sharing this with me, Guru Mahārāja. It is difficult for me, and it may get even more difficult, but I am not going anywhere; I am here with you. We'll be ready to go through whatever we have to go through, but I am here with you."

VRAJA-LĪLĀ DĀSĪ: Ekavīra was always there, always present. He was very attached to our *guru mahārāja's* following the discipline of the alternative care regimen, but sometimes our *guru mahārāja* wouldn't want to; he would want to eat something different or not follow the protocol strictly, and Ekavīra would get disturbed. It went on like that for a while, and one day I thought, "We have to end this somehow," because Ekavīra was getting frustrated that our *gurudeva* wasn't following some things, and Gurudeva was determined that he would do what he wanted how he wanted, and it was going back and forth like that. So one day I said, "Ekavīra, let's go discuss this." We went into Gurudeva's room, and I said, "Guru Mahārāja, we have a question for you. Is Ekavīra to understand that you will always follow the therapy the way it is prescribed for you?" He looked at me and took a breath. He seemed really happy that I had brought that up. Ekavīra, you can tell us exactly what he said.

Ekavīra dāsa: He immediately responded, "No, I am not going to follow the protocol completely. There are some things I just won't do, and you should understand that." At that point I said, "Okay, I'll just be here to offer the service, and if you choose to follow, okay, and if you don't, I'll understand." We learned a lot of lessons in detachment in that service.

Vraja-līlā dāsī: In Maryland Guru Mahārāja was really determined to bring everyone together, to create a family atmosphere with his disciples. That was his mood then: to create more harmony and openness. At night he would speak very openly and encourage his disciples to speak and inquire. He wanted them to be a part of what he was experiencing.

He requested them to systematically study Śrīla Prabhupāda's books, take shelter of *śikṣā-gurus*, take shelter of the holy names, and make sure to always care for each other. He also recorded several short videos about the importance of Śrīla Prabhupāda's books for the world.

Ekavīra dāsa: Mahārāja had always instructed his disciples to read Śrīla Prabhupāda's books in a scrutinizing way, but at the end he really emphasized—focused almost exclusively on—Śrīla Prabhupāda's books.

Vraja-līlā dāsī: During that time, Guru Mahārāja had his leg amputated and received a prosthesis, and that gave him some hope. The Hope Institute's philosophy is that with cancer sometimes you are up and sometimes you are down, and you can sometimes be up for long periods of time. So, once Guru

Mahārāja returned to Maryland he got hope again, and he was up for about three months. A major stress had been removed from his body, and also he was being energized by the devotees. After the leg was amputated, he was determined to walk with the prosthesis and even thought he might be able to go to Russia. He said, "Maybe Śrīla Prabhupāda will let me stay longer." For two and a half to three months, he underwent physical therapy and actually got to the point where he was walking with the prosthesis. But he didn't go to Russia. He relapsed.

Ekavīra dāsa: In late March or early April, more tumors appeared, and we could see that he probably wouldn't be with us in his physical form much longer. Guru Mahārāja, too, accepted that it was too much—the cancer had become quite aggressive—and he went to Gita Nagari to prepare for his departure. There his body deteriorated quite rapidly, and again he changed his focus—to making himself more publicly available and associating more with his godbrothers and godsisters and other devotees.

Vraja-līlā dāsī: It was a time for clearing things out—speaking lovingly and clearing up any misunderstandings or disturbing thoughts that anyone may have had in relation to him. Whatever discomfort or conflict there may have been in any relationship or decision or anything else in his lifetime of devotional service, he was now sending out messages of love, to anyone and everyone. Anyone who came to see him left in tears, because internally he had become a different person, an entirely loving being.

Ekavīra dāsa: Devotees were coming to see him every day. Bhaktivaibhava Swami came from Europe and stayed for several weeks, and Kāmagiri Mātājī came from Cleveland with her family. Radhanath Swami was a constant presence.

One day, some devotees came from New Vrindaban, and Bhakti Tirtha Swami spoke with them, and they were all in tears. After the devotees had left, Radhanath Swami said, "I have been trying to help these devotees for years. And Bhakti Tirtha Mahārāja, too, has tried to help these devotees before. But now, in less than two hours, he was able to affect these devotees' hearts on a level that I have never seen before. He is engaged in preaching in a way that I have never experienced."

Guru Mahārāja's mood was extremely loving. He was simple, like a little boy. He had said that when we make our transition, we have to give up the identity we had during this lifetime. He told us, "I am no longer Bhakti Tirtha Swami. I am not that same person."

VRAJA-LĪLĀ DĀSĪ: Another person who was very influential during this period, who had a deep impact on Bhakti Tirtha Swami, was Bhūrijana Prabhu. Bhūrijana Prabhu wrote him these really intense, caring letters, which I had the privilege of reading to him. He told Guru Mahārāja, "You have to give yourself permission to leave, because none of the devotees around you are going to want to let you go." He would send many quotations from scripture, often related to death and dying—about Bhīṣmadeva's passing away, for example—to help him face that eventuality, but he would always end up writing something very straightforward and direct.

I said to my *guru mahārāja*, "When Bhūrijana Prabhu writes, he is so direct, so straight with you about your leaving. Yet many of your godfamily don't want you to leave. They want you to stay here." He looked at me and said, "Yes, this is Bhūrijana's mood. He is straightforward." And then he said, "There are householders in our movement who are more advanced than some *sannyāsīs*."

After my *guru mahārāja* left, Radhanath Swami asked me, "So what are you going to do now?" I had been serving my *guru mahārāja* all of my life as a devotee. So, I said, "I am going to India. I am going to find Bhūrijana Prabhu and hear

Śrīmad-Bhāgavatam." And that's what I did, the first thing we did while waiting for the *samādhi* in Māyāpur to be completed. Bhūrijana Prabhu came to Māyāpur and taught the First and Second Cantos of *Śrīmad-Bhāgavatam*. In the First Canto, Kṛṣṇa leaves Hastināpura, and Queen Kuntī and the Pāṇḍavas—everybody there—are lamenting, and for the first time I got some relief. I realized, "Oh, this is what it all means." I got some understanding from the scriptures. The devotees in Hastināpura were lamenting, but there was a greater purpose to the Lord's plan—to benefit His devotees. That gave me a lot of relief, and I felt peaceful. This was the beginning of my healing, and it went back to my *guru mahārāja's* receiving those letters from Bhūrijana Prabhu.

EKAVĪRA DĀSA: Bhakti Tirtha Mahārāja always looked forward to hearing from Bhūrijana Prabhu. He would ask, "Did Bhūrijana Prabhu write? Have you received anything from him?" Radhanath Swami was there, and of course Guru Mahārāja relished his association very much.

As Vraja-līlā mentioned, during this period Guru Mahārāja wanted to make his experience more publicly accessible, and to do this he used the Internet. Everything, including photographs, was posted online. Before, although he had been a flamboyant, charismatic personality in public, Guru Mahārāja had still been a very private person. He had liked his space and hadn't let many people in. But now he just opened up and allowed everyone to come into his life and see what was actually going on, on a deeper level.

This mood had very far-reaching effects. I spoke with a man who had been in a supermarket in Washington, in line to buy groceries, and had overheard another customer talking about some spiritual group she was in. "I have been having this amazing experience," she had said. "We have been going online, following a swami who is leaving his body." They would watch and read what was posted online and then discuss it, and everyone in the group was benefiting from the experience. It was helping them go deeper in their spiritual process. They were talking about Bhakti Tirtha Swami.

So we understood that Guru Mahārāja was preaching on a level that we didn't see. We hadn't been aware of how much he was affecting people throughout the world, in all walks of life.

VRAJA-LĪLĀ DĀSĪ: So many people were visiting—all different levels of his godfamily. Some were scared, frightened; others wanted to know more about the process. Many just came to see him—to offer obeisances, show support, receive blessings, and just experience his love. It was incredible. People came from all over the East Coast and sometimes from far away, from Texas and elsewhere.

Sometimes Guru Mahārāja could barely speak, but he would make himself so available to everyone. Even in extreme pain, he would have the devotees carry him to a wheelchair and bring him to the temple so he could give class. It was an incredible experience for all of us to be so close to him and see this person leave his body—how dedicated he was, what it means to be dedicated to the spiritual master, what it means to accept what the spiritual master arranges even though it might not be what one wants. Guru Mahārāja accepted it completely, and in that process of acceptance all he had to do was show love to the devotees. That's all he wanted to do—show love to the devotees.

Then Guru Mahārāja withdrew, and he stopped giving class. He decided, "Okay, now no more."

EKAVĪRA DĀSA: *Nirjana-bhajana.* Guru Mahārāja chose to depart in Gita Nagari rather than Māyāpur or Vṛndāvana because, as he said, he wanted to raise the devotees' awareness that Śrīla Prabhupāda had established many holy *dhāmas*. Many devotees don't have the opportunity to travel to Vṛndāvana or Māyāpur, and he wanted to help devotees understand that even if we are not able to leave our body in Māyāpur or Vṛndāvana, we can still take shelter of these other *dhāmas*, which Prabhupāda established. Śrīla Prabhupāda is available to all of us, and his mercy is prominent in all of these places.

Bhakti Tirtha Swami wanted to serve the devotees and show them his love, and included in that was his desire that they have strong *sādhana*, really chant the holy names. He had said that he wanted his disciples to be known for strictly following the principles of Kṛṣṇa consciousness—following the four regulative principles, chanting their rounds, and serving the devotees, especially in terms of protecting women, children, and the elderly. Unless we followed the principles and chanted the holy names, he had always emphasized, there would be a mood of exploitation.

Bhakti Tirtha Swami himself had always had strong *sādhana*, and during the whole period of his illness he was chanting with great intensity. He usually liked to chant in his room so that he wouldn't be disturbed and could go deep into the *mahā-mantra* and connect with the holy names. As time went on, Guru Mahārāja began to lose his motor functions and couldn't move the *japa* beads. As a result, he was chanting eight, ten, even twelve hours a day. He would say, "I don't know why it is taking me so long to finish just sixteen rounds. I've always chanted . . ." He'd usually chanted more than sixteen rounds daily, and throughout his entire devotional life he'd never missed chanting at least sixteen. For some years he had chanted forty-two rounds a day. But now he said, "I don't know why it is taking me so long." One day he was up chanting until eleven p.m. and still didn't think he'd completed his prescribed rounds. We were encouraging him to take rest. He had trouble sleeping, so whenever he got tired we tried to get him to rest. This time he agreed, though to his mind he hadn't finished his rounds. So, we prepared him for bed and he lay down, and at about eleven thirty he finally went to sleep.

Then at twelve, twelve fifteen—I myself had just laid down—the buzzer went off. It was Dhruva, who was staying upstairs with Bhakti Tirtha Swami, calling me. So I went up, and he asked me to help him set Mahārāja up on his chair, because Mahārāja wanted to finish his rounds. So we sat him up and then sat and chanted with him for a couple of hours, until about two thirty. When Guru Mahārāja had finally finished, he lay down again and went back to sleep for a couple of hours.

That next day, I watched Guru Mahārāja while he was chanting and then asked him if he wouldn't mind taking his *japa* beads out of the bag so I could see them. What was happening was that he was chanting but not moving the beads. I said, "Gurudeva, you are thinking that you are not finishing your rounds, but actually you are. But when you chant the *mantra*, you are not moving the beads." And he said, "Is that it? You mean I've been chanting sixty-four rounds a day and didn't even know it?" He started tearing up. "Thank you," he said. "Thank you, Śrīla Prabhupāda."

A few days later, Guru Mahārāja couldn't move the beads at all anymore. He was chanting, but he just couldn't move the beads. It was very difficult, and it was causing him anxiety. "Guru Mahārāja," I said, "you don't have to do this for us anymore. You have been such an example in showing us how important it is to chant. Please don't be in anxiety about it. You can chant without chanting on the beads for us." And then he looked at me and said, "Let this be a lesson for you all—how important it is to actually chant the holy name." Through both his words and his example he was preparing us, teaching all his disciples, that our connection—with him, with Kṛṣṇa, and with each other—was through the holy name. And then he gave us his beads and stopped chanting on the *mālā*.

A few days before that, as Bhakti Tirtha Swami told Radhanath Swami, he had had a dream. In the dream Tamal Krishna

Goswami had come to him and asked if he was ready to depart. Bhakti Tirtha Swami had seen tears in his eyes and asked, "Why are you crying?" And he had replied, "Because I know what my disciples went through when I departed." In the dream, Bhakti Tirtha Swami had said that he was ready to leave but that he was concerned about his disciples. "My disciples aren't ready for me to leave yet," he had said. "I have to prepare them more."

That very day, or maybe the next, Bhakti Tirtha Swami's disciple Kalpa-vṛkṣa dāsa came from New Jersey. We all gathered around our *guru mahārāja*, who was in a chair. He was in a lot of pain. Kalpa-vṛkṣa started crying and said, "Guru Mahārāja, you should go. You've done so much for all of us, and we don't like to see you in so much pain. You go, and we'll come and meet you. Now we know. You have told us and you have showed us. Now you have to go, for us to come and meet you. You go, and we'll get prepared. You should go. It's okay." There were about five of us all gathered around, and he was really crying. It was a very intense moment.

VRAJA-LĪLĀ DĀSĪ: This was after Tamal Krishna Goswami had come to Guru Mahārāja, in his dream. Bhūrijana Prabhu had said that we wouldn't be able to let our *guru mahārāja* leave, and he was right. But Kalpa-vṛkṣa—maybe because he had a special connection with Guru Mahārāja, maybe because he was inspired from within—was able to give that permission. And when he did, we all realized that it was time. We knew, and Guru Mahārāja also knew, but we hadn't been able to tell him; we just couldn't. But somehow this devotee, Kalpa-vṛkṣa, was able to say it. And then Guru Mahārāja put his head back and said, "Okay. We'll find out in the next few days when."

EKAVĪRA DĀSA: This was the period of *nirjana-bhajana*. Our *guru mahārāja* had been extending—had always extended—himself to others, but now his focus was on internal activities, which were increased by hearing and chanting and by the association of Radhanath Swami. He designated Brāhma-muhūrta

Prabhu, one of his caretakers, as his "timekeeper" and would ask him, "What is Kṛṣṇa doing at this time of day?" In reply, Brāhma-muhūrta would consult scripture and answer in relation to Kṛṣṇa's *aṣṭa-kālīya-līlā*. Advaita Ācārya and Gopāla from Aindra Prabhu's *kīrtana* group in Vṛndāvana organized a twenty-four–hour *kīrtana* outside in the main room. Devotees would come from all over—from New York, Washington DC, and elsewhere—to participate.

One day Radhanath Swami informed Guru Mahārāja that the renowned Vraja-vāsī Ramesh Baba's main followers were in Harrisburg, PA, not far from Gita Nagari. "Would you like them to come and chant for you?" he asked. "Yes! Yes!" Guru Mahārāja responded enthusiastically, tears filling his eyes. Then he became grave and said, "I am so fortunate. I did not go to Vṛndāvana, but Kṛṣṇa is so kind, Śrīmatī Rādhārāṇī is so kind, They are sending Their devotees to Gita Nagari. Śrīla Prabhupāda is so merciful."

A couple of days later, we got a phone call from some devotees in Dallas; they said that they wanted to come and bring Tamal Krishna Goswami's little Rādhā-Dāmodara Deities. On hearing this news, Guru Mahārāja, speaking of Tamal Krishna Goswami, said, "He's coming. Now it will be only a few more days. They are coming for me." He became quite joyful. When the devotees arrived with the Deities, we thought we would have them come into Guru Mahārāja's bedroom, but he said, "No. I'll come out." "But Gurudeva," we said, "you are in so much pain you can hardly move." But he was insistent. "No," he said, "I'm going into the front room." So Ekavīra, Brāhma-muhūrta, and Dhruva wheeled him out in his wheelchair, and he greeted the devotees and took *darśana* of the Deities, and they had a short program. He became inspired and happy, and he even spoke—about prayer, how important it is to pray and how Kṛṣṇa responds based on what is in each individual's heart.

Vraja-līlā dāsī: Afterward, the little Rādhā-Dāmodara

Deities were set up in the front room, and on the altar was a small picture of Tamal Krishna Goswami.

Two days later, understanding that he would be leaving soon, our *guru mahārāja* asked to address all the devotees. Only with great difficulty was he able to speak. He said, "Kṛṣṇa is letting us know that our time is over. How wonderful and glorious this is." He spoke of his physical pain, which was becoming too much to bear. And he spoke of the pain of others—of devotees and of humanity—and how he had prayed to be of some use in alleviating their suffering. He was concerned about all the people who had no one to care for them. The whole experience was emotional for everyone. Then Gurudeva said that he did not know exactly when he would be leaving but that it would be soon—"today, tomorrow, a few days." And Ekavīra, Dhruva, and Brāhma-muhūrta wheeled him back into his room.

EKAVĪRA DĀSA: The next day, Bhakti Tirtha Mahārāja asked a devotee from South Africa, Bhāva-bhakti dāsī, to lead *kīrtana*. Lying on his bed while she was singing, he started whirling his arms like he had done when he was dancing. Although he couldn't get out of bed and dance, he was dancing internally.

VRAJA-LĪLĀ DĀSĪ: Guru Mahārāja appreciated the *kīrtanas* very much. He would close his eyes and chant along with the devotees.

Radhanath Swami read to Guru Mahārāja daily from *Śrī Caitanya-caritāmṛta*, and sometimes from the *Kṛṣṇa* book. One day he was reciting the pastime of Kṛṣṇa lifting Govardhana Hill and Guru Mahārāja became very happy and excited and said that he wanted to go on Govardhana *parikramā*.

EKAVĪRA DĀSA: Radhanath Swami said, "Mahārāja, it is difficult for you to walk right now, but Śrīla Prabhupāda, in Vṛndāvana, before he left the planet, asked to be taken by ox cart to Govardhana Hill to do *parikramā*, and we have Govardhana here. Girirāja is right here. Would you like to go on Govardhana *parikramā*? Your wheelchair can be your cart and

Ekavīra can be your ox." Bhakti Tirtha Swami smiled and said, "Yes, let's go. Take me on Govardhana *parikramā*." So Brāhma-muhūrta and Vraja-līlā, who both had *govardhana-śilās*, set up a Govardhana Hill on an altar in the middle of the main room, and we brought Bhakti Tirtha Swami and circumambulated Girirāja, with Radhanath Mahārāja leading *kīrtana*.

VRAJA-LĪLĀ DĀSĪ: Then it was only a matter of days. His body started deteriorating even more rapidly, and he went into internal consciousness. He wasn't speaking or eating or drinking—nothing. Madhvācārya Prabhu and Mother Saṅgītā, a hospice nurse and disciple of Śrīla Prabhupāda, informed us that Guru Mahārāja had twenty-four to thirty-six hours. Puruṣa-sūkta and Nanda-sūno sent the message out, and devotees came from everywhere. Radhanath Swami sat by Guru Mahārāja's side continuously. Many devotees were gathered outside. A video monitor had been set up so they could see what was going on. In this way everyone was present. Many, many devotees were there when, on June 27, at 3:35 p.m., he took his last breath.

Everything after that had been arranged—who would take care of the body, what would be done and how, the *sannyāsa mantra*—the whole thing. Brāhma-muhūrta had studied the process and the rituals, and Radhanath Swami was there to help with everything. Guru Mahārāja himself had actually been involved with many of the arrangements. He had picked out the urn and wanted to be involved with what would happen.

EKAVĪRA DĀSA: He had directed that his body be cremated rather than being brought to Māyāpur, because he felt that the cost of transporting it would be too great and that it would be a better service to Śrīla Prabhupāda if we used the funds to print and distribute more books. "Now, I know you guys might try to take my body to Māyāpur," he had told us, "but I want you to know that I do not desire you to do that and would not be pleased if you actually tried to." He made us promise.

VRAJA-LĪLĀ DĀSĪ: So it was all very organized and everyone

worked together. When the body was ready, the devotees carried it down to the temple in a *kīrtana* procession. Kalpavṛkṣa had carved a beautiful table, and the body was placed on it before the Deities for a last program. There was *kīrtana* and foot bathing and *ārati*. Flowers were offered—many, many garlands—and the devotees came forward to touch his foot. Radhanath Swami performed the *ārati*, and Dhanurdhara Swami and Candramauli Swami were also present. The temple was packed with sobbing devotees. The program went on for hours, until about one in the morning, when Ekavīra, Brāhma-muhūrta, Dhruva Mahārāja, Vṛndāvana, and Jagannātha Paṇḍita accompanied the body to the crematorium.

EKAVĪRA DĀSA: One amazing thing was that even though Bhakti Tirtha Swami had been in so much pain during his last days, after he departed and we had bathed his body and placed it on his bed before carrying it to the temple, we saw a smile on his face. You can see it in some of the photos. It just appeared naturally.

Bhaktisvarūpa
Dāmodara Swami

Hari-kīrtana—Scientific Knowledge in the Service of the Lord

A letter to Bhaktisvarūpa Dāmodara Swami written on October 8, 2006, six days after his departure.

My dear Mahārāja,

Please accept my humble obeisances. All glories to Śrīla Prabhupāda.

We are missing you terribly today, after your sudden departure from this realm of mortality to the service of Śrīla Prabhupāda in eternity.

My thoughts turn to my earliest association with you. I had been suffering from a relapse of jaundice in Bombay, and Śrīla Prabhupāda said that as long as I remained there I would be unable to recover. So I returned to the United States for treatment and after spending about five days in Chicago, proceeded to Los Angeles.

There, you were continuing to associate with the devotees and going on your famous morning walks with Śrīla Prabhupāda, discussing the principle of "life comes from life" and the importance of scientific preaching. As I gradually recovered from my illness, I was able to accompany you and Śrīla Prabhupāda on some of the walks and be in Śrīla Prabhupāda's room when you and sometimes Dr. Wolf-Rottkay came to meet him. Hearing your discussions, I was struck by your humility and simplicity—and by your open and intimate relationship with Śrīla Prabhupāda. He had so much love for you and put so much trust in you—and surely, his great hopes for you were not disappointed. Your obvious sincerity combined with your intellectual prowess were strong qualifications for understanding Śrīla Prabhupāda and his teachings and mission—and the specific mission he gave to you. You took all of his words to heart and were so enthusiastic to take up his call. Obviously, you were a very pure devotee from your birth, from your culture, and in Śrīla Prabhupāda's association your natural devotion was encouraged and manifested. It was like a jewel that Śrīla Prabhupāda mined and cut and polished—and then held out to sparkle for all the world's benefit.

Earlier in 1973, one of the most prominent scientists in the study of the origin of life had come to the university and given a lecture on how life had arisen from a combination of four primordial elements: carbon, hydrogen, nitrogen, and oxygen. With many technical words and diagrams and formulas, he had tried to establish that life had come from these material elements. At the end of the presentation you had stood and inquired, "If I give you these ingredients, will you be able to produce life?" And the scientist had replied, "That I do not know." Śrīla Prabhupāda was so pleased and proud of you that he spoke of the incident in his lectures and conversations—how "our Svarūpa Dāmodara" had challenged the scientist and defeated the notion that life came from matter.

Being with you and Śrīla Prabhupāda in that atmosphere, I became inspired by the idea of scientific preaching. Although I was not qualified like you—materially or spiritually—I did have some desire to participate. So one day I approached Śrīla Prabhupāda in his room, during his massage, and told him that I was willing to join in the scientific preaching. And in a relaxed, blissful mood, he simply smiled and said, "Your field is psychology." (He knew I had been a psychology major.) Still, he said I could apply that knowledge in the work of the Bhaktivedanta Institute. Then I told him that I had noticed that when he spoke about the scientists he used such words as "nonsense" and "rascals" and said that we should "kick them in the face with boots," and I asked whether when we preached to or met with scientists we should use such language. And Śrīla Prabhupāda replied, "No. You should speak like a gentleman."

Soon enough, I was able to recover my health and return to India (as Śrīla Prabhupāda had told me in LA, "Back home, back to Bombay") to work on the Juhu project. In time, the project developed and we were able to provide Śrīla Prabhupāda a facility on the fifth floor of the west tower, overlooking the Arabian Sea. There too, Śrīla Prabhupāda continued to emphasize the importance of scientific preaching and to encourage you in all respects. I was fortunate to be present with Tamal Krishna Goswami when Śrīla Prabhupāda asked him how much money the Bhaktivedanta Institute, the BI, needed for its work. Goswami Mahārāja wasn't sure exactly—he said he would have to consult with you—but he thought about $10,000 a month. And Śrīla Prabhupāda, without a moment's hesitation, responded, "Arrange immediately." He wanted you to have whatever you needed; he didn't want you to have to worry about money.

Śrīla Prabhupāda was also concerned that you should have proper offices in the new construction. Although he had instructed that in general our offices should be at the back of the property in the old tenement buildings, he insisted that the BI should be in the temple complex, in a prominent location. So you and I reviewed the architectural drawings and walked through the site and decided on the six rooms between the two towers on the second floor (in America, the third floor), three overlooking the temple courtyard and three overlooking the guesthouse entrance. Later, you created a room on the western end of the offices, overlooking the temple, for use as a conference room, and you got other rooms to use for residences.

In the 1970s you were still quite new to ISKCON's ways, and because of your humble and gentle nature—and your highly cultured (and different) background—you were often overlooked by ISKCON's leaders. Although I myself was not one of the big managers, at least I was able to speak with them on your behalf. Being attracted by your nature, and knowing how much Śrīla Prabhupāda loved and cared for you, I would often ask how you were doing and if you needed anything. And you, in turn, would approach me whenever you had some difficulty or needed to get some message through to the leaders. So I was pleased to present your concerns to them, or to arrange for you to meet with them and present your concerns to them directly.

In March of 1977 we arranged a *paṇḍāl* program for Śrīla Prabhupāda at Cross Maidan in downtown Bombay, and as part of the program Śrīla Prabhupāda wanted you to make a presentation. Although Prabhupāda was quite ill then (this proved to be his last public engagement) and remaining in the *paṇḍāl* for long was a strain for him, he was so keen on your work that he wanted to be there for your presentation. The programs began in the early evening, and after the first *kīrtana* and Prabhupāda's own lecture, when he usually left, you began your presentation about life coming from life, with slides and your own explanations.

Earlier, Śrīla Prabhupāda had commented that ordinary people can't understand what the scientists are saying but that they are impressed by the scientists' bombastic words—the complicated calculations and formulations and diagrams and jargon. So even if people don't understand what we are saying, if they see that we too have scientists who make presentations with technical language and scientific evidence—in favor of God and the philosophy of the *Bhagavad-gītā*—they will be impressed and think, "Oh, this is scientific; we can believe what they say."

So Śrīla Prabhupāda . . . I will never forget how happy he was. I had hardly ever seen him so happy. He was so pleased with your presentation that evening at Cross Maidan; he really felt that this approach could change the world. He knew that the scientists' ideas were guiding all of human society and that, unfortunately, most of the scientists were atheistic. On a morning walk in Juhu I had described to Śrīla Prabhupāda a news report about a scientist who had been in town and who, when asked where the ingredients for creation came from, had replied that he didn't know. "Then why do you talk nonsense?" Śrīla Prabhupāda had retorted, as if to the scientist. "Another rascal. You do not know from where the ingredients came. Our answer is that Kṛṣṇa reveals, *ahaṁ sarvasya prabhavo mattaḥ sarvaṁ pravartate* [*Bg* 10.8]: 'The ingredients come from Me.'" But the scientist had said more. So I had continued, "He replied that he didn't know but that he was sure that the answer wouldn't involve God." And Prabhupāda had responded, with sarcasm, "Still, he is a scientist. He doesn't know. He is a rascal, but still he is a scientist. Just see." Śrīla Prabhupāda considered the scientific preaching to be crucial, so that God would assume His rightful place in people's consciousness, in their understanding of the scheme of things, and their human lives would not be wasted in animalistic, materialistic pursuits.

Śrīla Prabhupāda wanted you to present the same philosophy of the *Bhagavad-gītā* in scientific language. Once, some devotees proposed to him that we use the name "Bhaktivedanta Research Institute," because research was so popular and people liked to give for it. But Śrīla Prabhupāda was emphatic: "No 'research.' The research is already done—*Bhagavad-gītā.* No research." He was pleased when you published *The Scientific Basis of Kṛṣṇa Consciousness.*

After the *paṇḍāl* program, Śrīla Prabhupāda spent some time in Juhu, and following a brief stay in Rishikesh retired to Vṛndāvana, where he was to spend most of his last months. There, with his encouragement and guidance, you organized a three-day international conference for that October—"Life Comes from Life." And Śrīla Prabhupāda, although so ill, took personal interest in every detail. He was pleased when he heard your reports about the meetings you'd had with various scientists and other leaders you'd invited, and he was even more pleased when he heard the reports, from you and from others, about the conference itself. In fact, he became ecstatic.

Earlier, at the end of August, Śrīla Prabhupāda had gone to England, and there he had called for you. In a most personal, private, and intimate encounter, he had appealed to you, "Please take me from here. I want to go back to India, back to Bombay." Many of the other leaders had other plans for Śrīla Prabhupāda—to take him to America, to Gita Nagari—and Śrīla Prabhupāda himself had said that he wanted to go there to establish *varṇāśrama-dharma*. But now he confided in you: "I want to go back to India, to Bombay. Please arrange."

Śrīla Prabhupāda wanted to see the Juhu temple open, and he returned to Bombay. But as fate would have it, he did not live to see the grand opening—although we are sure he was there in his spiritual presence. Anyway, after some time in Juhu he decided that he would go to Vṛndāvana, and we went with him.

There, you were in the inner group, serving Śrīla Prabhupāda personally. I had always been impressed by your simplicity and dedication and devotion. Although you were so qualified academically, culturally, and spiritually, you were always humble and unassuming. And you were a *brahmacārī* then, in the midst of many *sannyāsīs*. But you were very much there with Śrīla Prabhupāda. As stated in the *Bhagavad-gītā* purport (2.56), you were "daring and active."

When the controversy arose about whether Śrīla Prabhupāda should go on *parikramā* to Govardhana or other places, by bullock cart, you were in the group that wanted Śrīla Prabhupāda to stay and recuperate before he attempted to travel, and you were very strong about it. And I believe that your love—the love of all of you—prevailed. Your spontaneous desire to keep Śrīla Prabhupāda with us longer—to keep him from pain and danger and perhaps even death on the way—conquered his heart, and he agreed to stay.

In your humility, you often took the night shift. Śrīla Prabhupāda was always concerned about all the devotees, even when he was so ill, but I think he was especially concerned about you. Seeing you there at night, he was concerned that you were staying awake both day and night and not sleeping. You explained, "No, Śrīla Prabhupāda, we take turns. When others are here during the day, I take rest, and then I come at night." Then Śrīla Prabhupāda gave a very important instruction: "You must take rest. If you don't take care of your health, then later, even if you are enthusiastic to preach, you won't be able to."

Śrīla Prabhupāda left us at 7:26 p.m., November 14, 1977. After putting Śrīla Prabhupāda in *samādhi* in Vṛndāvana and carrying his flowers to Māyāpur for his *puṣpa-samādhi*, Tamal Krishna Goswami and I proceeded to Bombay to work for the grand opening of the Juhu temple, which took place on January 14, 1978, exactly two months after His Divine Grace's disappearance. We had many items to think about, and one was certainly the BI and the facility for it in the new complex.

It was a time of deep separation from Śrīla Prabhupāda and deep contemplation about the future of our lives, the future of ISKCON, the future of Kṛṣṇa consciousness in the world. And I was very touched when once you mentioned, with utmost humility, that we should give special respect to Tamal Krishna Goswami, because of his extraordinary service to Śrīla Prabhupāda in Prabhupāda's last days—some special position of honor and respect. That really touched me. So free from envy were you that without reservation you appreciated the service of another servant of Śrīla Prabhupāda's and were prepared to express your appreciation. Because of your deep, deep attachment to Śrīla Prabhupāda, all that really mattered to you was Śrīla Prabhupāda—his comfort, his service, his mission—and anyone who could serve him well was worthy of your respect and appreciation, admiration and love.

Much happened in the years that followed. You organized the extraordinary "World Congress for the Synthesis of Science and Religion" in Bombay, with presentations by renowned scientists, theologians, and historians. It was a tremendous effort with wonderful results. Because of visa problems, I was unable to be present to assist you in your endeavors or even attend the event, but after my return to India I heard reports about it and eventually saw the beautiful volume, *Synthesis of Science and Religion: Critical Essays and Dialogues*, with papers that had been delivered at the conference. From there you went on to plan and attend many other major conferences, and in 1996, to coincide with Śrīla Prabhupāda's Centennial Celebrations, you organized the "Second World Congress for the Synthesis of Science and Religion" in Calcutta, Śrīla Prabhupāda's place of birth.

In time you also developed the temple in Manipur. I was impressed, because it was one of the first temples other than the ones Śrīla Prabhupāda had constructed, that devotees in ISKCON had built from scratch, in a unique blend of Indian and Balinese architecture. At first, after Śrīla Prabhupāda left, you were not authorized to initiate, so you brought some of the early devotees from Manipur to Bombay to experience temple life, and to be trained and initiated by Tamal Krishna Goswami. I remember them—Ekanātha Prabhu and Banamali Prabhu—with great love and affection. My heart goes out to them in their separation from you, and I offer my services to them and to your project in Manipur in any way practical.

So revered and influential were you in Manipur that the royal family gave you a temple at Rādhā-kuṇḍa and an ashram in Navadvīpa. One year, at the time of the Navadvīpa *parikramā*, you hosted Tamal Krishna Goswami and a few of us at the facility in Navadvīpa and treated us to your wonderful association, Vaiṣṇava hospitality, and Manipuri *prasāda*.

You also brought the great Vaiṣṇava culture of Manipur to the world, through your Ranganiketan performances. I was fortunate to witness some of them on the summer Polish festival tour with His Holiness Indradyumna Swami.

And your own *kīrtanas* were legendary. My office in Juhu overlooked the temple, right under the BI (appropriate that I should be under your lotus feet, as your servant), and the sounds from the temple carried right into my office. Once, I heard your *kīrtana* but didn't know until later that it was you singing. I was astonished. The spiritual purity and potency of the sound completely captivated me. The sound entered my heart and captured my mind.

It was always a special occasion when you led *kīrtana*. One year in particular you led the *kīrtana* during the Ratha-yātrā in Bombay. That was truly an extraordinary experience—thousands of people around us, hundreds in the procession, wonderful singing and dancing and playing of *karatālas* and *mṛdaṅgas*, and you at the center of it all.

So we miss you.

Śrīla Bhaktivinoda Ṭhākura wrote in his inscription at Nāmācārya Haridāsa Ṭhākura's *bhajana-kuṭīra*:

> He reasons ill who says that Vaiṣṇavas die,
> When thou art living still in sound!
> The Vaiṣṇavas die to live, and living try
> To spread the holy name around.

And Śrīla Prabhupāda, in relation to the Bhaktivedanta Institute, often quoted the verse from *Śrīmad-Bhāgavatam* (1.5.22):

> *idaṁ hi puṁsas tapasaḥ śrutasya vā*
> *sviṣṭasya sūktasya ca buddhi-dattayoḥ*
> *avicyuto 'rthaḥ kavibhir nirūpito*
> *yad-uttamaśloka-guṇānuvarṇanam*

"Learned circles have positively concluded that the infallible purpose of the advancement of knowledge, namely austerities, study of the *Vedas*, sacrifice, chanting of hymns, and charity, culminates in the transcendental descriptions of the Lord, who is defined in choice poetry."

He related the verse to the purpose of the BI and concluded, "Science, philosophy, physics, chemistry, psychology, and all other branches of knowledge should be wholly and solely applied in the service of the Lord . . . to establish the glory of the Lord. Advanced people are eager to understand the Absolute Truth through the medium of science, and therefore a great scientist should endeavor to prove the existence of the Lord on a scientific basis. . . . Scientific knowledge engaged in the service of the Lord and all similar activities are all factually *hari-kīrtana*, or glorification of the Lord."

Thus, through the BI, through your followers, your *kīrtana* continues.

Like others, I wish I had done more for you while you were here—and had more of your association. But knowing that you are with Śrīla Prabhupāda, and that we have been left here to serve you both, gives solace. As Śrīla Prabhupāda instructed, "Please remember always the humble teachings that you have received from me, and that will make you always associated with me, and with your godbrothers. We should all work together for satisfying Lord Kṛṣṇa, and in that way the feelings of separation will transform into transcendental bliss."

Our hope now is that we can somehow serve you and please you in your physical absence, and we pray for your blessings that we may satisfy you with our efforts here, and one day again have the opportunity to serve you personally, in service to His Divine Grace Śrīla Prabhupāda.

Your eternal servant,
Giriraj Swami

Arcā-vigraha Dāsī

Adventures and Enlightenment

A talk by Kuntīdevī dāsī on Mother Arcā-vigraha's disappearance day on May 9, 2000, in Carpinteria, California.

My mind is so filled with memories of Mother Arcā-vigraha that it is difficult to isolate what inspired me about her, and what inspires me about her now. But I think that she embodied the two most important devotional principles—chanting the holy names and serving the Vaiṣṇavas—and she performed these activities with great determination and enthusiasm.

I miss her as a friend. She was, in Kṛṣṇa consciousness, the person with whom I had the deepest relationship. She was older than I, and more experienced, and I learned a lot from her training, instructions, and association, but we were also great friends, and I haven't really had another friend like her. I really miss her a lot. I often share thoughts and experiences with her in my mind—especially confidential things that I wouldn't share with anyone else. Or something happens and I immediately think of her—especially if it is funny, because we used to laugh at the same things. She is not there in the same way anymore, but in another way she is still there and very supportive as a friend and as a devotee.

I first met Mother Arcā-vigraha in 1985 in Durban, South Africa, at the opening of the Śrī Śrī Rādhā-Rādhānātha Temple. I had met the devotees and moved into the temple just two weeks earlier. Arcā, Aileen Lipkin—or "Angel," as she was then known—had come from Johannesburg to attend the opening festival, and we were part of a large group of women who shared a small room stacked with bunk beds, with a primitive shower in the corner.

I was struck by how Angel seemed to transcend her

surroundings. She was always beautifully dressed in gorgeous designer Punjabi suits, with a matching bead bag. Petite, with compact intensity and a colorful shock of red curls and bright, piercing brown eyes, she was attractive, sophisticated, and mature, and at the same time very sweet and funny and down-to-earth. And she was a perfectionist. Whatever she did, from making a salad to completing a painting or sculpting a piece of wood, she did with sharp focus. I never detected in her even a trace of laziness or sloppiness, and she never compromised on quality. I liked her immediately.

Shortly after the temple opening, I was sent to Johannesburg to do *saṅkīrtana*. There was a vibrant devotee community in Muldersdrift, a semirural area just north of the city, and there, at the temple, I again met Angel. We would often sit together and talk, but I was frequently traveling, so she and I also exchanged letters. Hers were works of art, written on huge pieces of drawing paper in beautiful, meticulous script, often accompanied by a small watercolor painting or pencil drawing. They were long, personal letters filled with wisdom and realization. I remember one that influenced me particularly—an account of Angel's meeting with a Buddhist nun who had taught her that a woman did not have to have many, or even any, children of her own; she could be the mother of all living entities, showing mercy and kindness to all.

Angel had known that she was different—and an artist—from an early age. As a child, she would spend hours drawing and would even dab turpentine on her wrists the way other girls would perfume. Her spiritual search had begun at the age of twelve. Angel's mother, with whom she enjoyed a very close, deep relationship, had fallen ill with cancer. Angel would sometimes come home from school and find her mother in bed, shaking with tremors, and she would lie down with her and take her in her arms, or lie on top of her to stop the shaking.

When her mother died, Angel was devastated. She would spend hours swinging back and forth on the front gate, gazing at the blue sky and feeling very alone. It was, she said, the first time in her life that she was confronted with death. Her father was grief-stricken and unable to take care of his children. So he handed them over to other families—Angel to the care of a Catholic lady, Mrs. Schneider, who lived next-door. Although Angel was Jewish by birth, Mrs. Schneider trained her in the Christian way—how to pray with folded hands and bended knees, how to call out to God and take shelter of God. She taught her, Arcā later realized, to develop a personal relationship with God, something that stayed with her for the rest of her life.

After high school, Angel apprenticed as a display artist in a Johannesburg department store, and soon thereafter she started her own commercial art studio and quickly built up a successful practice. She married, and later credited much of her success to her husband, Lee, who encouraged her to dedicate herself fully to her art. The couple had two children, but tragically, some years later, Lee passed away following a heart attack.

In the years after her husband's death, Angel found herself weary of the intense materialism that surrounded her. Even though she had two beautiful children and had accumulated wealth, success, fame, and popularity, she felt that her life was incomplete, that her soul was aching for release. She also longed for solitude, and the desert seemed the answer. So she traveled alone to Israel, and at the edge of the Sinai desert she joined a band of Bedouin nomads—the only woman, the only outsider, in the group.

The solitude of the desert, the natural surroundings, and the simple, rugged, detached life of the nomads had a profound effect on Angel; it was a turning point in her life. When, about two months later, she returned to "civilization," sunburned, relaxed, and revived, she determined to devote herself fully and relentlessly to her search for higher meaning.

Notwithstanding her professional and commercial success—her painting "Woman on a Donkey" was one of the best-selling poster prints of all time—her artwork had always been part of her inner search, a road map of her spiritual journey. And by the mid-'80s, she had explored many paths: the major religious traditions as well as others more occult, mystical, and philosophical—anthroposophy, Egyptology, and Kabala. She had read books by Rajneesh and visited Sai Baba in India, and learned from the Bedouins in the desert. She practiced and taught Tai Chi and fencing and was well versed in naturopathy, homeopathy, acupuncture, and Ayurveda.

But still she yearned for something more.

In 1984, while doing research for an art project at the University of Witwatersrand, Angel met the devotees and began attending programs. She and a friend would drive the hour or so from where she was living, in Yeoville, to the temple in Muldersdrift, pitch a tent, and stay the weekend. She had already been following a vegan and mostly raw diet, and she was attracted to the philosophy of Kṛṣṇa consciousness and liked both the austerity of the devotees' lifestyle and the whole spiritual atmosphere. The only thing she couldn't come to terms with was the quantity and opulence of the devotees' diet. So instead of honoring (eating) the *prasāda*, she would take it back to Johannesburg to distribute to "Twilight Kids," homeless boys living on the streets.

One highlight of the Sunday programs for Angel, and for me as well, was Bhakti Caitanya Swami's (then named Raghubir dāsa) *Kṛṣṇa* book classes. She was always eager to learn about the philosophy of Kṛṣṇa consciousness, and she loved to hear about Kṛṣṇa's pastimes.

Whatever path she had followed earlier, she had learned

whatever she could about it and practiced it very seriously. Gradually she rejected all the other theories and came to Kṛṣṇa consciousness. She realized that Kṛṣṇa consciousness was the process she had always been searching and yearning for. And when she joined and became a devotee, she already had had a lot of spiritual training and realization.

She wasn't conventional. She lived "outside" in her own house at a time when we all lived in the temple and were trained to be very, very strict. There were so many rules and regulations, and the slightest "deviation" had tremendous consequences, or so it seemed at the time. But she was so spontaneous, and in the beginning she couldn't get every detail right, like how many times to offer an incense stick or ghee lamp. Later I understood that the purpose of all the rules and regulations was to remember Kṛṣṇa and that she was remembering Him, so what was the problem if she made some small mistakes?

On May 3, 1987, Angel, I, and three other aspiring devotees received initiation from Giriraj Swami—his first disciples. Derek became Dāmodara dāsa; Paolo, Patraka dāsa; and Aditi, Vrajeśvarī dāsī. And Angel became Arcā-vigraha dāsī. Mahārāja explained how one devotee, an artist, had asked Śrīla Prabhupāda, "Of the nine types of devotional service, which is painting?" Prabhupāda had answered, "*Arcanaṁ*, decorating the form of the Lord." And from then on, painting the deities became one of Arcā's main services.

It was toward the end of that year that Arcā-vigraha was first diagnosed with cancer. But the doctors removed a lymph node in her right armpit and the cancer went into remission.

About a year later, Indradyumna Mahārāja organized a Ratha-yātrā festival in Durban, and he asked Arcā-vigraha to help paint the chariots, which she did in the most beautiful way. As usual, she worked very hard, taking time off only to chant her rounds. She would walk up and down in the parking lot in front of the Rādhā-Rādhānātha temple, chanting intensely.

At that time I was based at a new preaching center not far from Arcā's house. There was no facility for women at the center, however, so I stayed with her. She just opened up her home to me—and to ISKCON—and I ended up living there for two years, until we moved to India. She often held programs there and had the most beautiful temple room, with large Jagannātha-Baladeva-Subhadrā deities, covered from floor to ceiling in colorful Orissan cloth and adorned with sequined pillows and embroidered carpets. She attracted a different group of people—artists and intellectuals—and even the mayor of Johannesburg, with whom she was friends, once came to a program.

Arcā would get up very early every morning, around three o'clock, and she never failed to chant her sixteen rounds. We would go to the morning program at the center, and then she would get to work and I would go out and distribute books all day and then come back to attend the evening program. When I would finally get home, at about ten, ready to collapse, she would still be awake and would make some hot milk with molasses, and we would talk until late at night, sometimes reading from *Śrīmad-Bhāgavatam*. The next morning she would be up again at three, ready to start another day (though she would often encourage me to take a little extra rest).

Arcā always said that Jayānanda Prabhu was her model. It was his example that inspired her with the determination to always finish her rounds, no matter what. While taking Giriraj Swami's course on *The Nectar of Devotion* at the VIHE in Vṛndāvana, she commented that the real nectar of devotion was to do service. She had such a taste for service that she often said that she wanted to become like the Six Gosvāmīs, and she lamented that she had to sleep at night. Later, when she was painting the deities in Vṛndāvana, she would hardly sleep for days, sometimes weeks.

In Johannesburg, I would often read aloud to Arcā. She did not read so much herself, but she always enjoyed hearing. Sometimes, when she was working in her studio, I would sit in a chair in the corner and read from *Śrīmad-Bhāgavatam*. Sometimes we would listen to devotional recordings. We both found it all—the philosophy, the descriptions, the pastimes—incredible, mind-blowing.

Inspired by *Śrīmad-Bhāgavatam* and the *Bhagavad-gītā*, Arcā developed the idea of organizing some of their themes into a series of drawings. She had a vision of starting with charcoal drawings depicting different aspects of sinful, materialistic life and then gradually introducing more and more color as she moved into depictions of spiritual life. She planned to culminate the series with a gorgeous image of Goloka Vṛndāvana, all in color. She called the series "The Eye Opener."

Arcā worked on "The Eye Opener" for years, but the owner of the prestigious Goodman Gallery, where Arcā had exhibited throughout her career, did not like the spiritual dimension of her new work and refused to exhibit it. That was a blow to Arcā's professional career, but instead of being discouraged, she took it as Kṛṣṇa's mercy to further cut her ties with the material world. She had faith that eventually someone, somewhere, would exhibit her new work or use it in Kṛṣṇa's service. (Ultimately she never completed "The Eye Opener," partly because she got sick, partly because her other services demanded increasing amounts of her time.) Her art was her only means of livelihood, but she was so immersed in Kṛṣṇa consciousness that she just kept taking on more devotee projects—anything from designing incense packets to painting the personal deities of whoever asked.

Arcā's service to the devotees was incredible. She was fearless, and she never held back. She was everybody's friend, and she made everybody feel important and special and loved. She would greet you in such a way that you would feel that you meant everything to her. One day, before I lived with Arcā, I went to visit her. I knocked on the door, and when she opened it she exclaimed, "Oh, Kuntīdevī!" with such joy. I thought, "Wow, she really likes me!" Then, about an hour later, somebody else came and knocked, and when Arcā opened the door she greeted that person with exactly the same joy and enthusiasm. I was surprised and a little disappointed at first to realize that it wasn't just me whom she liked so much, but then I realized what a special quality it was to be so warm and gracious, not just as a social mannerism but from a genuine love and appreciation in her heart for all kinds of people. She really was happy to see each of us, and she really did like us both.

In the late eighties, Giriraj Mahārāja became very ill on one of his visits to Johannesburg. Arcā took charge of the situation and insisted on taking Mahārāja to the hospital. There, they told us that if we had brought Mahārāja five minutes later, he would have left his body. If Arcā, in her fearless, spontaneous manner, had not taken charge, overriding the indecision and hesitation of others, the incident might have had a very different outcome.

Arcā then insisted on taking Mahārāja back to her house, where she could administer the proper care. This kind of arrangement was unheard of, but Arcā knew what had to be done and just did it. A number of devotees moved in with her to help, and Arcā did not spare any cost or effort to take care of Mahārāja. She pushed all else aside. As she did with everything, she embraced the service of Mahārāja's care wholeheartedly, with full dedication and surrender, and poured every ounce of her being into it. She never held back from Kṛṣṇa or His devotees.

Mahārāja stayed at Arcā's house for many weeks, gradually gaining strength, and when he was strong enough to travel again, she accompanied him to Mauritius to make sure he would get the right kind of care and *prasāda*. She trained the Mauritian devotees how and what to cook for him. And more than that, she trained all of us to take care of each other. At that time this kind of love and care was not really emphasized in ISKCON; we tended to be a bit regimented in our service and often neglected ourselves and others. But Arcā brought her special quality of love.

Her cooking, like everything else she did, was superb. She was a very conscious cook, preparing food with the freshest, most wholesome ingredients and giving full attention to every detail. She never compromised on quality, even though she was sometimes criticized for spending extra money or discriminating between different kinds of *prasāda*. Her salads were big bowls of nutritious art, perfectly cut and gorgeously assembled. Everything was done to create healthy and delicious offerings, but also with the same beauty and elegance that characterized everything she did.

Arcā took equal care with her possessions. She had a juicer that she had received as a wedding present, thirty years earlier, and she took such good care of it that it was still in first-class condition, even though she used it every day. This was one of the first practical lessons I learned from her—after every use to immediately take the machine apart, wash every piece, dry every part, put it together again, and pack it away. I learned how to take care of things and how to perform even simple tasks thoroughly. This may not seem like a very profound lesson, but Śrīla Prabhupāda said that Kṛṣṇa consciousness means to be conscious, and she taught me to become conscious of details.

Arcā was also a friend with whom one could talk about anything and freely reveal one's heart. She never indulged in gossip, and, in addition to being a good listener, she gave excellent advice. Many devotees, young and old, took shelter of her and confided in her, and she had the ability to see the uniquely beautiful qualities in each. She knew that we all were capable of reaching higher and said, "We should just use this one little incarnation for Kṛṣṇa." If she saw the need, she could also speak sternly to someone about correcting his or her behavior. No matter what, she spoke from her own conviction. Finally, in the end, Arcā really had only one message: full surrender to *guru* and Kṛṣṇa—there is no time to waste.

Arcā's devotion to Kṛṣṇa was wonderfully spontaneous; she just followed her heart. Sometimes, while offering *prasāda* to her deities, she would stop and say, "Wait, Lord Jagannātha, wait! I have something else for You!" Then she would run back to the kitchen, cut up an apple, and run back to the altar to complete the offering. She knew that *bhakti* was the most important offering of all and understood that the first principle of Deity worship was to remember that Kṛṣṇa was a person and that we should treat Him with love. If something disturbed her, she would call out loud, "Kṛṣṇa!" and when confronted with a difficult problem, she would say, "I will speak to Kṛṣṇa," and then she would talk to Him just like she would talk to a dear friend. We weren't quite sure how to understand her spontaneity, but her relationship with Kṛṣṇa was indisputably real.

She would befriend all kinds of devotees, even if they were unpopular or ostracized. Later, for example, when we were in Vṛndāvana, Arcā made friends with one devotee who was considered offensive, a renegade in ISKCON, and welcomed him into her house. At first I was really concerned and could not understand why she had befriended him, so I asked Govinda Mahārāja and Giriraj Swami what we should do about her association with this devotee. But eventually I realized that Arcā was just following her heart, so full of purity and spiritual realization.

In the late eighties Arcā traveled to India often and fell in love with Vṛndāvana. On one trip, she bought a plot of land and decided to build a house—one of the first Western devotees to do so. It was a struggle, and being a Western woman, she was cheated and taken advantage of, but still she persevered, selling paintings in the West and returning to India, and in this way, with her going back and forth, the construction progressed.

Then, on Nṛsiṁha-caturdaśī in 1991, at a program at the Hillbrow temple in Johannesburg, Arcā felt some pain just beneath her collarbone—she knew that the cancer had returned. Medical tests confirmed it, and the doctors' prognosis was that she had only another seven to nine months to live.

Arcā was devastated. We just sat in her kitchen and pondered it all. She wanted to speak to her spiritual master, so we tracked down Giriraj Swami in Portugal. "Let go of everything," he told her. "Go to Vṛndāvana and let Śrīmatī Rādhārāṇī take over."

Arcā took her *guru mahārāja's* words to heart and wholeheartedly surrendered her life to his instruction. Over the next few months, she wound up her affairs in Johannesburg, and in September 1991, she, her daughter Sara, and I left for Vṛndāvana—Arcā-vigraha for good, Sara to help with the move, and me to be with Arcā for what I thought would be a few months.

When we arrived in Vṛndāvana, Arcā's house was not yet ready, so for the first few months we lived in the old temple guesthouse, in a dark, unheated room with a cold-water shower, at the far end of the outside passage. A group of aggressive monkeys lived on the adjacent boundary wall, and it was frightening even to step outside.

In time, the house was completed and we moved in. We were on a secluded lane nearby the temple and just off the *parikramā* path, diagonally across from Balaram Baba's ashram, where the sound of *kīrtana* could be heard twenty-four hours a day. There was a small *gośālā* on the one side, and Śivarāma Swami and B. B. Govinda Swami shared a house on the other. It was perfect.

From the beginning, Arcā intended the house to be not just for herself, but an offering to her spiritual master, a place for him to stay during his visits to the holy *dhāma*. She would work and live on the ground floor, and the second floor, with a separate entrance and quarters, would accommodate Guru Mahārāja. That was her mood: to offer everything to her spiritual master and Kṛṣṇa.

Arcā was already a well-known figure in Vṛndāvana, and all the devotees were aware that now she had come to leave her body. Several, especially Bhaktisiddhānta Prabhu and Mother Vidyā, helped her settle in, and there were many serious devotees absorbed in cultivating Kṛṣṇa consciousness who were also eager to help Mother Arcā-vigraha attain her spiritual goals. Our lives became completely surcharged with the spirit of Vraja.

B.B. Govinda Mahārāja (at first still Ayodhyāpati dāsa) became Arcā's spiritual guide. He would take us all over the *dhāma*, to all the holy places, in his big brown Food for Life van, and through him we got to experience Vṛndāvana and Kṛṣṇa's pastimes in a very real and tangible way.

Govinda Mahārāja came to see Arcā almost every day. He had so much love and compassion and had been living in Vṛndāvana for so long that he was able to advise us both spiritually and practically. He would read to Arcā, chant *bhajanas* for her, cook for her, and bring his deities over to stay with her. He was the best possible friend and benefactor, with his blend of down-to-earth humor and wisdom. Sometimes, when I would find my service challenging, he would tell me to just shower Arcā with "love bombs." Without his help and support and encouragement, I never could have accomplished my service to her. And Arcā adored Govinda Mahārāja, who helped guide her over the threshold of material life into transcendental service.

Despite the dire prognosis handed down by the doctors in South Africa, Arcā still had some health and vitality, and initially, for the first year or so, she continued to live a fairly normal life. She attended the full morning program at the temple, and almost every morning after *maṅgala-ārati*, together with Bhaktisiddhānta Prabhu, we would do Vṛndāvana *parikramā*, taking a bath in the Yamunā along the way.

We often went to Delhi to purchase household items for the new house, or to Jaipur for service or *darśana*—once even as far as Bombay, where Giriraj Swami was based. One time, Govinda Mahārāja arranged that we have *darśana* of Śrī Govindajī and Śrī Gopīnātha in Jaipur and Śrī Madana-mohana in Karoli all in one day, because it is said that if one has had *darśana* of all three Deities on the same day, one has seen the complete form of Kṛṣṇa. At that time, Arcā still wore beautiful, colorful saris, and her short hair remained a rich reddish color. But these experiences were drawing her deeper and deeper into spiritual consciousness.

All the shopkeepers and rickshaw *wallas* in Vṛndāvana knew Arcā and respected her for leaving her comfortable life in the West to prepare for her departure in the holy place of Vṛndāvana. At times some of the Vraja-vāsīs would invite us to their homes for lunch, and we always accepted. People of all types and walks of life wanted to know Arcā and serve her in some way. Everyone accepted me as her daughter, even though we explained that that was not our biological relation. To the Vraja-vāsīs, serving her *like* a daughter meant that I *was* her daughter, and I was afforded a degree of respect, even honor, for serving Arcā this way.

Arcā was always seeking ways to employ her skills and talents to render devotional service. Śrīla Prabhupāda had said that by tradition in India, women did not go on the altar. So the idea of Arcā painting the temple deities there was unheard of. But Bhaktisiddhānta Prabhu, who was serving as head *pūjārī* in Vṛndāvana and was also an artist, had arranged for her to paint

Śrī Śrī Rādhā-Śyāmasundara secretly at night. He was the first to arrive at the temple in the morning and the last to leave at night, so he was able to open the doors and let her in and out without anyone knowing. In Juhu also, after being requested, she would paint the deities at night; no one knew who was doing the beautiful work.

When Arcā served like this, she would hardly sleep for weeks on end. I think that is one of the reasons she got so sick. She would be up all night on the altar and busy during the day. She was always very controlled, never sleeping much and eating only healthy food and even then not too much. But when she was absorbed in service, she would forget eating and sleeping entirely. And she couldn't refuse any devotee who asked her to paint their deities or help with some project. This in turn endeared her even further to the devotees, with whom she forged close friendships.

She still wanted to complete some of her own projects too—to finish "The Eye Opener" and do something big for Śrīla Prabhupāda. Bhūrijana Prabhu once preached to her that not even Śrīla Prabhupāda had been able to finish his work of translating *Śrīmad-Bhāgavatam*, and this comforted her a little. But she never let up.

Over time, Arcā was able to use her artistic talent in the service of some very special projects. Once, a Gauḍīya Vaiṣṇava at Rādhā-kuṇḍa wanted to renovate Śrīla Kṛṣṇadāsa Kavirāja Gosvāmī's *bhajana-kuṭīra* and was looking for an artist to paint a new portrait. It would be served and worshiped like a deity, nondifferent from the transcendental personality it represented, and since Rādhā-kuṇḍa was one of the most important holy sites, visited by millions of pilgrims every year, the painting had to look exactly like the one it was replacing, and the artist had to be carefully chosen. So, this young Vaiṣṇava, who was friendly with Bhūrijana Prabhu and his wife, Mother Jagattāriṇī, asked them to help him find the right person—"but not a foreigner and not a woman." So Bhūrijana and Jagattāriṇī asked Arcā-vigraha to do the service secretly—she couldn't even sign the painting or reveal herself as the artist.

On the day of the *bhajana-kuṭīra's* reopening, the painting was unveiled for all to see, and everyone thought it was wonderful. Then someone pointed to Arcā-vigraha, who was sitting at the back of the assembly, and exclaimed, "And here is the artist!" We froze on the spot. But the local *bābājīs* were so enchanted with the painting that they no longer cared who had painted it. In fact, they requested Arcā to also paint Jīva Gosvāmī, and Ananta dāsa Bābājī, Rādhā-kuṇḍa's chief *mahānta*, requested a meeting with Arcā to thank her personally. Both paintings are still there at Rādhā-kuṇḍa, installed and worshiped.

Another wonderful service opportunity came when Govinda Mahārāja arranged for Arcā to paint a large *govardhana-śilā* for the Houston ISKCON temple. We had never seen such a large *śilā*, and it stayed with us for several weeks, while Arcā contemplated how to paint the features. She was a perfectionist and never rushed a task, no matter what. She painted Girirāja with gorgeous, full lips and expressive lotus eyes. I had never seen a *govardhana-śilā* painted quite like that. Usually *śilās* had conchshell eyes and a simple, linear, half-moon smile. But Arcā infused so much transcendental personality into the deities she painted. All her hearing and meditation on Kṛṣṇa's name, form, qualities, and pastimes were translated into her art.

Even before we arrived in Vṛndāvana, Arcā had already decided that she did not want chemotherapy or any other conventional cancer treatment. She decided to accept Ayurvedic care and eventually settled on that, but at first she was also open to a variety of alternative approaches, and strangers often approached her with claims of a cure. One local *bābā* claimed that the cancer was the result of a Muslim ghost and prescribed a black rubber band to be worn around Arcā's waist; another recommended mantras and talismans invoking Hanumān, another one those invoking the lower spirits. Ananta-śānti dāsa, Śrīla Prabhupāda's first disciple in Russia, who had endured many hardships and was now wandering around India, an emaciated ascetic with his blonde hair in a topknot, insisted that she go to the Himalayas to fast and submerge herself in icy cold water every day for forty days.

Initially we also injected an experimental homeopathic drug from Switzerland directly into the tumor. Due to the lack of proper medical facilities and personnel, I would often administer the injections myself, despite my lack of training. Eventually, with the help of a young Ayurvedic doctor—the son of a more established physician—she settled on a regimen of treatments that for a while seemed to soften and shrink the tumor. But whatever the treatment, Arcā was adamant that she wanted to maintain a clear consciousness right until the moment of death.

In 1992 Arcā contracted hepatitis, probably from drinking contaminated water, and as a result she could not tolerate any medicine. Then, while still struggling with the hepatitis, she developed a severe case of pneumonia. It was a battle for her life, and a great setback in her fight against the cancer. After this incident, we realized that there really was no hope of a cure or even an extended remission. More and more, Arcā accepted the inevitable.

Despite the steady decline in her health, Arcā continued to work at her art until almost the very end. She took inspiration from the verse *tat te 'nukampāṁ su-samīkṣamāṇo*—that if one is suffering but takes the misery as the mercy of Kṛṣṇa, tolerates it, and takes the opportunity to become more serious about Kṛṣṇa consciousness, he or she can earn the right to enter the kingdom of God. Although she was in such extreme pain—every doctor said that the type of cancer she had was the most painful—she never begrudged it but always took it as Kṛṣṇa's purifying mercy upon her.

Sometimes the local Vraja-vāsīs would affectionately joke about that "tough English woman" and say that she had been a yogi in a previous life. Many people thought that Arcā was a very wealthy woman, but the truth was that she still had to work to earn the money she used for the house and her medical expenses. She would paint floral still lifes, for which there was a demand in South Africa, and her daughter, Sara, who served as Arcā's agent, would travel back and forth between India and South Africa, collecting the paintings, selling them, and bringing back the payment and more art supplies.

Although Arcā was very sick at that time and the pain in her arm was almost unbearable, somehow she would still paint. I would go into the fields and to different places in Vṛndāvana to collect flowers for her to paint. It wasn't so easy to find flowers on stems in Vṛndāvana, because people there grow flowers mainly for garlands. So sometimes I would go to Delhi, to a nice flower market at Khan Market, and I would pick out some beautiful flowers for Arcā and bring them back to Vṛndāvana. We would arrange them in one of her colorful Rajasthani ceramic vases, and then she would just paint for days. It was a momentous effort every time. But she was so determined. Then we would have to package the paintings so that Sara could sell them. Arcā was very particular about the packing. She did it with great care and precision and artistry, the way she did everything. I would watch her and help her, and eventually I was entrusted with doing the packing. When a person who is such a perfectionist and has such fine taste entrusts you with something so dear to them, it really means a lot.

Although I fall far short in every respect, I have often thought that my service to Mother Arcā-vigraha prepared me for my service to my *guru mahārāja*, because he is also a perfectionist with very sensitive and refined taste, and he also has an artistic temperament.

In addition to being an amazing devotee, Arcā was just a wonderful person. Nowadays we often speak about devotees being "balanced." I feel she was balanced—as a human being and as a devotee—in that she was very deep in spiritual life, deeply absorbed in Kṛṣṇa consciousness, but was not fanatical or dogmatic. She often said that we should see the divinity in everyone. She had great respect for all living entities—even the dogs. When she saw dogs suffering in Vṛndāvana, she would cry. Sometimes she would say that she was crying for the whole world. Of course, her emotions were heightened by her particular situation, but she was always very sensitive.

And she was also adventurous and fun, even when she was sick and dying. At one stage we were going all over India, seeing different kinds of doctors and healers and going to different hospitals (I think I saw every cancer ward in Bombay and Delhi). But through all of this, which was a very heavy experience, Arcā always had a sense of humor. Looking back on it now, I can see how incredible it was for her to have maintained this spirit under such circumstances. But then we just saw it as an adventure—not only a physical adventure of traveling through India, but also a spiritual adventure, a journey. It was a very dynamic time. All these things, unusual things, would happen to us, and it was a great experience.

Arcā also still had commitments to her children. Her son, Michael, a brilliant and successful advertising executive in Canada, had had a nervous breakdown, and Arcā was very concerned about him and tried to help him through his struggle with stress and depression. Eventually he was able to overcome his problems and became a successful author and motivational speaker, often referring to her in his talks and books.

While Arcā was still able to go out, we went on *parikramās* whenever we could, visiting the holy places. She had a special affinity for Vṛndādevī, and we often drove to Kāmyavana for Vṛndādevī's *darśana*. Later on, when Mother Daivī-śakti and Dīna-bandhu Prabhu began the renovation of Vṛndā-kuṇḍa, they arranged for Arcā to paint the deity there. (Later, after Arcā left, Giriraj Swami, Govinda Mahārāja, and a few close devotees visited Vṛndā-kuṇḍa, and Guru Mahārāja mentioned to the *pūjārī* that Arcā was sorry that she could not finish her work on the deity. The *pūjārī* smiled, pointed upward, and replied, "Her service to Vṛndādevī will be complete there.")

All the while, Arcā was aware that part of her process was to let go of her remaining material attachments, even natural, loving attachments like family and friends, and subtle ones like art—her paper, brushes, and paints. One of her final attachments, she said, was color. She clearly understood how all the tastes and impressions we gather throughout a lifetime become imprinted on our hearts and how eventually we have to let them all go.

In the summer of 1993, when Arcā's frail health could no longer tolerate the intense heat in Vṛndāvana, where there was still no air conditioning and even electricity was sporadic, we flew north, to Kullu-Manali, in the Himalayan foothills near India's border with Tibet. While we were staying in the small village of Kullu, one boy invited us to visit his family, high on the mountain slopes. The only way to reach their village was by foot, a steep, three-hour climb from Kullu, and there was no way Arcā could make the trek, but she insisted I go. One morning the boy and I set out. The ascent was magnificent, with beautiful vistas of the surrounding mountain peaks and the river below. I knew Mother Arcā would love it and resolved to take her as well.

First our friend offered to carry her on his back. Then he said he could take her on a mountain horse, but she was too frail for such a bumpy ride. Reluctantly, we gave up the idea. At nine o'clock the next morning, however, our friend burst into our room and said, "Come, let's go!" He had four other men with him, and they had crafted a special palanquin, or *pālki*, for Arcā, complete with curtains and a roof to shield her from the sun. For a reasonable sum, they would carry her up and down the mountain.

Arcā loved the *pālki* and was excited about the adventure. Not wanting to miss the beautiful scenery, she had us take down the curtain and the roof, and she made herself as comfortable as possible, sitting cross-legged, sketching. The palanquin bearers carried her with the utmost care and respect—she had that effect on people: everyone recognized her as someone special, and wherever we went around Kullu, people would offer respect and address her as "holy mother."

Eventually we reached the village. First we visited the village temple, where there were a deity of Lord Rāmacandra and a *śiva-liṅga*. Then the boy took us further up the mountain to his family home. They lived in a simple log cabin, with sheep downstairs and the people above, overlooking groves of almond and apple trees. Huge hemp bushes grew wild.

Arcā was fascinated by the villagers' simple, self-sufficient way of life. They grew their own wheat, dal, and vegetables; herded sheep for wool; and kept short-legged Himalayan cows for milk. They ground their own *āṭā* and spun and dyed the wool to weave their famous Kullu shawls and tunics. Using the hemp they made shoes.

With classic Indian hospitality, the mother offered us lunch. Quickly, she gathered bundles of wheat, ground them in a stone grinder, and with this freshly-ground *āṭā* hand-formed thick rotis. Then, squatting on the floor, with her baby playing in a corner, she cooked dal and a *sabjī* of fresh, tiny eggplants with chili-masala stuffing. It was simple and delicious.

After lunch, we drank glacier water from a mountain stream. According to legend, the Pāṇḍavas, as well as many sages and *ṛṣis*, had spent time in the area, and it wasn't difficult to imagine these great devotees living there, drinking fresh water from the streams, eating fruits and berries from the trees, and meditating on God.

Arcā gained a lot of inspiration from that trip up the mountain. She saw it as a symbolic journey—surveying from above the world she was leaving behind and embracing the world beyond.

One morning, while we were still in Kullu, Arcā woke up with intense pain. The cancer, we knew, had spread, so we immediately returned by bus to Delhi—a fifteen-hour journey winding down steep, narrow mountain passes. In Delhi we went straight to Batra Hospital to meet Dr. Ghosh, an oncologist whom she had previously consulted. He was very straightforward and told her that the cancer had come to a critical point.

Arcā was shaken; she did not have long to live. The only thing she could do was try to manage the pain through radiation therapy. So we went back to Vṛndāvana for a few days, before returning to Delhi, to Batra Hospital, where she would receive a series of treatments.

She wanted her art equipment with her—her pencils and brushes and paints and papers—in case she felt inspired to work. We also took a portable kitchen—stoves, pots, and dry goods. And her special pillow, sheets, and personal effects.

The taxi left us at the hospital, and there were throngs of people. Struggling with all our luggage, we took our places in a long line leading to the front desk and eventually reached the admissions clerk. Our idea was that I would stay under Arcā's bed and cook for her and take care of her. But the hospital refused. Hearing that, Arcā turned around and walked out.

"We're going to Kaya Maya," she declared—to a nearby

Ayurvedic clinic. So we piled into an auto rickshaw, with Arcā in the back on top of the luggage and me squeezed in next to the driver. When we arrived at Kaya Maya, however, we found that the facility was just a day clinic. Still, the manager agreed to give us a place to stay—a small dark room full of cobwebs, with a simple tap-and-toilet bathroom and another room, a crude cement structure with a tap and a basin, to use as a kitchen.

Every day people would come to consult "Guruji," the clinic's famous Ayurvedic *kavirāja*, and as they waited for hours in the courtyard, they would come right up to our door and window and stare at Arcā and me. And Arcā, also intrigued, would return their gazes, noting something unique and beautiful about each person, no matter how ordinary he or she seemed.

But she was very sick and in great pain. We had no transport to get back to the hospital, where she was receiving treatments, so every day I would walk down to the main road to hitchhike. When a car stopped I would tell the driver, "Just wait, I have to call my mother," and run back up to get Arcā.

Arcā was so refined, and she had been accustomed to having the best of everything, but here she was, far from country and family and modern facilities, accepting rides to a mediocre hospital. There, we met people from all over India and Nepal, some with huge tumors, like footballs, protruding from their bodies. All of it was hard to even imagine.

When the series of treatments was complete, we returned one last time to Vṛndāvana, where Arcā became more and more absorbed in Kṛṣṇa consciousness. She was like a great saintly person, finishing up her life on earth, and other saintly personalities came to see her, both to bless her and to receive her blessings. Giriraj Swami came to Vṛndāvana to be with her, and despite his duties in Bombay, he stayed with her until the very end. (Arcā's experience during this time convinced her of the need for a hospice in Vṛndāvana, and Mahārāja promised her that he would complete one.) Govinda Mahārāja still came every day, positioning his *govardhana-śilā* in Arcā's line of vision and helping her focus on Kṛṣṇa's pastimes by recounting them and reading aloud. Tamal Krishna Goswami came every morning to read from the portion of *Śrīmad-Bhāgavatam* known as the *Veṇu-gītā*. Bhūrijana Prabhu also came daily, and Śivarāma Swami and Keśava Bhāratī Mahārāja visited often. Sometimes they would all read to her from the *Lalita-mādhava*, each reciting the part of a different character. She had retained her great taste for hearing and absorbed it all with enthusiasm. Sometimes, as she listened to the beautiful pastimes of Kṛṣṇa in Vṛndāvana, her heart would melt and she would cry. Nārāyaṇa Mahārāja also came to bless her, as well as other senior Vaiṣṇavas, and some of the senior female devotees would visit regularly. The atmosphere was deeply surcharged with spiritual energy, and as Arcā in this way became more and more absorbed in Kṛṣṇa consciousness, her focus shifted from her life and service in this world to her life and service in Goloka Vṛndāvana.

By Gaura-pūrṇimā of 1994, Arcā was no longer able to eat. The tumor was pressing down on her food pipe and she couldn't swallow. She wasn't able to keep her Ayurvedic medicine down and was becoming increasingly dehydrated and weak; we were afraid she would fall into a coma. Just then, a wonderful devotee doctor from France—Gopasvāmī Prabhu, who had a certificate in hospice care—arrived in Vṛndāvana, and with his help we learned how to manage the different symptoms of her failing body. There was no hope or chance of recovery, but Gopasvāmī Prabhu showed us how to keep Arcā's body comfortable enough that she could remain conscious, in keeping with her desire. She was often in great pain, and her body was barely more than a skeleton. But she still relished hearing Kṛṣṇa's pastimes—sometimes laughing, sometimes crying.

Arcā had always said that she wanted only five devotees

present at the time of her passing. For the previous few weeks, we had screened her visitors, allowing only her closest friends to visit. But on the night before she left her body, we sensed that the time was near, and there was an all-night *kīrtana* and vigil to which everyone was welcome. Many devotees came, and everyone who wanted to serve her got the chance to do so. We took turns crushing ice and putting small amounts into her mouth.

Late the next morning—Jahnu-saptamī, May 18—only Giriraj Swami, Nāma Cintāmaṇi, Rasikānanda, Kṛṣṇa Kumārī, and I were present.

At around noon Mother Arcā-vigraha breathed in deeply a few times, flung her right arm backwards, and took her last breath. One tear ran from the corner of her right eye. There were *tulasī* leaves on her tongue and forehead, and she was surrounded by sacred objects. Giriraj Mahārāja was chanting *japa*, and the recorded sound of Śrīla Prabhupāda chanting filled the room.

Govinda Mahārāja, who had been called away to attend to something urgent at the temple, returned moments later; then, after a few minutes, the door flew open and devotees poured in. Dīna-bandhu Prabhu, Gaurī dāsa and the *gurukula* boys, and so many other devotees entered, and there was a beautiful *kīrtana*. We bathed Arcā's body in water from Rādhā-kuṇḍa, decorated it with *tilaka*, painted the names of Rādhārāṇī on different parts of her body, and dressed Arcā's body in a fresh white sari. The body was placed on a palanquin and decorated with garlands. Everything was so beautiful and auspicious.

The men then took Arcā's body on a procession to all the main temples in Vṛndāvana, starting at the Kṛṣṇa-Balarāma Mandira, and finally to the cremation ghat on the banks of the Yamunā. Arcā's closest friends and well-wishers—her *guru mahārāja*, Govinda Mahārāja, Bhūrijana Prabhu, and others—lit her funeral pyre and stayed for hours, until it was all over.

By her own example, Mother Arcā-vigraha taught us about wholehearted, unflinching faith and surrender to *guru* and Kṛṣṇa. She showed us how to live with grace and dignity, and she showed us how to leave in the same manner. Her last few months had extracted from her the ultimate in surrender and purification, and by the time she passed away, her consciousness had become highly exalted.

Arcā had taken her spiritual master's instruction, "Just go to Vṛndāvana and let Rādhārāṇī take over," completely to heart. Her faith in *guru* and her love for Vṛndāvana had assured her complete victory, and there is no doubt that she entered the eternal pastimes of Rādhā and Kṛṣṇa.

Earning Entry into God's Kingdom

From a talk on June 16, 1994, in Johannesburg.

tat te 'nukampāṁ su-samīkṣamāṇo
bhuñjāna evātma-kṛtaṁ vipākam
hṛd-vāg-vapurbhir vidadhan namas te
jīveta yo mukti-pade sa dāya-bhāk

"My dear Lord, one who earnestly waits for You to bestow Your causeless mercy upon him, all the while patiently suffering the reactions of his past misdeeds and offering You respectful obeisances with his heart, words, and body, is surely eligible for liberation, for it has become his rightful claim."

—*Śrīmad-Bhāgavatam* 10.14.8

* * *

In spite of all difficulties, if one is sincere and has no desire other than to serve *guru* and Kṛṣṇa, and follows the four principles, chants sixteen rounds, and fully engages in devotional service, one can go back to Godhead. And Mother Arcā-vigraha serves as an example.

Mother Arcā-vigraha was very qualified. She was always thinking of Rādhā and Kṛṣṇa. About a week before she left, I asked her, "Are you thinking of Śrīmatī Rādhārāṇī?" And she replied, "Oh, yes. All the time. All the time." And maybe three days before she left, after she'd just gone through an extremely difficult bout with pain—she was always in great pain, but sometimes the pain became even more excruciating—she mentioned that she just wanted her mind to be filled with one thing: *tavaivāsmi tavaivāsmi na jīvāmi tvayā vinā/ iti vijñāya devī tvaṁ naya māṁ caraṇāntikam.* That was Raghunātha dāsa Gosvāmī's prayer to Śrīmatī Rādhārāṇī: "I am Yours, I am Yours, I cannot live without You. Understanding this, please bring me to Your lotus feet." (*Vilāpa-kusumāñjali* 96)

She was always thinking of Śrīmatī Rādhārāṇī and Kṛṣṇa, even when she wasn't able to chant aloud, because of being so weak. The cancer was gradually closing her food-pipe, so for about two months before she left she couldn't eat. She could only drink, and drinking also became increasingly difficult. She commented that she had gradually given up all material attachments—and the last was eating. But because of not eating she became very weak, and even speaking or chanting aloud was difficult. Still, within her mind she was always chanting or praying. And she had a dream that she was a young girl, playing in the forest with her girlfriends; then she heard the sound of a flute, and they all ran toward the beautiful sound. Around the same time, Rañcora Prabhu had the same dream about her. And when I came from Māyāpur to Vṛndāvana, I had a similar dream.

So, she had an idea what her destination was, and she was always thinking of it.

Actually, when one comes to the stage of *prema*, one generally can't continue in this body. The symptoms of *prema* are too intense for the body to bear. When *prema* actually comes, without being conscious of it one sheds the body and enters the pastimes of Kṛṣṇa. Śrīla Viśvanātha Cakravartī Ṭhākura describes this in *Mādhurya Kaḍambinī.* Generally, within this world or within this body, we can progress only up to *bhāva. Bhāva-bhakti* means that one is still living in this body and sometimes has glimpses of Kṛṣṇa and His pastimes and sometimes is conscious of being in this world. In the case of Arcā-vigraha, there are many indications that she was thinking of Rādhārāṇī and

Kṛṣṇa at the time of death and attained Their eternal service.

If somebody thinks about the pastimes of Kṛṣṇa at the time of death, he or she can go to the pastimes of Kṛṣṇa. But unless we are advanced in Kṛṣṇa consciousness, there is a chance we won't think about the pastimes of Kṛṣṇa at the time of death. Even when we chant, our mind may be somewhere else. And what counts most is the consciousness, not the lips and the tongue. So if we are chanting and thinking of something else and then die, our thoughts will determine where we go, not our show of chanting. "Show" means we are chanting as a routine, chanting rounds but not actually hearing.

The extraordinary mercy Mother Arcā-vigraha received can be seen from different angles. When I returned to Vṛndāvana from Māyāpur and entered her room, I was immediately struck by the spiritual atmosphere. She had an altar, and from her bed she was always gazing at the deities. There was a small deity of Śrīla Prabhupāda, deities of Rādhā and Kṛṣṇa and Gaura-Nitāi, and a picture of Vṛndādevī from Vṛndā-kuṇḍa.

Sitting in front of the deities, by her side, so many thoughts came to me. She had done two extraordinary services for me. One was that when I became very sick and almost died, she had served me literally day and night and nursed me back to life and health. And the other was that she had built the house in Vṛndāvana as a facility for me to stay there. So the impression I got from the deity of Śrīla Prabhupāda was that because she had served me in the mood that I was his representative (although I am so insignificant compared with him), he was as pleased with her service to me as he would have been if she had done the same service for him directly. You can imagine how pleased Śrīla Prabhupāda would have been if someone had served him like that. Therefore he wanted to give her his full mercy. And the result was that for many months so many advanced devotees constantly visited her. Govinda Mahārāja and Bhūrijana Prabhu came every day, and when Tamal Krishna Goswami, Śivarāma Swami, and Keśava Bhāratī Prabhu were in Vṛndāvana, they also came and read to her, and Mother Kartā and others also came.

So this is Śrīla Prabhupāda's mercy. And I don't say that Prabhupāda was pleased with only those two things. She did so much exceptional service. She was always concerned about the devotees' welfare, always trying to help them in any way she could. Selfless service to the Vaiṣṇavas is a great qualification.

Another thought came in relation to the verse in the Tenth Canto of *Śrīmad-Bhāgavatam*, *tat te 'nukampāṁ su-samīkṣamāṇo.* If one is suffering but accepts the misery as the mercy of Kṛṣṇa, tolerates it, and takes the opportunity to become more serious about Kṛṣṇa consciousness, he or she earns the right to enter the kingdom of God, just as a son has the right to inherit the property of the father. So I thought of that too. Although she was in such extreme pain—every doctor said that the type of cancer she had was the most painful—she never complained, never begrudged it; she always took it as Kṛṣṇa's mercy upon her to purify her, and she did everything that the verse said. She took advantage of the opportunity, gave up all material attachments, and became completely serious and absorbed in Kṛṣṇa consciousness. On the basis of that verse, she earned the right to enter into the kingdom of God.

An Exalted and Exemplary Vaiṣṇavī

Bhūrijana dāsa's Vyāsa-pūjā offering to Śrīla Prabhupāda in 1994.

My dear Śrīla Prabhupāda,

Please accept my humble obeisances. All glories to you. We pray that your powerful preaching potency continues forever.

As I write this, Mother Arcā-vigraha is still alive. By the time this offering is read by the devotees, she will be gone. She now lies bedridden within her Ramaṇa-reti house; her thin, almost white hair is cropped close and with *śikhā*. The May Vṛndāvana heat glares, and her body burns as if filled with poison from one thousand scorpions. Only her left arm near the shoulder is fat, for there the cancer spreads from her lymph gland. The rest of that arm lies thin and useless at her side, like the arm of a doll, but burning with pain.

"'Good' and 'bad' in the material world are the same thing. [They] are our mental creations. All is actually distress, for we must die. Human life is meant for Kṛṣṇa consciousness. Why should we lose this chance? A Kṛṣṇa conscious person is not under the laws of material nature." (All quotes are from a 1969 New Vrindaban lecture by Śrīla Prabhupāda.)

Arcā-vigraha was a famous South African artist. She took initiation from His Holiness Giriraj Swami years ago and developed deep faith in you, her *guru mahārāja*, Kṛṣṇa consciousness, the holy name, Vṛndāvana-dhāma, and the Vaiṣṇavas. Now, in her final days, her face is gaunt; deep crevices rim her eyes. Yet she is neither miserable nor morose nor fearful. Mother Arcā remains either silently Kṛṣṇa conscious or jolly.

"One who is Kṛṣṇa conscious is never afraid or disturbed in

any condition of life. This is the effect of Kṛṣṇa consciousness. Therefore Nārada is trying to convince Vyāsadeva, 'You preach Kṛṣṇa consciousness. Whatever you have so far written is useless. Now you write something that by reading, one will become immediately Kṛṣṇa conscious.' *Śrīmad-Bhāgavatam* is so nice that by reading, immediately one can capture the Supreme Lord within his heart. Our whole program is that Kṛṣṇa is very kind, always kind upon us."

She hasn't eaten any solid food for about seven weeks and has been subsisting on less than 500 milligrams of juice a day. Her life has been sustained by *kṛṣṇa-kathā*, which she longs to constantly hear. And Mother Arcā still preaches. Despite her pain, as long as she can speak, she greets all with good spirits, encouragement, and Kṛṣṇa conscious advice: "Most problems don't seem important from this perspective, do they?" "The body is useless, isn't it?" "*Jaya jaya* Śrī Rādhe-Śyāma!" Devotees approach her to offer solace but find shelter in her Kṛṣṇa conscious strength.

"The pure devotees, if they are put into difficulty, they think, 'This is Kṛṣṇa's grace. It is Kṛṣṇa's grace.' They take it in this way. 'I was to suffer hundreds of times more due to my bad activities in my past life, but You are only giving me a little of it. So it is Your grace.' "

We do not know when Kṛṣṇa will actually take Mother Arcā. She almost left just after Gaura-pūrṇimā, and we rushed to her bedside at 11:00 p.m. to find her gasping and wheezing and unable to breathe. The cancer is gradually closing off her windpipe. But Kṛṣṇa wouldn't take her then. She is now quite ready to go and awaits His call. She chants more or less constantly in her mind.

"Hypnotized. It is so nice, hypnotized! Otherwise, why are these boys working so hard? They can earn money, but they are hypnotized here. Kṛṣṇa is so nice. He is all-attractive.

He hypnotizes His devotee. Just like the Pāṇḍavas. They are all Kṛṣṇa's friends. Nārada met Kṛṣṇa, and because he was a devotee, he could speak to Kṛṣṇa with a little criticism: 'My dear Kṛṣṇa, by becoming Your devotees, have Your Pāṇḍavas become happy? They have lost their kingdom. Their wife has been insulted, and now they are banished for twelve years. Is it a very good thing? But the wonderful thing I see, in spite of all these inconveniences, they have increased their love for You!' So Nārada is asking, 'What kind of hypnotism You do I don't know. In spite of being placed in so many inconveniences, their love for You has increased.' That is the position of a *bhakta*."

Both her breathing and swallowing are now strained and painful. I used to ask her if she had anything remaining to accomplish within the world of matter. Her last anxiety was spiritual, to finish the remaining true-to-size drawings for the 6' x 3' panels at the back of your *samādhi-mandira*. She wasn't physically capable, but she strained and sat up and directed the remaining work to its end. "See, I told you I'd finish!" No further work remains for Mother Arcā-vigraha within this world.

"Anyone who has associated with Kṛṣṇa consciousness, he cannot forget . . . He cannot give it up. If one once surrenders sincerely, 'Kṛṣṇa, I am Yours,' Kṛṣṇa will never leave you. He will protect you."

Prabhupāda, you have already bestowed your mercy on this fine devotee, Mother Arcā-vigraha. We, out of affection for her, nevertheless pray to you for her eternal welfare. We also beg you to continue giving us the association of exalted and exemplary Vaiṣṇavas.

Praying to serve you eternally,
Bhūrijana dāsa

"I Just Have to Fix My Mind on Kṛṣṇa"

A talk by Bhakti Bhṛṅga Govinda Swami on Mother Arcā-vigraha's disappearance day on April 25, 1996, at Hare Krishna Land, Phoenix, Mauritius.

Today is Jahnu-saptamī. On this date two years ago, according to our Vaiṣṇava calendar, His Holiness Giriraj Swami's disciple Arcā-vigraha devī dāsī passed away from this world and returned back to Godhead.

Actually, Mother Arcā-vigraha and I were very good friends and had been friends for a long time. We first met in 1986 when she came to Vṛndāvana. Then, in 1987, I went to South Africa with Indradyumna Swami and we had some programs at her home in Yeoville.

Arcā suffered from cancer. She got the news in late 1987, but she had some treatment done, and the doctors seemed to think that it had cleared the cancer up, but then she became affected again. So, she took some small treatment in South Africa, but by nature she wasn't inclined to take a lot of heavy medications. She felt that she should depend more on her *guru* and Kṛṣṇa. She wasn't inclined to take heavy treatments that were likely to disturb her consciousness. That was a big factor for her: she didn't want her Kṛṣṇa consciousness to be affected. She wanted to always try to have a clear mind and consciousness so that she could meditate on the holy name and meditate on the instructions of her spiritual master. She didn't take the chemotherapy and other treatments they like to give in Western countries, which generally have the tendency to destroy a person suffering from such a disease.

Arcā started coming to Vṛndāvana, and by the grace of

Śrīmatī Rādhārāṇī and Kṛṣṇa she was able to buy a plot of land in Vṛndāvana and build a house. She wanted to pass her final days there. I would say to her, "There are so many people in South Africa—twenty or thirty million—and out of them, how many have been blessed by Rādhā and Kṛṣṇa to come to Vṛndāvana, purchase a piece of property, build a house, and live in that house in Vṛndāvana?"

So, she started staying there, and she took up service in Vṛndāvana, and because she was such a fine artist, she was always involved in different art projects. The last service that she was given was to do the artwork for the large carved marble panels to be placed at the back of Śrīla Prabhupāda's *samādhi*.

Arcā-vigraha was very serious about her work. In her final days she was in terrible pain, and her left arm was useless; the cancer was affecting her whole left side. Then the cancer grew and intruded upon her windpipe and esophagus, the food pipe, and eventually she couldn't eat. She just stopped eating and was only drinking. She had no energy, and she became just like bones with some skin on top. But what would she do? She would ask the devotees caring for her to prop her up in her bed, and then she would say, "Bring me my artwork," and they would bring it to her. She was determined to do this service for Śrīla Prabhupāda and the Vaiṣṇavas. She would sit there, and with whatever little energy she had she would draw the designs of Prabhupāda for those back panels. They were big panels, and she would cut out sections and put them together. Sometimes she could work for only five minutes and then have to take rest, but then she would get up again, have the devotees bring her artwork back, and start all over again. She had so much transcendental determination.

Arcā was like a different species of person. Sometimes I look at our present generation, and I have to admit that our generation is not very good. The postwar generation really went down fast—lack of honor, lack of credibility. The word I like to use most is *integrity*. If you look at the world today, it has just become lost for want of integrity. People lie—say anything to achieve their end, to achieve sense gratification. They'll say or do anything to get what they want as quickly as possible. I see this particularly in India, where I live, but I know it goes on everywhere. In India, I go mad at the lack of integrity. In contrast, when you look at Śrīla Prabhupāda's generation, they were people who would die for principle. They would give their head for principle, they had so much integrity. Arcā's generation was like that too. We find that generally the older people we meet are men and ladies of integrity and honor. And she was like that. She was a phenomenal person. And even though she was suffering from cancer and was in pain, she always held her head high. Her mentality was never that she wanted people to just come and pet her and give her consolation. What was her mentality? She was always trying to do good for others. Devotees were constantly coming to her. She would be suffering so much, but when devotees would come, she would immediately set herself upright and start preaching, preaching straight Kṛṣṇa consciousness. She had so much character. She was so noble. And then the people would leave, and she would collapse again. And then more people would come, and she would preach, "We are not this body. We should not identify with the pains and pleasures of this body. We should fix our mind on Kṛṣṇa, fix the mind on the goal."

After Gaura-pūrṇimā 1994, some young people from Bulgaria were in Vṛndāvana. They had become attracted to a famous yogi there. They had heard about him and come to Vṛndāvana because they thought, "He is our *guru*." In Vṛndāvana they stayed with this yogi and they found out how terrible he was—very angry at times and screaming and doing erratic things. So, these Bulgarians said, "We came all the way here, and we thought this guy was our *guru*, but he's not." They didn't know what to do. They were coming by the Kṛṣṇa-Balarāma temple, and they met the devotees there and somehow the devotees introduced them to Giriraj Mahārāja. So they started coming over to listen to Giriraj Mahārāja speak. They would come over to Arcā-vigraha's house, and we were doing a lot of reading there. There would often be *kīrtana*, and on different occasions Arcā would have the devotees sit her up and she would start preaching to these Bulgarian people. So much character. She had so much faith in Kṛṣṇa and so much faith in the holy name. She was a unique personality.

I was Arcā's next-door neighbor, and every evening I would go over at about eight o'clock to check on how she was doing and how the day had passed. Up until Kārtika 1993 she had been on her feet and was still moving and doing all right. But one evening at eight o'clock I walked in her house and what I found was not so pleasant. Arcā was sitting on her bed and crying and crying and crying. I had never seen her cry before. So I walked over and asked what was wrong. "This pain is increasing every day," she said. "I don't know what to do." I said, "You're sure you don't want to go to Delhi to take some treatment?" She said, "No, I don't want to go that way; I don't want my consciousness to be disturbed." I used to argue with her about that, because I am the type that if I get a headache I take an aspirin. She wasn't like that. She was tough. I used to argue some, but it got to the point where it seemed that my arguments were exhausted. She was crying and saying, "I don't know what's going on with this pain. I don't know what's going to happen to me. I just don't know. I just don't know."

Then I realized that the only thing to do was to speak about Kṛṣṇa. So I got out the *Kṛṣṇa* book and started reading about Kṛṣṇa's pastimes in Vṛndāvana. I said, "Mātājī, there is no other medicine than this, so you just have to fix your mind on Kṛṣṇa's pastimes." And I started reading to her about Kṛṣṇa's pastimes in Vṛndāvana. And I saw the most amazing thing: a person who just five minutes earlier had been weeping and crying—she just started listening to the pure recitation of Kṛṣṇa's pastimes, and her mind became absolutely absorbed. She was a phenomenal person, and she was an artist. She had an artist's mind, and whenever she heard a beautiful description of Kṛṣṇa, she could keep that impression in her mind. She would paint the whole scene within her mind and remain fixed on it.

So I read her some stories about Kṛṣṇa, and she became absorbed. When I started, she was crying, but when I finished, she was ecstatic. Then I went back to my place to take rest. The next day after the morning program, I came back to see how she was doing, and she told me that she had become so absorbed in hearing about Kṛṣṇa—she had become so ecstatic from what we had read the previous night—that she couldn't take rest and had stayed up until one o'clock just thinking about what we had read and discussed, and chanting *japa*. One amazing thing she said was, "When I was chanting *japa*, all I could think about was what you had read me from the *Kṛṣṇa* book. It was the best *japa* I have ever chanted in my life, because I was chanting Kṛṣṇa's holy name and thinking about Kṛṣṇa at the same time." She became completely enlivened. It reminded me of when Śrīla Prabhupāda came back to Vṛndāvana for the last time before he passed away. He said, "My diet is *caraṇāmṛta*, and my medicine is the holy name." So that became her principle and policy too. Her diet became practically nothing, and her medicine became Kṛṣṇa's holy names and pastimes.

Because Arcā was such a fine person, a lot of people in the Vṛndāvana community had a lot of love for her. So it was non-stop—from morning to night—that people were coming to her house to have the opportunity to be able to just sit and read from Prabhupāda's books for her. There was practically a queue, and for Arcā it was exhausting. Here was a cancer patient who was going through her final stages, so she wanted to have some time to rest during the day, but from morning to night people were lining up to come and see her and read for her. So she would invite everyone and listen. Braja Bihārī would read from *Śrī Caitanya-caritāmṛta*, and I would read from *Kṛṣṇa* book and *Śrīmad-Bhāgavatam*, and different devotees would come, and they just wanted to read for Arcā, because her mentality was, "I have to fix my mind on Kṛṣṇa, I have to fix my mind on Kṛṣṇa, I have to fix my mind. The best things for me to fix my mind on Kṛṣṇa are the names and the pastimes of Kṛṣṇa." She just wanted to hear. She became very greedy and enthusiastic simply to hear about Kṛṣṇa. That went on through the course of the winter.

One time, Arcā put me in a predicament. In January of that year (1994), I had prepared everything to go abroad for a preaching tour. Everything was arranged, and I had told Arcā that I was going, because I had really been helping her a lot. Then the night before I was to leave, she took her medicine as usual, but because the pipe in her throat was closing up, she started choking. She practically choked to death—but she survived. She became very nervous. When I went to see her the next day, I was getting ready to leave, and she said, "My *guru mahārāja* can't come here at this time. I'm really worried that I might die very soon, and I'd like to have one of my spiritual authorities here (she saw me as a *śikṣā-guru*) when I pass away. Please don't go now on your preaching tour." For me it was a big shock. I had everything arranged, and I was ready to just get on the plane and fly. She said, "Please don't go now, because I may die at any time." So I didn't know what to do.

I consulted some senior devotees at the Kṛṣṇa-Balarāma temple and explained the situation, that I had been requested to stay, and asked them, "What is your opinion?" Three or four different devotees came back with the same opinion, that we are continually traveling throughout the world and preaching to people that they should become devotees of Kṛṣṇa, and so many people are surrendering and becoming devotees of Kṛṣṇa, and once they surrender and give their lives to Kṛṣṇa, at that last moment of their life when they need help as well, we shouldn't abandon them. So these devotees, whom I considered my authorities, requested, "Perhaps you should stay on here in Vṛndāvana and help." So I chose to do that.

Things were going on. I had service in Vṛndāvana, so I stayed and did my service, and I was helping Arcā-vigraha. This was more or less the way things were going. Her condition was going down day by day, but she always maintained, "I have to hear." Despite how bad she was, "I have to hear about Kṛṣṇa, I have to hear about Kṛṣṇa." She was becoming like a materialistic person who is eager for money, but she was becoming eager for Kṛṣṇa: "I just have to hear about Kṛṣṇa." That continued until Gaura-pūrṇimā.

At Gaura-pūrṇimā her situation really started to decline. Her condition just went down and down, and she was becoming weaker and weaker, with more pain and more pain. Between Kārtika and close to Gaura-pūrṇimā, Giriraj Mahārāja had not been able to come to Vṛndāvana. Finally, immediately after the GBC meetings in Māyāpur, he came, with the idea to spend some time. It was interesting, because when Arcā-vigraha had been asking me about her spiritual position I had spoken to her as I had heard Śrīla Prabhupāda preach: "Simply fix your mind on Kṛṣṇa and understand Kṛṣṇa, and *punar janma naiti*—there'll be no more birth and death, and you'll go back to Godhead. Just fix your mind on hearing Kṛṣṇa's names and pastimes, and you'll go back to Godhead." So, when Giriraj Mahārāja came and in one of his first meetings with Arcā-vigraha asked, "How are you doing?" she replied, "Everything is fine. The material situation is hopeless, but spiritually everything is fine. I'm fixing my mind. I'm going back to Godhead." When Giriraj Mahārāja heard his disciple saying, "I'm fixing my mind, I'm going back to Godhead," he might have felt that was a bit bold, or presumptuous. She was thinking, "I'm getting enthused, I'm getting determined, I want to go back to Godhead, I want to get out of this material world, I want this to be the last time."

So he came over to my house, and he was in one of those very deep, deep, deep, thoughtful moods. He wasn't really saying anything. When eventually I asked, "What's up, Mahārāja?" he replied, "I just went to see Arcā-vigraha." "So, what's up?" "She's thinking that she will go back to Godhead." I looked up and said, "Yes, I think she'll go back to Godhead, too. Don't you think she'll go back to Godhead?" He said, "But I've heard that Mādhavendra Purī was crying and Rūpa Gosvāmī was crying and Raghunātha dāsa Gosvāmī was crying, just hoping against hope to go back to Godhead, to attain the service of Rādhā and Kṛṣṇa, and here she is—she's chanting and she's hearing, but she's just assuming that she's going to go back to Godhead. It doesn't seem like she has the right mood." I said, "Well, I think that Kṛṣṇa has a special plan for each and every one of His devotees. For us, people who have taken up Kṛṣṇa consciousness from the West and are following Śrīla Prabhupāda and his instructions, we should constantly hear about Kṛṣṇa. I think Kṛṣṇa will construct a special program just for Arcā-vigraha to take her back to Godhead."

Then I asked Mahārāja, "What thing enlivened you the very most in your entire life?" He thought and then replied, "The thing that enlivened me the most was when I would sit before Prabhupāda and hear him speak Kṛṣṇa consciousness." Giriraj Mahārāja was already planning to spend some time in Vṛndāvana, so I said to him, "I think that your prime responsibility and duty now, as Arcā-vigraha's spiritual master, is to sit with her and discuss with her about Kṛṣṇa." Mahārāja was very serious. "I have to go now," he said. And he left.

Mahārāja took our discussion quite seriously, and he devised a schedule by which he was able to spend a great deal of quality time with Arcā-vigraha. And what was he doing when he was with her? He would sit there with *Śrīmad-Bhāgavatam*. Any of you who have been to Vṛndāvana may have seen the big red chair in Arcā-vigraha's room. He would sit there in the red chair and the rest of us would sit nearby—and from morning until night he would read *Śrīmad-Bhāgavatam* or *Śrī Caitanya-caritāmṛta*. He was just pouring the nectar of Kṛṣṇa into the ears of his disciple. It was nonstop, incessant. I would come over from my place twice a day. The reading would have been going on for many hours, and I would come in to be with the devotees and we would start having *bhajana* and *kīrtana*. That would go on for a few hours, and then the reading would start again. A big program was developed for just hearing about Kṛṣṇa. Hearing about Kṛṣṇa is the real medicine, the medicine to relieve us from birth and death, and that was her program.

There was another interesting time. Śrīla Rūpa Gosvāmī wrote some dramas, which are discussed in the *Caitanya-caritāmṛta*. He wrote one called *Lalita-mādhava* and one called *Vidagdha-mādhava*. *Vidagdha-mādhava* is about Kṛṣṇa's activities in Vṛndāvana, and *Lalita-mādhava* is about His activities when He left Vṛndāvana and went to Dvārakā—a super beautiful play, the most beautiful play you could ever read in your life. One day someone may make a dramatic presentation of that play, and it will be beautiful. There are so many feelings of separation. It's a ten-act play. In the first act Kṛṣṇa is in Vṛndāvana and then, in the third act, Kṛṣṇa leaves Vṛndāvana and goes to Mathurā, and all the Vṛndāvana people are just cast into a terrible ocean of separation. And then through so many dramatic devices, Śrīla Rūpa Gosvāmī describes how all the people who were in Vṛndāvana rejoin Kṛṣṇa in Dvārakā. So much intrigue, so many funny words, so many funny jokes. Rūpa Gosvāmī is the most beautiful, fantastic poet that has ever existed.

So, that play, *Lalita-mādhava*, has many different characters. And we did one thing for Arcā-vigraha. Giriraj Mahārāja, my friend Śivarāma Swami, Keśava Bhāratī Mahārāja, and Tamal Krishna Goswami, who were all in Vṛndāvana, all went over to Arcā's house and started reading *Lalita-mādhava*, and we would each take a different character in the play, like we were actually performing the play. We were all assuming different voices and trying to read with feeling, and this amazing drama was being enacted right there in the house of Arcā-vigraha. We read the whole play. It was something amazing.

So, we would just go on like that, reading and reading and reading and reading. And I could see that Arcā would never tire of hearing about Kṛṣṇa. It is described that this is the mentality of a devotee. A devotee never becomes satiated hearing about Kṛṣṇa. Sometimes because we have the diseased type of mentality described by Rūpa Gosvāmī as jaundiced, it is as if our tongue has jaundice and cannot taste the sweetness of Kṛṣṇa's name or pastimes, but when that jaundice is cured, we can just go on relishing more and more. So that was the situation. It was a high, high intensity program of simply hearing about Kṛṣṇa, hearing the philosophy of Kṛṣṇa, hearing the pastimes of Kṛṣṇa, and hearing *kīrtana* of the holy name of Kṛṣṇa. This is how Arcā spent her final days in this world.

Even though Arcā's suffering was becoming more and more intense, she was actually very peaceful.

At a certain point we came to realize something: because her throat was closing up, she couldn't drink, and the thing that would actually finish her life was not going to be the cancer but dehydration. At one stage she did become dehydrated, so I called the doctor and he put her on a drip. She became resuscitated and full of life again. Then we had a little discussion that putting her on the drip had improved the quality of her life and her situation. She said, "The quality of life may be there, but then the pain also comes back." Later, she was becoming dehydrated again. My principle in dealing with her was that she was in control. I never made decisions about her independently. So when it became obvious that we would have to give her another drip, we asked her, "What is your decision?" She said, "Now I'm ready to go." So we didn't give her the drip. We fed her water by spoonfuls, and at the end of her life she couldn't take even water; her caregivers would crush ice and put little bits in her mouth, and it would melt and trickle down her throat. And she very peacefully lay in her room hearing about Kṛṣṇa from morning until night.

At that point all of us had more or less been staying up all day and all night, so it was becoming difficult, but on the night before Arcā passed away, some devotees organized an all-night *kīrtana*. The next morning, Giriraj Mahārāja came down and started preaching to Arcā and reading from *Śrīmad-Bhāgavatam* and discussing Kṛṣṇa's activities in each section. Later he simply sat next to her bed and chanted *japa*. I was called over to the temple to do some work in the Food for Life office, and at about eleven o'clock in the morning, while I was standing in the office, someone came over to tell me to come quickly to Arcā's house, because she was having difficulty breathing. When I arrived, Giriraj Mahārāja was chanting the names of Kṛṣṇa, and when I looked at Arcā-vigraha, she had already left her body.

It was actually a very auspicious situation.

The ladies prepared Arcā's body to be carried to the Yamunā. The devotees from the temple came, and we had *kīrtana*. The devotees lifted up Arcā's body, and we performed *parikramā* of the Kṛṣṇa-Balarāma Mandira. We put Arcā's body at the gate of the temple with her head facing the feet of Śrī Śrī Kṛṣṇa-

Balarāma, Śrī Śrī Gaura-Nitāi, and Śrī Śrī Rādhā-Śyāmasundara. We had *kīrtana* there for some time, and then we set out for the Yamunā. In India when there's a funeral procession the ladies stay back, so the ladies stayed back. We went by all the major temples of Vṛndāvana with a big *kīrtana* procession. Then, on the banks of the Yamunā, we had the cremation ceremony of Arcā-vigraha, and then we all took bath in the Yamunā and returned to the temple in the evening.

Arcā was not an ordinary person in any sense of the word. She was a famous artist in South Africa, and her nickname there was "Angel," because she was such an angelic person. You always think an angel wants to do good for you, and that was Arcā's mood. She never wanted to stop doing good for the devotees. She was like the best mother you could ever have. I used to joke with her—she was born in a Jewish family, and there are so many jokes about the characteristics of Jewish mothers. I used to joke with Arcā that I had preached in Israel and had done so many things in relationships with Jewish people, but I had never had a Jewish mother, and now Kṛṣṇa had arranged it. She was always caring for the devotees. She never stopped preaching or trying to encourage people. Her life was exemplary.

Today, as I think about Arcā, there are two things that strike me: one, how she cared for other people and didn't care for herself; and two, how fortunate she was to leave her body in Vṛndāvana and go through that high-intensity program of hearing about Kṛṣṇa. When Śrīla Prabhupāda came to Vṛndāvana to leave, he said that to be born in Vṛndāvana is good, to live in Vṛndāvana is better, but to die in Vṛndāvana is best. He had been on one last tour, and the devotees had brought him back to Bombay, and he was lying there in his new quarters in Juhu. He was very weak. Sometimes the devotees would meet around Prabhupāda's bed and discuss what to do, and Prabhupāda would pretty much just lie there silently, not saying anything. Then one day after they had been discussing what to do—"Should Śrīla Prabhupāda go to Vṛndāvana or stay in Bombay?"—one of my godbrothers, Kulādri, said, "Śrīla Prabhupāda, it seems to me that you are waiting for Kṛṣṇa to make some decision on whether you stay or go. If you are going to wait for Kṛṣṇa's decision, that might as well be in Vṛndāvana." Thereupon Śrīla Prabhupāda smiled and said, "Yes, that is very good advice." And then the devotees arranged for his travel back to Vṛndāvana.

So I think that Arcā was so fortunate. She wasn't born in Vṛndāvana, but at the end of her life Kṛṣṇa gave her the opportunity to live in Vṛndāvana, and He gave her the opportunity to die in Vṛndāvana. And Kṛṣṇa gave her that opportunity because she was such a fine person. She was always making endeavors to help everyone else, and at the end of her life, Kṛṣṇa allowed her spiritual master to stay there and help her. It was a very wonderful situation, and she was a very wonderful person.

On days like this we should remember Arcā-vigraha and pray for her mercy, that we may develop the quality to always be able to help other people and the quality to always be able to hear about Kṛṣṇa and have great faith in Kṛṣṇa's names and Kṛṣṇa's pastimes.

Abhirāma Ṭhākura Dāsa

The Glories of Abhirāma Ṭhākura

A talk at Śrī Śrī Rādhā-Gopīnātha Temple in Chowpatty, Mumbai, on October 17, 1999.

When we hear of the glories of devotees, we may think that "glories" applies only to pure devotees like Śrīla Prabhupāda, or to the ones mentioned in books like *Śrīmad-Bhāgavatam* or *Śrī Caitanya-caritāmṛta*. But even within our own times and in our own lives, among our contemporaries, we may meet great devotees. Unfortunately, we may not be able to recognize them. I have been away from India for a while, and while I was gone one great devotee, Abhirāma Ṭhākura, or Abhirāma Gopāla, as he was affectionately known, left this world.

Abhirāma Ṭhākura was born in East Pakistan, which is now Bangladesh. He was in the Air Force and happened to be posted in West Pakistan, and when Bangladesh declared independence, he decided to stay in West Pakistan with his family. He used to say that he was the only Bengali *brāhmaṇa* in West Pakistan. Shortly after Śrīla Prabhupāda left this world in 1977, I began to visit Pakistan to preach. One time I went there, Amoghalīlā told me he had met a nice Bengali gentleman named Anup Kumar Bhattacarya who was very eager to read Śrīla Prabhupāda's books.

After hearing about Anup Kumar, I had the opportunity to meet him. He was a wonderful person. He wanted to read and read and read whatever Śrīla Prabhupāda had written. Whatever books by Śrīla Prabhupāda we could smuggle into Pakistan, he wanted to get and read, and I would bring new books especially for him.

As we got to know each other better, Anup Kumar began to tell us about himself. As a small boy in East Pakistan, he used to go to a nearby temple to play. He had no idea about the significance of the temple, but his friends would say, "Let's go to the Mahāprabhu temple and play there." So they used to go to the temple and run and play. Only years later, when he met the devotees in Pakistan and got *Śrī Caitanya-caritāmṛta*, did he come to know who Mahāprabhu was. But he was so fortunate and so pious that even as a child he used to visit the temple of Mahāprabhu.

Anup Kumar was the manager of a big international company, but from reading Śrīla Prabhupāda's books he understood that the purpose of life is to serve Kṛṣṇa and preach the message of Caitanya Mahāprabhu, especially under the guidance of Śrīla Prabhupāda. He had a wife and children, and somehow he got the idea that he could make some arrangement for them and come and live in the ashram and devote himself fully to Kṛṣṇa consciousness. We used to give advice according to our experience, which wasn't very extensive, so we said, "Yeah, come on!" So he moved into our little ashram, which was really just an apartment in a building in Karachi, and he lived with us just like a *brahmacārī*. He was so devotional; he loved to serve the devotees, especially by cooking. He would study *Śrī Caitanya-caritāmṛta* and find recipes for preparations that Caitanya Mahāprabhu would have, and with great pleasure he would make those preparations for us. There was one called *lāphrā*, a very simple preparation—basically just five kinds of vegetables boiled in water with some spices. It is mentioned in the *Caitanya-caritāmṛta*, and he took great pleasure in preparing it for the devotees, serving it to the devotees, honoring it with the devotees, and relishing it with the devotees. And because it was so simple, it was even more relishable, because we were living very simply.

We were enjoying life chanting, speaking about Caitanya Mahāprabhu and Śrīla Prabhupāda, and trying to spread Kṛṣṇa consciousness in a very difficult place. And we were enjoying each other's company. But his wife was not very happy, and she used to come to the ashram in the middle of the night and bang on the door. Anup Kumar was detached, but he was also very dutiful. So just as he had immediately left his family when Amoghalīlā advised him to stay in the ashram, he immediately left the ashram when we advised him that maybe he should go back to his family. And when he went back, although personally he was detached, he was very dutiful and wanted his family to become Kṛṣṇa conscious. In the years that followed, his wife also became a great devotee, and some of his children also became nice devotees. So he stayed with them, did his duties, and supported them materially and spiritually. Eventually the situation in Pakistan became so bad that he took the opportunity to bring the family to India. But while he was in Pakistan he was one of our main supporters.

Most of the Hindus in Pakistan are from what are called the Harijana communities. Anup Kumar was not only from a higher caste, but he had an important position as the manager of an international company, and he was able to help the movement. For us, even to make phone calls was sometimes a problem. But we could go to his office and use the telephone. Another, bigger, problem was getting books into the country. But his company dealt with imports and exports, and so, after great difficulty, he was able to get us permission to import a huge shipment of Prabhupāda's books into Pakistan, which everyone else we consulted had thought was impossible. Even he said that it would not be possible for him to repeat the feat.

I feel that at one stage I may have committed a subtle offense against Anup Kumar, who by then had been initiated. In order to open a bank account, we needed to have a registered society. And because Abhirāma Ṭhākura was a very respectable and responsible person, we asked him to be one of the members of the society, one of the directors, and one of the signers on the account. Although he was very busy, he did take some time out one day to come to the bank. Karachi can be very hot and humid, even hotter than Bombay, and the day we went to the bank was very hot. You didn't want to be in the sun at all, but if you were in the sun for more than a few minutes, you really felt it. I had a little puffed-up idea that I was doing Abhirāma Ṭhākura a favor by engaging him in Kṛṣṇa's service and giving him a chance to be a trustee or a signer, but when I think in retrospect of how great he was and also how busy he was and how much of a gentleman he was, I feel sorry . . . And the banks there! The banks in India are quite time-consuming, but the ones in Karachi were even worse. So the whole thing took a long time, and in retrospect I feel sorry that I made him spend so much time in the heat, and also with the formalities. Superficially I was polite, but at the time I didn't fully realize or appreciate whom I was dealing with, and so I must appeal to him to forgive me.

Later, Abhirāma Ṭhākura relocated to India, and because of certain circumstances in my life I couldn't come to India for many years. Then, after about seven years of being away and also of not meeting him, I returned. I guess it was Kṛṣṇa's arrangement that I was to go to Pune at the same time as the Pune *yātrā*. I thought I'd attend for just a few hours. But those few hours were very wonderful. I ended up spending most of my time at the *yātrā*, and there I met Abhirāma Ṭhākura again. He was living with his family in Pune. He was very softhearted and would cry very easily. Just from the quality of his voice and his laugh, you could understand how softhearted he was.

One of the most unforgettable moments of my visit was at the train station, when the Bombay devotees were leaving to go back to Bombay. His Holiness Radhanath Swami and I were standing in the doorway of the train and reciprocating with the devotees on the platform. Radhanath Swami had put his arm around me, in his affectionate way, and the devotees on the platform were doing *kīrtana*. Abhirāma Ṭhākura was standing on the platform, looking at the two of us, and he was just crying and crying—out of joy. He had been very attached to Amoghalīlā and me because we were the first ones who had met him and associated with him in Kṛṣṇa consciousness. Then, because of circumstances or fate, he was separated from the two of us and he became associated with the temple and devotees here, and with His Holiness Radhanath Swami. And I believe that within himself he felt torn, because he was actually attached to both groups of devotees. Then, by Śrīla Prabhupāda's great mercy, we all came together. And there we were, Radhanath Swami with his arm around me, and I with my arm around him, and the devotees doing *kīrtana* on the platform, and Abhirāma Ṭhākura was just looking at the two of us and crying and crying. I could see that in one sense it was the perfection of his life, that the devotees or groups of devotees he was attached to, who had been apart from each other due to circumstances, were now together. I guess his heart, in a way, had been broken, because it had been pulled in two different directions. And now we all were united, and so his heart was united, and he was just so happy. That is my most vivid memory of Abhirāma Ṭhākura in India.

Then his wife passed away. As I mentioned, she had also become a great devotee. Now Abhirāma Ṭhākura Prabhu was ready to come back to his old life in the ashram. And I think the *brahmacārīs* here were fortunate to have the maximum association with him. Although he was elderly and respectable in every way, he didn't want any special facility. He just wanted to sleep on the floor in the hall with the *brahmacārīs*, and he was actually happy to live simply with them and to serve the devotees. I didn't witness all of it, but I heard that just as much as he used to take pleasure in cooking for Radhanath Swami—and sometimes he would cook for the two of us—he would also take pleasure in cooking for the *brahmacārīs*. He would wait up at night until the *brahmacārīs* who were out came back, and he would insist that they take *prasāda*. He would cook for them, and he wouldn't rest until everyone had taken *prasāda* and been properly received and satisfied.

I was not here during Abhirāma Ṭhākura's last months, but we heard that he was afflicted with a very painful disease. He had internal bleeding, and his stomach would fill up with blood and it would come out of his mouth. But throughout everything, he never complained. And I am not talking just about his last days. I am talking about his whole life. As far as I know, he never complained about anything. That's why I feel so bad that I dragged him to the bank in the heat of the summer.

He never complained, because he was doing everything in the mood of service to *guru* and Gaurāṅga and the Vaiṣṇavas. Here I think of an incident when Śrīla Prabhupāda said something that nicely summarizes Abhirāma Ṭhākura's mood. At the time, I was staying in the Calcutta temple. The temple president had somehow become preoccupied with doing business—for the temple, but doing business nonetheless—and he wasn't taking care of the devotees. Most of the devotees were quite disturbed. We weren't getting proper food, we were new in India, and we depended on the temple president to make many arrangements for us. The devotees were just waiting for Śrīla Prabhupāda to come. When Śrīla Prabhupāda did come, many devotees approached him and complained about the conditions in the temple and about the temple president. Eventually Śrīla Prabhupāda called a meeting with all the devotees, and he heard all of their complaints. He listened very sympathetically, very patiently, and then he made a managerial arrangement. He formed a committee, and he said that the committee should meet every week and that whatever they decided should be recorded in a book that everyone should sign. And then, whatever they decided, they should do. But then Śrīla Prabhupāda's mood changed and he started talking about his own struggles—and I would say his own sufferings—in bringing Kṛṣṇa consciousness to the West and spreading Kṛṣṇa consciousness: two heart attacks; some buzzing in his brain in New York, as he explained it; and suffering in so many ways to spread Kṛṣṇa consciousness. "I don't even wish to discuss how much I suffered," Śrīla Prabhupāda said, "but I never complained, because my policy was always 'Everything for Kṛṣṇa and nothing for myself.' "

When I reflect now on Abhirāma Ṭhākura, I think he must have had the same policy: Everything for Kṛṣṇa and nothing for himself. And in the end he was rewarded with the highest blessing of leaving his body in full Kṛṣṇa consciousness, thinking of Śrīmatī Rādhārāṇī, and I am sure that he has gone to serve Mahāprabhu and Śrīmatī Rādhārāṇī and Kṛṣṇa. And I also believe that because of his advanced Kṛṣṇa consciousness he is still available to us if we remember him and want to serve him and please him. I am sure that if we remember his ideals and try to fulfill them, he will reciprocate with us and bless us.

So, on this occasion, feeling the presence of His Grace Abhirāma Ṭhākura here at Śrī Śrī Rādhā-Gopīnātha Mandira, I would like to thank him for being such a wonderful devotee and servant of Śrīla Prabhupāda and the Vaiṣṇavas. And I ask him—of course, I think he would actually object, but I ask him—to kindly forgive me for not properly recognizing him or appreciating him fully when he was present. I am sure that in his usual good humor he will tolerate my request and smile and laugh. And I pray that his memory and his spirit and his mercy will live eternally in this temple and in the lives and hearts of the devotees, that we can try to serve him by living up to the ideals that he cherished and exemplified, and thus become better servants of Śrīla Prabhupāda and Śrī Caitanya Mahāprabhu and all the devotees.

Kīrtidā Dāsī

A Saintly Life of Service

Talks by Giriraj Swami and Sārvabhauma dāsa on Mother Kīrtidā's disappearance anniversary on June 21, 2009, in Montgomery, Texas.

GIRIRAJ SWAMI: Mother Kīrtidā was born in South Africa, where she was trained as a nurse. Later, she came to the United States and began to visit the Dallas temple. She developed a relationship with the main Deities, Śrī Śrī Rādhā-Kālachandjī, and became Their devoted servant. She also heard His Holiness Tamal Krishna Goswami lecture, and she became his disciple. And she fully engaged in the process of devotional service.

Her preparations for leaving her body became the focal point of the whole Dallas devotee community. The whole community united and gathered around her, having *kīrtana* in her room. At retreats and festivals we also experience coming together to chant the holy names, but with Mother Kīrtidā there was the added element of her impending departure, that particular time of life when one is preparing for death, which itself creates a special, sacred atmosphere in which the experience of one's spiritual practices is intensified.

Much could be said about Mother Kīrtidā and her exalted state of consciousness. His Grace Sārvabhauma dāsa has written a book—*Servant of Love: The Saintly Life of Kīrtidā Devī*—and many devotees have been profoundly influenced by reading about her. Now I shall request Sārvabhauma dāsa to speak.

SĀRVABHAUMA DĀSA: Mother Kīrtidā came to devotional service relatively late in her life. She was about forty-eight. She had experienced some severe health problems, and she had almost died a few times. She had lost nearly 90 percent of her stomach in different surgeries and was living on intravenous feeding. She would work long shifts at a Dallas hospital in her position as a surgical nurse. At night she would hook herself up to these tubes, and a few times they got infected and she almost died. Usually if someone gets three or so of those infections, there is a good chance they will die, but she got five.

One day she decided to commit suicide. That was before she became very involved in Kṛṣṇa consciousness, though she used to sometimes just visit the Dallas temple. She came from a very pious, devoted family, so she had always had some impressions of Kṛṣṇa consciousness with her, but in her life she was mainly devoted to her career as a nurse, and in doing that she gave up getting married and many of the normal things that people do. She was extraordinary in her service to other people, even before she became a devotee.

So, she almost died a couple of times, and she got depressed and was determined to commit suicide. So she decided to go to the temple. She knew it wasn't a good or pious thing to do, but she had just had enough with the way her life had been going. So she went before the Deities and was in a sense asking permission to leave this life, and she actually got some kind of a vision of the Deities speaking to her. They said, "You didn't create life, so you cannot take life." She wasn't expecting to get this message, and it was an extraordinary turning point for her. She was already a selfless servant, but from that point on she decided to give all her devotion—her entire life—to Kṛṣṇa.

So she started doing service for the temple. She was still working ten- or twelve-hour shifts as a nurse, but she would come to the temple and do very simple services in the restaurant and for the Deities. She would cut fruit and do many different services.

Then the devotees told her, "You should retire. You are going to leave your body any time. You may not live very long, so you should go to Vṛndāvana." So she was thinking about that, and then she met Tamal Krishna Goswami. He also encouraged her in that direction, but she wanted to tie up her affairs gradually. So it wasn't until a couple of years later, in 1993, that she actually moved to Vṛndāvana.

When she went to Vṛndāvana she decided to leave her body there. Although she had brought all these bags of intravenous food, when she got there she felt that was artificial; she just wanted to depend on Kṛṣṇa.

On the day before Janmāṣṭamī she had her catheter removed in the hospital in Vṛndāvana. She—and the doctors—thought she would die quite soon, that without her having the intravenous feeding and the catheter, her departure would be accelerated. She was only occasionally drinking juice and things like that. Then the day after Janmāṣṭamī, Śrīla Prabhupāda's appearance day, there was a feast offered to Prabhupāda and she took some of the *mahā-prasāda*. She felt that she got a little appetite, so she began to eat and gained some energy from that. At first in Vṛndāvana she could hardly walk and see the deities, but then, as the months went on, she just kept on living in Vṛndāvana and got more and more strength.

When Kīrtidā gained a little more strength she did some service. Instead of working as a nurse, she served in the dispensary for the *gurukula* boys. One day she wanted to go on Govardhana *parikramā*. She was going to go on the *parikramā* by rickshaw, not walking, but then she just got off and said, "I am going to walk." It took her a very, very long time, but she actually made it the whole way around.

Then, after maybe another six months, she got so much strength back that she was able to walk very quickly. She would take devotees on *parikramās* herself. She would go around in close to four hours, which was very quick.

In a sense, Kīrtidā got a rebirth in Vṛndāvana. From the point when she almost committed suicide, she decided to give up everything for Kṛṣṇa. That's what we are trying to do when we chant and serve, but we always have some struggles in that regard. It seemed that she just got off the mental platform. She was always in the mood of service, whether she was chanting or taking people on *parikramās* or helping devotees. She helped many devotees who had health issues, and devotees who were passing away. She helped many of them, including Indradyumna Swami's disciple Vraja-līlā, and she also helped a bit with Giriraj Swami's disciple Arcā-vigraha.

She was planning to leave her body in Vṛndāvana, but she was just always in the mood of a servant, and her service to her *guru mahārāja*, Tamal Krishna Mahārāja, Śrīla Gurudeva, became the focal point of her service to Kṛṣṇa.

At one point Śrīla Gurudeva asked her to come out of Vṛndāvana to England. Sometimes in spiritual life we get attached to some facility—like living in Vṛndāvana, which was a perfect situation for her—but he asked her to come to England. He had just recovered from his surgery and wanted her care. So, it was very difficult for her to leave, but she surrendered to that and spent several years in England.

Then Kīrtidā came down with some type of cancer in the throat area, and she had surgery in London and then decided to go to Dallas to recover, because the Deities there, Śrī Śrī Rādhā-Kālachandjī—and the devotees in the Dallas community—were so dear to her.

So, she went to Dallas to recover, but then it was discovered that the cancer was terminal. It was summertime, and it was quite hot. Tamal Krishna Goswami advised her that she didn't have to worry about going to Vṛndāvana to leave her body; there were so many nice devotees to take care of her in Dallas. He also thought that her passing in the West would be a valuable service to the devotee community. We sometimes hide death, to make it easier to enjoy the material world. So Tamal Krishna

Goswami felt that she was an elevated devotee and that if she left her body with the support of the devotees, showing them—both the adults and the children—how someone who has lived her life in Kṛṣṇa consciousness leaves her body, it would provide a very nice example. Her passing became a service to her *guru*. And Dallas became her *prabhu-datta deśa*, the place given by the spiritual master for service. So, she had wanted to be in Vṛndāvana, but then she accepted the idea of leaving in Dallas.

One of the qualities of advanced devotees is that they inspire in others faith in the holy name, and just her presence there when she was leaving her body unified the devotees in *kīrtana*. During the twenty-four hour *kīrtanas* that took place in Kīrtidā's room in the time before her departure, different devotees would take shifts, chanting from two to four, four to six—all through the night—and it created a very intense spiritual atmosphere. It became a life-transforming experience for many devotees. Even guests were crying. Because of her mood of service and her spiritual master's request that she leave amidst the devotees in Dallas, the whole situation became auspicious and gave a boost to everyone's Kṛṣṇa consciousness.

Kīrtidā had always been a very quiet person, but when devotees came to cheer her up, they found that she was completely ecstatic, and she was actually uplifting them. Devotees would ask her, "How do you feel?" and she would say, "I've never felt so wonderful, so happy, in all my life." She was very confident that she was under Kṛṣṇa's protection. She felt that she would be with Rādhā and Kṛṣṇa. She wasn't a big scholar or such an experienced devotee, having come to Kṛṣṇa consciousness later in life, but she had great faith in Kṛṣṇa and her spiritual master and the *paramparā*. She was not mental.

After she passed away, a number of devotees spoke about her, and Tamal Krishna Goswami said, "I have no doubt that she went to the spiritual world, because she had no material desires; she had only spiritual desires." So, sometimes we may wonder what our fate is, but we should have confidence that if we surrender to Kṛṣṇa, Kṛṣṇa will take us back home, back to Godhead.

I think that not so many people know about Mother Kīrtidā—even now—but her spiritual master wanted something written about her, to be part of the literature of the devotees in our Kṛṣṇa consciousness movement. So on the day that she passed away he asked us to write a book about her. I always saw her as a wonderful devotee, but from what I heard when I interviewed many people about her, my appreciation for her increased. I came to understand that she was very advanced in Kṛṣṇa consciousness. And I became purified writing about her. I was very fortunate to have been involved in this project.

Exemplary in Life and Death

Talks by Giriraj Swami, Guru-bhakti dāsī, and Rasikendra dāsa at Mother Kīrtidā's memorial program in Carpinteria, California, on August 6, 2001.

GIRIRAJ SWAMI: We have gathered to glorify Mother Kīrtidā and, in the process, to purify our hearts. So, I shall request the devotees to speak about whatever they want—some pastimes they remember or some of her qualities.

RASIKENDRA DĀSA: To speak about Mother Kīrtidā, I need to be empowered by her. So let me pay my obeisances to her. May whatever I speak increase her glories.

I met Mother Kīrtidā around 1994. I noticed her because of her spotless white sari and her very gentle manner. I can't remember the first meeting exactly, but when I got to know her there was a certain bond between us, which developed very quickly. I think there must have been some kind of previous connection.

I always noticed that she never spoke about herself. There is a tendency for all of us to speak about ourselves, but she never did. Despite there being so many things to say, she never spoke about herself, and she always made everybody around her feel that she was just an ordinary person. She never really revealed her greatness. I think that is a mark of a great Vaiṣṇava. There was no self-aggrandizement. She always talked about the greatness of other devotees—how this devotee is so saintly, how this person is so wonderful, how this devotee dresses the Deities so nicely. But I can't recall once when she spoke about her own greatness. To the contrary, she would say, "I've got so far to go, I am suffering so much in this world, I think I must have been very sinful"—things like that. She always downplayed her own qualities.

As time went on, I noticed that she was very attached to making sure that Rādhā-Kālachandjī had the best things we could get. She arranged that for every festival, we offer a brand new outfit from Vṛndāvana, and because I knew a lot of congregation members, she kept pushing me: "Rasikendra, you have to get this. We need a new outfit for Gaura-pūrṇimā—for Ratha-yātrā, Janmāṣṭamī, Rādhāṣṭamī, Diwali; we need to offer at least five brand new outfits to Kālachandjī. We need to get Him new flutes." She was always absorbed in trying to serve the Deities. Although she never directly served the Deities on the altar, she always made sure that all the devotees serving the Deities had everything first-class to serve Them.

She was always in the background, moving the pieces. So nobody really noticed her. Devotees never actually realized her greatness until Goswami Mahārāja told us, "You need to have continuous *kīrtana*" and he came and the relationship between him and Mother Kīrtidā thickened in front of everybody. Then people started to see how great a person she was. Goswami Mahārāja had not displayed this kind of intense affection for any of his disciples, at least from what I know, and the way the love between them grew to such an intense flavor really bewildered the devotees, because this was very unlike Goswami Mahārāja. So that was a small glimpse into the great story that was about to unfold, page by page, as the days drew on.

Mother Kīrtidā had never taken care of her health, and she never complained about anything. There were sometimes devotees who, for some frivolous reason, tried to find fault with her. But anyone who knew her knew that she was actually faultless. No matter how much you might try to instigate something or find some negative quality—you could not. Just like when I was watching one video on Śrīla Prabhupāda, one businessman, who went on to surrender to Prabhupāda . . .

GIRIRAJ SWAMI: Oh yes, Śrī Nāthajī dāsa.

RASIKENDRA DĀSA: He mentioned the same thing about

Prabhupāda: "I have done business with so many people. A businessman finds the weakness in the other party and takes advantage of that weakness. I tried so hard to do that with Swamiji, but after some time I just came to a dead end. I saw that there were no bad qualities in this person. In fact, everything was so wonderful about him—'Let me surrender to him.' " So, in the same way, you could never find any bad qualities in Mother Kīrtidā.

She even went to the extent of lying to get outfits for the Deities. I thought this only made her greater. One couple, Vrajanātha and Gaṅgā, who have become my godfamily—definitely by her mercy—used to sponsor an outfit every Janmāṣṭamī. There came a time when we had one extra outfit, so Mother Kīrtidā said, "Let's offer this outfit and take the money from them and apply it toward next year's outfit. Then we'll give a first-class outfit to Kālachandjī." It was only a matter of time before they would find out, because word would get around that it wasn't their outfit that was being offered that year. So I thought I would break the news to them before they got very upset with me and left the temple or something. Because I was meditating on this and it disturbed me very much, I called Mother Kīrtidā: "You put me in this spot. What should I do?" She said, "Just tell them that I did it." So I told them. They were quite upset with me, and they did not understand Mother Kīrtidā's greatness. They thought we had told them some mundane lie. But that actually increased her glory.

One other incident was quite extraordinary. About a year after Goswami Mahārāja's *TKG's Diary* came out, while he was in Cambridge, devotees were trying to raise funds for his expenses there. So, Mother Śyāmalā Sakhī and Mother Kīrtidā had an idea: "We'll take all the copies of Gurudeva's *TKG's Diary* from Dallas. We'll ship them to the UK, and we'll sell these books for twenty-five dollars and raise some money to help pay the bills." I thought it was a great idea. But they did not consult with Goswami Mahārāja. She was so intent on serving Goswami Mahārāja—Mother Śyāmalā too—that without consulting with Goswami Mahārāja she called me and said, "Rasikendra, Śyāmalā and I are going to wire some money to you. Take the money to Kāmadhenu, who is in charge of Goswami Mahārāja's affairs, and buy all the books. Don't tell her where the books are going; just buy all the books."

There were probably twelve, thirteen hundred copies. Kāmadhenu, of course, was very excited about the whole thing. She said, "Wow, this is a great opportunity to sell the books."

But Mother Kīrtidā and Śyāmalā did not know that Viṣṇu Mūrti Prabhu already had exclusive rights to sell these books in the UK and Europe. So, Kāmadhenu told me, "He already has these rights. Where is this shipment going? I hope it's not going to the UK." I said, "Don't worry; it is going to some place." I did not want to tell her the truth. So I shipped the books. When Goswami Mahārāja found out, he was furious—so furious. Then he discovered that Mother Kīrtidā and Śyāmalā Sakhī had done this, but I took the brunt of the whole thing. But this again showed that she was taking extreme measures to please her spiritual master.

She was always thinking about Gurudeva's welfare; she was always thinking about the Deities' welfare. She used to tell me that all the devotees who had served Gurudeva so selflessly had become very dear to her—like Guru-bhakti's husband, Sārvabhauma Prabhu; and Rādhā Kṛṣṇa Prabhu. She always used to talk about them. She used to say, "Despite Gurudeva being so heavy, these devotees have served so sincerely; I fall at their feet and take the dust from their feet."

She started calling me "Son," and I started calling her "Mother." Over the years we developed such a bond. All the time, she was nourishing me with so much. She used to call me from the UK, and Pādadhūlī and I used to call her. When she was going through the surgery, we were talking every day. Her sister was beside her then.

And she had a very dear friend in Dallas, Jayshree, a nurse who had known her for forty years. Kīrtidā was trying her utmost to make her into a devotee. She told me, "I do not know if she'll become a devotee in this lifetime, but you please take care of her. She is very dear to me. Please try your best, you and Pādadhūlī, to make her a devotee." Even up to the last day, she was always thinking about Jayshree's welfare.

Mother Kīrtidā was always thinking about every devotee's welfare, except her own. She was always giving; she was such a magnanimous soul. Even toward people who had tried to find fault with her—when they came, in the last days, she never held any malice in her heart. And she gave freely; she gave herself completely. This is another sign of her greatness: she was always giving, always serving selflessly. I think all this is just a small glimpse into her greatness, which is yet to be fathomed. I think I could try for many lifetimes and not be able to fathom her greatness. And she was so good at keeping her greatness to herself; she never advertised. This is another sign of her greatness.

Giriraj Swami: Yes, after she left, Keśava Bhāratī Prabhu and I discussed what had brought her to such an exalted position in devotional service. In retrospect, we could appreciate her devotional qualities, but in some ways, she hadn't seemed so extraordinary compared with other devotees. So I asked him what he thought had brought her to such a position, and he immediately replied, "Selfless service."

She gave herself fully to the service of others: to her spiritual master, Tamal Krishna Goswami; to her beloved Deities, Śrī Śrī Rādhā-Kālachandjī; and to the Vaiṣṇavas—devotees in ISKCON, and also Vraja-vāsīs. For example, in Vṛndāvana she was particularly attached to Lalitā-devī in Unchagaon—the Deities of Rādhā and Kṛṣṇa, and Lalitā-devī. Every year she would sponsor new outfits for the deities and a feast for Lalitā-devī's appearance day. Every month she would donate for *bhoga* for the deities—for rice, dal, flour, vegetables, and ghee. And she even brought medicine for the local Vraja-vāsīs. She was a very loving and caring person.

Rasikendra dāsa: When Goswami Mahārāja was sick, she used to come back to the house to take a bath, and she would sit down to take the french fries my wife used to make, which were her favorite. Goswami Mahārāja had become so dependent on Kīrtidā because he felt so comfortable with her. He couldn't stay away from her for a moment. And while she was having a shower, the phone would ring. The servant would say, "Gurudeva wants Kīrtidā up there." She would come out; she wouldn't even take her meal. And I would get very upset: "Why don't you tell Gurudeva that you have to take your meal. Only when you take your meals can you care for him. Gurudeva will understand." She would say, "No, no. I have to go. Gurudeva needs me there." So she used to skip her meals, and she used to skip her sleep. I couldn't have lasted two days doing what she did. She lasted for six months, day and night, with Goswami Mahārāja, practically without sleep. Guru-bhakti used to tell us how intense it was up there with Goswami Mahārāja. It was very painful for me to even see Gurudeva walking with his tubes. He used to go for a walk sometimes with Ṛtadhvaja Swami and Mother Guru-bhakti. It was an unbearable sight. And I used to ask Kīrtidā, "It is so intense. How can you stay?" And she would reply, "I know it is very intense, but this is my service. I have to do it. Whether I die or I live, I have to do this service."

Her intensity in her service to Gurudeva and her total faith, her magnanimity, and her selflessness and tolerance are just inconceivable. I have never seen a more tolerant person. She could take so much austerity and not speak one word about it—very, very great; inconceivable.

One thing happened that is interesting. When Kīrtidā's

relatives came, there was some misunderstanding about how to partition her will. We were getting quite upset that even at this time, things like this were happening, which were causing her stress. She was a person who never wanted to hurt anybody. There was one time when even Keśava Bhāratī Prabhu got upset with Kīrtidā's relatives because they were always trying to capitalize on the situation. He raised his voice because he couldn't stand that she was put under this stress, and they got quite affected by that; they were a little offended. Then she requested Keśava Bhāratī Prabhu, "Please apologize to them, because they don't understand devotees' dealings. They might think this is some mundane bout or tantrum you have shown." We were thinking it was not proper for Keśava Bhāratī Prabhu—such a senior devotee—to apologize. I don't know, maybe it might not have worked in her relatives' interest if Keśava Bhāratī Prabhu had had to go and apologize to them. But Keśava Bhāratī said, "I will be very glad to apologize." And he did apologize to the relatives, in front of them all.

She was so expert that she could see that this was the only way to make her relatives more Kṛṣṇa conscious. From then on, there was no tension, and the whole atmosphere became surcharged. They started to appreciate devotees more and more until they came and said, "Actually, we cannot do 10 percent of what you all are doing. We thought that she was not in good company, but after coming here we can see that actually this family is so wonderful. We cannot provide what you all are giving."

And every one of them left very happy, without any kind of bad thoughts in their hearts. Then I realized that what she had asked Keśava Bhāratī Prabhu to do had actually been in their interest. It is not that she had felt that he had offended them, but it had been for their benefit, so that their hearts could warm to the devotees. And they started chanting sixteen rounds, and her brothers started going every day for *maṅgala-ārati*. About four of them were chanting sixteen rounds every day.

Another amazing thing was that the nurse who had come to care for Mother Kīrtidā got so attracted by the whole thing that she too started chanting sixteen rounds. There was another nurse from the Caribbean; she got so attracted by it that she started chanting. And there was another nurse—Afro-American, Jerry—who started chanting. She was watching Goswami Mahārāja's videos while she was at work. And then a doctor, Christina, was totally blown away by the situation. These people were Christians, and they said that they had never experienced such a joyous occasion when a person was leaving her body, completely untouched by the fear of death. This shows that Mother Kīrtidā affected people's lives so deeply, and all of them were so attracted to her.

If you go to an old folks' or a nursing home, the people are skin and bones, and they are so miserable. And Mother Kīrtidā was skin and bones, but she was so blissful. She told Goswami Mahārāja, "I have never been so happy in my life. These are the happiest moments in my life, and I am very excited to see what the future holds for me." Goswami Mahārāja answered, "What are your thoughts about leaving your body?" She said, "I am very excited about what is on the other side."

She told us very confidential things that she was witnessing and experiencing. She was experiencing the most far-out things. She once told me, "Rādhā-Giridhārī—you know what *Giridhārī* means?" I said, " 'Kṛṣṇa who lifts Giri,' 'the lifter of Govardhana.' " She said, "No. Actually, *Giridhārī* means Rādhārāṇī." I was very confused. I didn't clarify that with her. She said that actually *Giridhārī* meant Rādhārāṇī.

Then Girirāja came in my dream and said, "You are not feeding me properly." Because we were so much into caring for Mother Kīrtidā, we were not cooking. We were just giving him simple fruit offerings. Then a week or nine days before she left her body, Girirāja came in my dream and said, "You all are not feeding me properly." I forgot about the dream, but two days before she left her body, while I was taking my shower, I remembered the dream. Then I told my wife, "We have to cook. I forgot about the dream. I didn't tell you." I think Mother Kīrtidā was also waiting for that to take place before she left her body. She wanted to see Girirāja. We fed him and all the devotees who had come to the house, and I felt purified by the whole service. She didn't tell me, but I think she was also waiting for that to happen.

I have never seen anybody so close to Goswami Mahārāja. This is something that drew a lot of disciples even closer to him—because they had always seen him as a very caring person but very strict and careful about details. But when they saw this exchange, it just melted their hearts. It melted everybody's heart. In the last days she became like a friend to him, literally a friend. Sometimes she was even telling him what to do. And we could see that this was a completely transcendental relationship. We cannot see anything like it in the material world. We couldn't fathom what was happening. I am very grateful that she came into our lives and affected us so deeply.

Afterwards, when we went to cremate her body, it was a hot, hot summer day, and the crematorium had just a zinc roof. We were there for about five hours, from about noon to 5:30. We were just chanting, and we never felt any fatigue. For five and a half hours in the heat, seven or eight devotees were chanting continuously while her body was being cremated. She looked so beautiful in her sari. We couldn't see that this was a dead person. Her body was glowing. We had never seen any dead body like that. I have seen many dead bodies, but her body was so effulgent. And everybody who came to her last rites commented, "This body doesn't look dead." She looked exquisitely beautiful.

After her body was burned, the ashes and some bones were left and they had to be put into a machine and be broken up. So the guy picked up all the unburned things. There were certain metals in her body, a substantial amount of metal—clips and such—from her surgery. And he picked up seven Rādhā-kuṇḍa beads. During her last days Mother Kīrtidā had worn a *mālā* of 108 of these beads, which are made from hardened mud from Śrī Rādhā-kuṇḍa. Somehow, after the cremation exactly seven of the beads were left intact. There were seven devotees there, and I had this clear realization that even at this moment she was distributing her mercy. Every one of the devotees who was there got one bead from her. Even at that point she was giving. I was very moved by that. Only since she left have I begun, little by little, to fathom her greatness. And I think I will keep on trying to fathom it for many, many lifetimes.

Thank you, Mahārāja, for allowing me to speak.

GIRIRAJ SWAMI: Thank you for this flow of nectar. Mother Guru-bhakti, would you like to say something?

GURU-BHAKTI DĀSĪ: I didn't know Mother Kīrtidā very well until we served Goswami Mahārāja in his illness. Before he went to the hospital and during the time after the surgery, we served him together for about two weeks. After that, I went on to work, and she continued taking care of him for six months. She was practically living there in his quarters, and any problem he had she would try to appease his anxiety. She had this nature that she would always like to please him. So sometimes, if she had something unpleasant to tell him, she would tell me and I would be the mouthpiece. This happened many times. She just didn't have the heart to tell him something he didn't like to hear. And sometimes also, because she was a nurse, he would just ignore her and say, "Oh, what do you know? You're just a nurse." And then she would tell him, "Then let's ask her, because she is a doctor. She can tell you." And then I would have the task of telling him what he didn't want to hear.

It became very evident that her love for him was unconditional. She never failed him. And I think that was her unique characteristic. No matter what he did, she never failed him. And that is what made him so devoted to her—her love for him.

Goswami Mahārāja was very dependent on Mother Kīrtidā, particularly in the years after his surgery, when he was in Cambridge. She would call him every day and inquire how he was doing, inquire how the servants were doing. And then she would try to make peace between them. And because she had gone through her own illness, that illness and suffering put her in a position where she could actually use the suffering in his service. The knowledge and experience she gained from the suffering actually helped her to help him. So it gave a lot of meaning to her life at that point—that she was able to help him in that way.

Later on, after she passed away, many devotees said that this was her characteristic, that she had such *guru-niṣṭhā*, steadfast devotion to the spiritual master. Goswami Mahārāja said that Mother Kartā had told him that she had seen many *sannyāsīs* and devotees both in ISKCON and in the Gauḍīya Maṭha but that she had never seen anyone who had as much *guru-niṣṭhā* as Kīrtidā did.

And after her passing away, it was amazing how Goswami Mahārāja was always lamenting about not having her association or not having her around to take care of him. The thing is that she actually understood his desire, and whatever he wanted she would do to please him. When he was in a position where he was very dependent, she nurtured him in his need to be dependent. Whereas some of us encouraged him to not be so dependent—which he didn't like at all—she really understood what he wanted and was able to nourish him. And by that nurturing, he recovered. Because that's what he needed to recover.

Giriraj Swami: That is what he told me too.

Guru-bhakti dāsī: I had this realization later, that this was actually what he needed and what won his heart, because she gave him what he needed without questioning his need for it.

Another characteristic was that she never found fault with anyone. She always saw the good in everyone, no matter what insignificant amount of good there was. So that was a very nice Vaiṣṇava quality she exhibited. She could find one little thing that was nice about a person and she would always glorify that good quality.

She took absolutely no care of herself. When we were taking care of Goswami Mahārāja, in order for her to eat I had to tell her that I would eat only after she did. That was the only way she would eat. Otherwise, if I ate before her, she would never eat. And she would never drink. I had to remind her to drink. As it was, she couldn't eat much.

Her nature was like his: high-strung and anxious. When he was anxious, she would become similarly anxious, and then her health would suffer. She would have diarrhea, or she would not be able to eat, because she had nausea.

At one point Kīrtidā practically had a breakdown—when Goswami Mahārāja had to be admitted to the hospital for the second time, after he had complications from the surgery. It was the night they found out that he actually had a blockage in the kidney. That was unexpected. When the surgeon tried to correct the blockage and failed, he would not admit that it required surgery to correct it, not just a simple procedure. So the night Goswami Mahārāja was supposed to stay in the hospital, no one slept. At that time we were having a big festival in Houston, so Kīrtidā would call every day and we would get some reports. Goswami Mahārāja was always asking me to come, and I was trying not to. I was telling him that he should not become so dependent, because the nature of an illness is that sometimes people get into this mode of being sick, and this may actually hinder the recovery. But then later Ṛtadhvaja Mahārāja said that I had to come, not for Goswami Mahārāja but for her, so that she would get some time off and recover—because she had such bad diarrhea and was really very nervous. So, one weekend I couldn't stay, and Goswami Mahārāja instructed her that she should sleep in his quarters—eat and then sleep—and maybe that way she would recover. And actually that gave her a little strength to continue for the rest of the few months that she was there.

Also, I thought that how she passed away was very characteristic of her. Her nature was that she never asked for service from anyone. But she did ask Goswami Mahārāja to be there when she passed away, which in some ways was uncharacteristic, because she always wanted to serve him rather than have him serve her. Before she passed away, two times there were false alarms. She had said that she would pass away at *brāhma-muhūrta*, and when some auspicious day, such as Ekādaśī, was coming up, we thought she would pass away that night. So the devotees stayed up all night chanting. It was so intense. The atmosphere was so thick. Nobody in that room wanted her to leave without hearing the holy name. It was so intense. There was no escaping that sound. Twice this happened.

Then the last day, all the medical signs were there that she was passing away. But because there had been two false alarms, and because I had a relationship with her as a friend and not just as a doctor, it was hard to be objective about her symptoms. I could feel her pulses starting to go one after another, and I could see that this was going to happen. But I did not want to call Goswami Mahārāja, because I thought that every time he came into the room she would get increased strength. Her pulse would be very thin, and she would not be doing so well, and as soon as he came in, after two minutes, she was strong. All her vital signs would improve. So I was thinking, "If I call him now, he is not going to sleep any time after that, and she may just come around; and then he will be up all night, and it will just be too much for him." So I kept waiting.

And it was so amazing, because there were certain devotees who . . . like, there was this friend of hers with whom she intended to retire. She was from Holland. She was initiated by Goswami Mahārāja just before Mother Kīrtidā passed away—Jaṭilā dāsī—right in Kīrtidā's room, actually. Jaṭilā would stay up every night. She would come in several times in the night to see how Kīrtidā was doing. She was a very selfless devotee. She would always make sure that the devotees who were taking care of Kīrtidā were taken care of. That was her service. She would always take care of everyone else. "Have you eaten? Have you slept?" She would massage them and take care of their needs. "Is there anything I can do?" And she would spend very little time with Mother Kīrtidā. She would hardly come close to her. I would actually have to tell her, "Come and be with her." And that night, for some reason, Jaṭilā was not there.

Rasikendra and Pādadhūlī were in the next room. And even me—we were doing this every day, so I was very tired. The previous day when we had had an alarm we had stayed up all night, and I was so tired. Then Goswami Mahārāja told me that I should go and sleep. I would usually take the night shift because there were fewer devotees then. But I told him that after all that I couldn't go to sleep. So he asked me, "Can you sleep here?" I said, "Yes, I can sleep here." So I sat there and slept for forty-five minutes. When I woke up I was completely refreshed. I just sat there, and then I said, "Let me just sleep for a few more minutes." Then one of the girls said, "Look, Mother Kīrtidā's breathing is slowing down." And after that it was just three breaths.

Every stage of her leaving her body took about half an hour, forty-five minutes. She lost one pulse, then half an hour, forty-five minutes later she lost another pulse, then half an hour, forty-five minutes later she lost another pulse. But this last time, it was so . . . When I saw that, I told one of my godsisters, "You have to go and call Rasikendra. Call Rasikendra to get Gurudeva." She didn't understand. She thought we had to call him on the phone. I said, "No, you go get Rasikendra to go get Goswami Mahārāja." By the time she went to get him, Pādadhūlī came into the room. That day, somebody had brought a garland, and there was a last *tulasī* leaf on her head. It was right there on her head. So I just put the *tulasī* leaf in her mouth. And there was Rādhā-kuṇḍa water there. I put that in her mouth. And as Pādadhūlī walked into the room, Kīrtidā went.

She wanted Girirāja on her head. When I asked for Girirāja, there were only two devotees chanting. Durāśayā always took the graveyard shift. Nobody came for that shift, between midnight and two. It was the hardest shift to cover. But he would continue until the next person came, always chanting just Hare Kṛṣṇa, straight. He sang so many different tunes that we had heard ten, fifteen years ago.

RASIKENDRA DĀSA: Beautiful ones, exceptionally sweet—he was singing for Mother Kīrtidā.

GURU-BHAKTI DĀSĪ: Mother Candrāvalī was accompanying him. They were singing. He would sing once, and then she would sing once. So, I said to Candrāvalī, "I need Girirāja." After I told her two or three times, she realized what was happening, so she brought Girirāja and put him on her. By then she was gone.

Then I was thinking, "This was her final request, and I did not fulfill it." She had wanted that Goswami Mahārāja should be there, and that Girirāja *śilās* should be on her chest and on her head when she passed away. And I was feeling very bad. So I told Goswami Mahārāja, "You know, this was her last request, and I feel I failed her."

In my experience, I have seen that when people pass away—this was my first time to see a devotee pass away—usually the person who loves them most will either be away or asleep. For some reason, they don't leave in front of their loved one. I guess it is to decrease the pain of separation. The loved one will either nod off for a minute or step out of the room, and the person will pass away. And it was exactly like that. I had been telling Goswami Mahārāja, but he had said, "No, that won't happen here. She is a devotee, and she says she'll tell us when she is ready to go." But she tricked all of us.

Now he gave me a very nice explanation. He said, "Actually, you have to understand the person's desire. Her first instruction to you was that you should take care of me. And you did the right thing by not calling me too soon." He said, "The only reason you would have called me was if she was in pain, and this just proves she wasn't in pain—that she passed away peacefully." So, that made me feel a little better. But I always wonder whether I did the right thing in not fulfilling her desire.

One thing she was afraid of was the pain. When she went to India in 1993, she was thinking she was going to die. And when she was sick there, she was really in a lot of pain. Then, during her surgery for cancer in London in January of 2001, she still had a lot of problems with pain, to the extent that she had to take very high doses of pain medicine, and it was actually interfering with her consciousness. She understood that there was a trade-off between pain control and her consciousness. At that point, also, she wasn't strong enough to bear the pain. She became kind of depressed. She felt that she had no control over the pain and that she just had to give in and take the medication. But then in Dallas, during that spring, when she found out that the cancer had recurred and she was deciding what to do, I told her, "Whenever you need me, I'll come." So when she was admitted into the hospital, in late April, she asked Pādadhūlī to call me to come. Then we talked about options for her treatment, and we went through the options. The cancer was actually choking her windpipe. It was so bad that she could not even lie flat, because even trying to swallow saliva she would choke. And that was very painful for her—and for the devotees. It's like—I don't know if anyone has had asthma, or a near-drowning experience—it's like dying at every moment, like you are going to leave your body. So, there were various means by which she could die. Then we thought the best approach for her would be to take some chemotherapy. At least she would die from something that wasn't as painful as the cancer, which would allow her to be in better consciousness.

She was very afraid that she might have pain. So I promised her that I would make sure that she wouldn't be in pain. But at the same time, I told her that it would be a trade-off: we would give her enough pain relief that it would not be so intense, but not enough to cloud her consciousness—because we agreed that the consciousness was most important. And I think that once that assurance was given she was quite peaceful. And also she had to face the fact that she could overcome the pain by her own Kṛṣṇa consciousness, and by being able to tolerate. She was very tolerant. And it was amazing that with all the pain she had, she never required more pain medicine than just a base-line rate, which never interfered with anything. So she actually overcame that.

I was thinking that Kṛṣṇa gave her so many illnesses and so many setbacks in her life but that with each physical ailment she got stronger and stronger. Even when she had the surgery for her cancer she wasn't perfect. But every experience made her stronger, and when she was perfect, Kṛṣṇa took her away. You could actually see her going through the process of purification. And so she attained perfection. Kṛṣṇa gave her so many chances, and when she was perfect, He took her. And she was such a good example for everyone to see, to the very last moment.

I just feel very fortunate that, for some reason, I had told her

I would be there. When I saw how she served Goswami Mahārāja, neglecting everything else, I was thinking, "She doesn't have anyone; she is an older person who is so sick. Who will take care of her?" So I told her, "When it's your time, I'll come to take care of you," and somehow she accepted. And when she was to have the surgery, I told Goswami Mahārāja that I would like to go and be with her, and he agreed. So I was glad that she gave me that opportunity to do some service. And even since she passed away, she has been giving me the opportunity—although I can never fill her shoes. But she has helped me to understand Goswami Mahārāja's desire in a better way.

While we are talking about this, I was going to ask you, Mahārāja . . . When she was going to leave, Goswami Mahārāja had such a hard time letting go because he was so dependent on her. So I was wondering, and I asked him, "When Prabhupāda left, how did you manage with that loss? How did you cope with it?" I was so shocked when he said, "I never expected Prabhupāda to leave." And that's what he actually meant: he never expected Prabhupāda to leave. And then after Prabhupāda left, there were so many things to do, that Goswami Mahārāja never actually had time to grieve. Then I asked him, "What about some of your godbrothers?" The loss that came to mind was when Mother Arcā-vigraha left. So I asked him, "How did Giriraj Mahārāja feel when she left?" He said, "It's not the same, because I was actually dependent on Kīrtidā. He wasn't." So there was very little we could offer. But then he said that the only way he could bear her loss was to always have her remain active in his life. And in that way he could come to terms with the grief.

So I was wondering, Mahārāja, How did you deal with the passing away of Mother Arcā-vigraha, or any of your close disciples?

Giriraj Swami: I thought you were going to ask about

Goswami Mahārāja, and so I will speak first about his talk with me a few days before Mother Kīrtidā left. He phoned, extremely upset about the prospect of losing her. He was saying, "Life is so cruel—you become attached to a Vaiṣṇava, and Kṛṣṇa, or destiny, just takes the Vaiṣṇava away." He was very upset.

So we spoke for some time. I happened to be in the car, and somewhere along the way the cell-phone connection got broken. It was sort of a natural time for the conversation to end, and he didn't phone back. Of course, I was very concerned. However, the next time he phoned he was in a different state of mind, and he said that he just got into the mood of serving her. And by being in the mood of serving her, his sense of loss was mitigated.

But there was another pastime that took place. As you know, up until Goswami Mahārāja's Vyāsa-pūjā Mother Kīrtidā was very positive and energetic. She was drinking coconut water, and we thought she was going to continue to live for a long time. I had thought of coming to Dallas, but I had some binding commitments in California for some days. And Keśava Bhāratī Prabhu, who was visiting me in Carpinteria, was planning to go back to Texas after a certain time, and he also had a commitment, to go to Sacramento first.

After Vyāsa-pūjā, Kīrtidā seemed so weak; she stopped taking the coconut water, and she was in the mood to leave. Before Keśava Bhāratī Prabhu came back from Sacramento, I had phoned and found out what was happening, but I didn't want to tell him immediately, because he was sort of excited from his trip and we had to take *prasāda*, and it didn't seem like the right time. But when I did tell him, he got upset. He said, "Mother Kīrtidā promised me that she would wait until I got back to Dallas."

Something inside both of us opened up, really opened up—very strong feelings of love for Mother Kīrtidā, and somewhat of a feeling of being dependent on her. We didn't want to lose her. We didn't want her to leave. And we weren't sure why she had changed her mood, whether someone had sort of put the idea in her mind, or where the idea had come from. So we decided we would phone her and just speak what was in our hearts. What was in our hearts was basically that we wanted her to stay. When we phoned her, however, she seemed to be in the mood to go—but she didn't want to say directly, "I am sorry, but I'm not going to stay."

So, she told Goswami Mahārāja about our phone call. Then Goswami Mahārāja phoned me. "She's determined to go," he said. "And even if the traffic signal is red, she's going to run the light. She will go ahead anyway. She's determined." Then he explained, "She's a nurse, and she knows what happens as one approaches the time of death. She knows that if she stays in this body much longer, symptoms will set in that will make it hard for her to think of Kṛṣṇa. So she has decided to leave now. And she is not eating or drinking." She didn't want pain, but at the same time she also didn't want to have to take painkillers that would affect her consciousness. She was going to have to leave soon in any case, but by fasting she could leave before the pain became worse. Goswami Mahārāja understood that we had our individual relationships with her, and he invited us to keep speaking with her, but he wanted us to be aware of her medical condition and to take that into consideration. So I conveyed to Keśava Bhāratī Prabhu what Goswami Mahārāja had told me, and then we decided that we would take some time and then phone back.

So I went for a walk.

I had some deep realizations on the walk; my main one was, "Just as I am able to feel her association here while she is in Dallas, why couldn't I also feel her association here when she is in Goloka Vṛndāvana? It's just an extension of the same principle." There were other thoughts, but that was the main one.

In the meantime, Keśava Bhāratī Prabhu also had his thoughts. Basically, he came to the same conclusion: we should not ask her to stay. So, we both phoned her, separately. I think he actually encouraged her in her determination. I wasn't ready to encourage her, but I was ready to accept her departure.

The other thing was, I felt a very strong sense of her presence here in this *kuñja* (the altar here, like a forest bower at Govardhana). Then I also told her that I felt she had a place here and that even after leaving her physical body she would be here and perhaps her presence would be felt even more strongly.

Then maybe a day passed when I didn't phone her.

The next day, Goswami Mahārāja phoned and said, "Mother, Kīrtidā would like to speak to you." And as you mentioned, in the end they had become friends. It was almost like Goswami Mahārāja was acting as her secretary, getting me on the line and then passing the phone to her.

She got on the phone and was in such an ecstatic mood over the picture of Gāndharvikā-Giridhārī, our Deities here. She was not seeing a picture of *śilās*; she was seeing Rādhā and Kṛṣṇa, and she was seeing the whole *kuñja*. She was in such high ecstasy. She just went on speaking about Them and Their associates. It was just wonderful—wonderful that she was seeing, "This is Gāndharvikā and Giridhārī, and this is Their *kuñja* at Govardhana." And she said, "Now I know why you don't want to leave this place. You are fully protected here." And she appreciated Kuntīdevī's service of arranging the *kuñja* and serving the Deities. That was really wonderful.

After that she wasn't able to speak so much. She became more withdrawn. That was when I started to phone and just listen to the *kīrtanas*. One *kīrtana* in particular was just so extraordinary, one that Rādhikā led; Gurudeva was also there.

But we didn't have a picture of Mother Kīrtidā. Then, soon after she departed, Cakrī and Viṣṇupriyā came. They had managed to get three snapshots of her before they left Dallas, and Viṣṇupriyā let me choose one. So I chose the one now on the altar. At first we didn't have a frame; we just kept the photo there. I was so elated when I put the picture there. I felt, "This is the best thing we have ever done"—with the altar.

By then, Goswami Mahārāja had returned to Cambridge, so I wrote to him there. I just knew I had to tell him: "I have placed Mother Kīrtidā's picture at the lotus feet of Śrī Śrī Gāndharvikā-Giridhārī here. I feel it is the best thing I have done. Her presence fills the house and our hearts." He was pleased, and he wrote back, "This is clearly where she is meant to be."

Cakrī dāsa: I remember when we put the picture there. I said, "She looks right at home there." She looked like she belonged there.

Giriraj Swami: I think that from the first time I spoke to Mother Kīrtidā after she came back to Dallas, something awakened in my heart that I hadn't felt for her before. It was something that I have never really felt for anyone in the same way. And it surprised me. But it was very real, and I accepted it. And I allowed myself to be impelled by it. Goswami Mahārāja said that she had "opened up our heart chakras"—not just ours, but many devotees'—and so there was this strong flow of love and feeling of intimacy, and confidence in her as a mother. We felt that we could speak to her in confidence, without reservation, that she was like a well-wishing, loving mother, who was very close to Kṛṣṇa and to the entire spiritual world. When later I spoke with my *vaidya* about this, he said that Āyurveda and the *Cāraka Saṁhitā* speak of the *hṛd-puṇḍarīka*, the heart lotus, which surrounds the soul, the consciousness, and sometimes opens and sometimes closes. When we are in pain, it closes, to protect the soul, to keep it, ultimately, from leaving the body. And when we experience bliss, and feel safe and secure, it opens, more and more.

Soon after Mother Kīrtidā's departure, Goswami Mahārāja and I discussed her leaving and its effect on him, and

Prabhupāda's leaving and its effect on him—and the effect on me of Prabhupāda's leaving. And he made a point that I think is quite valid: Mother Kīrtidā left after Goswami Mahārāja and all of us had matured a lot. When Prabhupāda left we weren't as mature as devotees, and we hadn't realized our spiritual individuality as fully—that we are persons, and Vaiṣṇavas are persons, and we have personal relationships with them, and it's not just regimented.

When Prabhupāda left I cried a lot for many days. Whenever I saw anything that reminded me of him, I would just start to cry. I was in a different position than Goswami Mahārāja. Because he was—and he said years later that he liked to be—the responsible eldest son. He was in that position. And he said that I liked to be the pet child. I was in that position. So, after Prabhupāda left he really was empowered—the way he dealt with all the ceremonies, the way he distributed some of Prabhupāda's personal effects to different devotees. He gave exactly the right item to each disciple of Śrīla Prabhupāda. It seemed like in everything he did, he was empowered.

I didn't really have any responsibilities in the ceremonies, although (and I am glad) I did get an opportunity to write something about Śrīla Prabhupāda soon after he left, which was published. So I was sort of free. I remember that once, I felt, "I am not doing anything," and I asked Goswami Mahārāja about it. He said, "There will be service for you, but not right now."

That was difficult, in a way. But I was so young, I couldn't really, in one sense, assimilate what had happened. And then there was just so much to do. We went to Māyāpur for the *puṣpa-samādhi* ceremony, and from there we went to Juhu for the temple opening. So we were very busy.

We were taught from the very beginning about the importance of *vāṇī*, of association through transcendental sound. "He lives forever by his divine instructions, and the follower lives with him." So we knew that was the process.

In Mother Arcā-vigraha's last days, or months really, it was the same thing: we hadn't realized her position before. So many senior devotees would come. It wasn't the same type of cohesive community as Dallas, but there was definitely a circle of devotees who were friends and would come and read to her, including some very senior devotees, such as B.B. Govinda Swami, Bhūrijana Prabhu, Keśava Bhāratī Prabhu, Śivarāma Swami, and Goswami Mahārāja himself.

She also became like a friend to me at the end. She maintained her position as a disciple, but she became a confidante. And she encouraged me. It came to the point that whatever it was, I would just go and speak to her, and she would listen, and give very wise advice.

Although I was much younger and healthier then, still, a few years before she left I had pneumonia in South Africa. And really, I could have died then if she and others hadn't taken me to the hospital just in time. I could hardly breathe, and in the same way as Guru-bhakti described, I felt like I was dying. I didn't know if I would be able to breathe. And gradually she nursed me back to health.

After she left, I thought, "Who is going to take care of me now?" I was still relatively young and inexperienced, and I condemned myself: "How could I have such a selfish desire?" I didn't think it was at all becoming. But it was there; it was definitely there.

So, coming back to Guru-bhakti's question, I do think that because of our increased maturity, Goswami Mahārāja and I could relate more personally than before with devotees like Mother Kīrtidā and Mother Arcā-vigraha, and thus feel more separation.

But right now, at this moment, I feel Mother Kīrtidā's presence so vividly, and (not to speak of it lightly) her grace. And I knew earlier in the day that she was in the mood to give mercy. I am sure she is always in the mood to give mercy, and you all have experienced her mercy. But I felt she just wanted an excuse, and the gathering here was just an excuse for her to give us more mercy.

So I think both have increased with maturity now: our ability to open our hearts and really feel love for a Vaiṣṇava, and our ability to appreciate the spiritual presence of a departed Vaiṣṇava.

RASIKENDRA DĀSA: She used to have a picture of Gāndharvikā-Giridhārī, and she would tell us, "Look how Rādhārāṇī is melted into Kṛṣṇa. Are you seeing all the *mañjarīs* in the groves? Do you see how Rādhārāṇī is melted into Kṛṣṇa?" She was telling this to everybody who came. "Do you see how Rādhārāṇī is melted into Kṛṣṇa?" We said, "Yeah, She is melting into Kṛṣṇa." She said, "No, She is *melted* into Kṛṣṇa." She said, "Can you see the *mañjarīs*? They are hidden there in the groves." She was literally seeing the spiritual world right in front of her. And we were trying to see what was happening there—but she could see everything. It was very amazing. We had that picture enlarged immediately and put it up there.

MAÑJARĪ DĀSĪ: She used to keep that picture with her before you put it up.

RASIKENDRA DĀSA: Yes, she always had it with her—on her chest.

MAÑJARĪ DĀSĪ: So she could see it. And then one day she told me, "After I have gone, this is yours."

RASIKENDRA DĀSA: Also, she had special love for Mother Kulāṅganā. She used to tell me, "She is so beautiful. Look at her. She has served Rādhā-Gokulānanda so wonderfully. She is so beautiful. Just look at her, Rasikendra." And Kulāṅganā was the only one who actually saw her leave her body. She told me, "I saw her taking her last breath. She opened her mouth, and I saw something rising, and she left." She said it was a very intense experience. And Goswami Mahārāja said that Kṛṣṇa had rewarded Durāśayā Prabhu and Mother Kulāṅganā. He rewarded Durāśayā because he was a selfless servant, just like Kīrtidā. He was chanting for her when she left her body. And Mother Kulāṅganā, also selfless in her service, would always rise early, at 2 a.m.—without fail—to come and chant for Mother Kīrtidā. And Kṛṣṇa rewarded her for that service.

Mother Kīrtidā's Mercy

A talk at Mother Kīrtidā's disappearance festival on July 8, 2002, in Dallas.

Before coming to the program here, I took the opportunity to visit Mother Kīrtidā's last room in Rasikendra Prabhu's house and hear from him and Mother Pādadhūlī about their experiences with her. But it was really after they left the room—after everyone left the room for a few minutes—that I was able to have my own experience with her. Then, alone in the room with her, I felt like crying, and the words to a song came in my mind.

The song has great significance to me. Its lyrics, written by Jāmadagneya dāsa, are in English, and it was set to music and sung by our godbrother Maṅgalānanda Prabhu many years ago. At that time I used to listen only to the songs that Śrīla Prabhupāda had given us, the ones in *Songs of the Vaiṣṇava Ācāryas*, but someone had handed me Maṅgalānanda Prabhu's tape. Around April of 1977, in Bombay, I became very sick. Śrīla Prabhupāda was there at the time, living in his new quarters on the top floor of the west tower in Juhu. For two or three days I was practically just lying on the floor in my little office, and I thought, "Let me listen to the tape." So, there was one song that very much affected me, and after I heard it the first time I would listen to it again and again.

During that period Śrīla Prabhupāda himself was very ill, and we knew that he would probably be leaving soon. I was thinking, "What will happen after he leaves?" Once I even thought, "What will happen to *me*?" Prabhupāda had always protected me. In his own way, Tamal Krishna Goswami Mahārāja had also protected me, but at the time Goswami Mahārāja wasn't the GBC there anymore. So I was thinking, "What will happen to me after Prabhupāda leaves?" and I would listen to the tape over and over again.

So, when the other devotees left and I was alone in Mother Kīrtidā's room, the song came back in my mind. The words are about going back to Godhead. In 1977 when I would hear the song I would think of Śrīla Prabhupāda going back to Godhead. I would also feel happiness, because obviously he was going back to Godhead—although in one sense he was already back to Godhead. And I also felt, "This is also my destination. One day I am also destined to go to the same place." But after that period in 1977 I never listened to the song again, because I was afraid it would bring back the memory of those days too strongly, and even until today I haven't listened to it again. But when the devotees left Mother Kīrtidā's room, the words to the song came to me. It begins with a wonderful description of what devotees are like, what they—we—do, and what happens to us, what result we get:

Selflessness relieves distress
Gentle rains of happiness
Put out the burning fire of life
Transport the soul beyond all strife
Past starry night and cruel death
For those who give their living breath
Upon their lips the holy name
In praise of he who came
To them a store of bliss is known
And hidden worlds to them are shown.

And then there is a beautiful description of the spiritual abode, the life that is our goal:

Where the Supreme Lord fills every eye
Sweet jubilation fills the sky
As dancing milkmaids and cowherd boys

Play in forests green with joys
Of bael and jackfruit lily white
An endless full-moon nectar night
Of dancing magic loving smiles
And gopī damsels' playful wiles
They sport in lotus lakes with He
Whose glances taste of ecstasy.

That is the song, and in 1977, when Prabhupāda was so ill, I would listen to it again and again. I knew Prabhupāda was going, and I knew this was my goal and destination, but I had no idea when I would reach it. Then, somehow, at that moment in Mother Kīrtidā's room this morning, I felt, "Yes, it is possible at the end of this life"—which seems inconceivable to me, because of all my disqualifications and attachments. But now, reflecting on how it is possible that someone like me could get such an idea from Mother Kīrtidā, I got an answer: It is by her mercy and the mercy of her lords and masters. But it's all by her mercy; her mercy is so strong that it is even more powerful than my attachment to the material world. At that moment, by her mercy, I felt that somehow I was gradually letting go of that attachment to—loosening my grip on—the material world. And I feel confident that anyone who takes shelter of Mother Kīrtidā and, through her, shelter of her *gurudeva*, Tamal Krishna Goswami Mahārāja, and, through him, of Śrīla Prabhupāda—anyone who does so can definitely go back to Godhead and be with them in the spiritual world at the end of this very lifetime.

How Ill Health and Misery Became a Blessing

Kīrtidā dāsī's Vyāsa-pūjā offering to Śrīpāda Tamal Krishna Goswami on June 9, 2001, at Śrī Śrī Rādhā-Kālachandjī Dhāma, Dallas.

nama oṁ viṣṇu-pādāya kṛṣṇa-preṣṭhāya bhūtale
śrīmate tamāla kṛṣṇa gosvāmin iti nāmine

Dear Śrīla Gurudeva,

Hare Kṛṣṇa. Please accept my most humble obeisances on this most auspicious moment of Vyāsa-pūjā *tithi.*

Even though I cannot physically pay obeisances, I am paying obeisances with my mind and heart. I cannot describe in words how indebted I am to you. I was swimming in an ocean of misery before I came to you, but you were the expert captain of the ship, who picked me up from the ocean out of your causeless mercy and gave me this most invaluable treasure, Kṛṣṇa consciousness. They say that *guru* and Kṛṣṇa's mercy are causeless. And I think I can proclaim that I have experienced causeless mercy from *guru* and Kṛṣṇa. Today I want to speak about the mercy of Śrī Guru.

Before I go on, however, I would like to give a brief history of my past, for those who do not know it. I believe that from my life's example, everybody here will realize the futility of material existence and the importance of taking shelter of Śrī Guru. I left home when I was fifteen years old to go to nursing school in South Africa. I trained for six years, and my ambition in life was to earn a good living and live very comfortably. My parents were very religious, and they gave me good guidance and instructions in life. My early religiosity was due to my parents' influence.

After nursing school, I worked for six years and came across an advertisement for a nursing career in the United States. I applied, and was accepted in March of 1972. I was alone and did not know anyone in this foreign land. While working during the day in the hospital, I was pursuing a nursing degree in the evening, driving ninety miles each way to college. I graduated with a nursing degree and had a successful career. Materially I was doing very well. I enjoyed the so-called fine things in life. For instance, I had a cooking set that cost $3,500, which I rarely ever used. But my health started failing because I used to work practically day and night in the operating room and my nourishment was basically Coca-Cola.

Meanwhile, I came to Śrī Śrī Rādhā-Kālachandjī Dhāma occasionally, just as a religious obligation.

I was diagnosed with duodenal ulcers, a very painful condition that eventually led to the removal of my stomach in 1980. After the removal of my stomach, my health took a turn for the worse. I had to have further surgeries to rectify my worsening condition. Even then, I was working day and night in the operating room.

All these miseries made me reflect on the purpose of life. "Is life simply meant for suffering?" I used to ask myself. Although I was materially well-situated, I was feeling miserable. I was beginning to realize that no amount of money can buy happiness, and even the friends I had didn't fill up the vacuum in my heart. My health was so bad in 1988 that I couldn't eat anymore, and the only nutrition I had were the chemicals I was intravenously feeding myself at night, after a full fifteen hours of work during the day.

I came to such a desperate, miserable condition that I decided to end my life. Just before attempting suicide, I came to the temple to beg forgiveness from the Lord for the act that I was about to perform. When I gazed at Śrī Śrī Rādhā-Kālachandjī I received a clear message from Them: "You do not create life, so you do not take life." This really awakened me from the ignorance I was in. I changed my decision about suicide.

It dawned on me that all my material things were of no use to me and that there was much more to life than just taking shelter of matter. I started coming to the temple more often as my miseries increased.

Now I can appreciate Queen Kuntī's prayers to the Lord to keep her always in distress so that she may never forget the Lord. Of course, Queen Kuntī is an eternally liberated soul, but she was playing the part of a conditioned soul.

Now that I look back on all the miseries, they were actually instrumental in helping me to think of and take shelter of Lord Kṛṣṇa. I started attending Sunday feasts regularly and developed a taste for the philosophy. Devotees approached me and asked me to take initiation, but I refused. I was chanting some rounds, but without any commitment, due to my long hours of work. I attempted to do some devotional service, and this gave me happiness. This gave me an impetus to go forward in Kṛṣṇa consciousness. I felt very much at home when I was at the temple. I was beginning to realize the value of performing devotional service.

I first met you, Śrīla Gurudeva, in 1990, when it was advertised that you would be in Dallas and giving discourses. I was very uplifted by your classes and developed more "greed" for Kṛṣṇa consciousness. Whatever you preached, I realized to be the truth in my life. At times I felt that you were personally addressing me in the class. I used to wonder how you knew so much about me.

In 1991 I went to Vṛndāvana during Kārtika, when you were there. After avoiding initiation for many years, I could not avoid being initiated by you in Vṛndāvana on the first day of Kārtika.

You made me call the devotees in Dallas and inform them that I was initiated. The devotees were very pleased that I had taken such a crucial step in my life.

In 1992 my health had deteriorated to the point where my doctors gave up hope. You gave me the instruction to give up my job and go to live in Vṛndāvana. I was thinking at that time that I would go to Vṛndāvana and give up my body within a month. By some extraordinary mercy of Śrī Guru and Gaurāṅga, my health improved by living in the *dhāma*, and I was amazed at how well I had become. I started to perform *parikramā* of Śrī Govardhana. My health returned to normal, and I was able to do service in the *dhāma*.

By this time I was deeply convinced that without total surrender to *guru* I would not attain the goal of life, *kṛṣṇa-prema*. From then on, I decided I would fully dedicate my life to you, Śrīla Gurudeva. Your instruction became the most important thing in my life—*guru-mukha-padma-vākya, cittete koriyā aikya*. After taking this vow to surrender to your lotus feet, there were no more anxieties in my life.

I stayed in the *dhāma* for six years and developed friendships with many wonderful devotees. At that point I felt I could not live outside of Vṛndāvana, and I also realized the invaluable benefit I received from residing in Śrī Vṛndāvana-dhāma.

All this would have been impossible without your causeless mercy.

Now that I reflect on my life, I can see that these so-called unfortunate events in my life were actually fortunate and auspicious, because they drove me to take full shelter of *guru* and Kṛṣṇa. Now in this materially debilitated state, I am so happy and blissful. This is all because of your mercy on me.

Above all, there is one thing I would like to share with everyone. It is this: Without taking full shelter of Śrī Guru one cannot receive the mercy of Kṛṣṇa and attain the goal of life.

I would like to thank all the devotees here for their association and prayers, which have sustained my life. I am deeply indebted to them. This debt cannot be repaid, just as Kṛṣṇa told the *gopīs* that He could not pay His debt to them.

Thank you very much, Śrīla Gurudeva, for all that you have done for me. Thank you for making me realize the Supreme Absolute Truth.

Begging to remain your servant,
Kīrtidā devī dāsī

Epilogue

Meeting in Separation

Meeting and separation are integral parts of the eternal dynamic of Kṛṣṇa consciousness. Even in the spiritual realm, devotees are always meeting with Kṛṣṇa and being separated from Him. But in all circumstances, whether in meeting or separation, the central point is Kṛṣṇa, and the emotional feeling is ecstasy—manifest in different ways.

The feelings of meeting and separation experienced by devotees in the material world are also part of Kṛṣṇa consciousness. Śrīla Prabhupāda explained, "To feel separation from the spiritual master or Kṛṣṇa is very good position. That means one who is in pure love with Kṛṣṇa and His representative, spiritual master, he thinks always of them. And this thinking process is Kṛṣṇa consciousness. If we can think always of Kṛṣṇa, even in separation, that is Kṛṣṇa consciousness. And on the absolute platform, there is no difference of separation and meeting. The separation is also meeting; rather, in separation one relishes the loving relationship more tasty. So don't be disappointed that you are separated from me. I am also always thinking of you how you are making progress there." (Letter dated October 21, 1968)

He elaborated, "So there is no cause of becoming sad. Our meeting and separation in the material world is like the flowing tide of the river. During the flowing tide of the river, so many different floating articles meet together, and with the flowing, they again become separated by the movement of the waves. That is the way of the material life. But our separation, although it resembles exactly in the material way, it is completely different. In the spiritual world, separation is more relishable than meeting. In other words, in spiritual life, there is no separation. Separation is eternal, and meeting is also eternal. The separation is simply another feature of meeting." (Letter dated April 3, 1969)

In separation, one naturally wants to meet one's loved one. And for devotees in the material world, such association is achieved through *vāṇī*, transcendental sound or words—remembering and following the teachings one has received. Therefore Śrīla Prabhupāda wrote, "Please be happy in separation. I am separated from my *guru mahārāja* since 1936, but I am always with him so long as I work according to his direction. So we should all work together for satisfying Lord Kṛṣṇa, and in that way the feelings of separation will transform into transcendental bliss." (Letter dated May 3, 1968)

And to another disciple he instructed, "You write to say, 'I really miss Swamiji and my godbrothers' association so much.' But I may remind you that I am always with you. And so wherever I am there, you are there, all your godbrothers are there. Please remember always the humble teachings that you have received from me, and that will make you always associated with me and with your other godbrothers." (Letter dated August 24, 1968)

Not only is our relationship with our spiritual master eternal; our relationships with our godbrothers and godsisters, who are associated with him, are also eternal. When one of Prabhupāda's disciples became confused about his relationships with his godbrothers and sisters, thinking that they, too, might be illusory like ordinary, mundane relationships, he wrote to Prabhupāda, "There are times when I take all my relationships within ISKCON and the pleasures and difficulties as something like a dream only. I am reminded of the time you explained to me that there is no reality in this world save and except the Divine Name and service to Him. In the *Śrīmad-Bhāgavatam* I have also read that all this having to do with past, present, and future is a dream only. I am understanding, 'Yes, even these relations as my wife, my children, or my friends or close godbrothers in Krishna consciousness, ISKCON, are like sticks meeting in a stream, to be separated in time but with the same end of

Krishna *bhakti*, back to home . . .' It was raised that 'No, our relationships formed here in ISKCON with one another are eternal in themselves, in addition to the service. That ISKCON and we members as we are known now shall be known there.' . . . All this I was unable to support scripturally, and lest I make an offense and direct error, I place this before you."

Śrīla Prabhupāda replied clearly to dispel his disciple's confusion: "As to your question concerning whether relationships between devotees are eternal, the answer is 'yes.' This is confirmed by Śrī Narottama dāsa Ṭhākura: *cakhu-dān dilo yei, janme janme prabhu sei*—he is my lord birth after birth. In this way you have to understand, by studying carefully the philosophy. We have got so many books now, and I want all of my disciples to read them carefully. Soon we shall be instituting Bhakti-sastri examinations, and all *brāhmaṇas* will have to pass. So utilize whatever time you find to make a thorough study of my books. Then all your questions will be answered." (Letter dated January 7, 1976)

Studying the dynamic in the spiritual world, we find that when, after a long period of separation, Kṛṣṇa met the *gopīs* in Kurukṣetra, He told them that He is attained only by pure loving service:

mayi bhaktir hi bhūtānām
amṛtatvāya kalpate
diṣṭyā yad āsīn mat-sneho
bhavatīnāṁ mad-āpanaḥ

"Rendering devotional service to Me qualifies any living being for eternal life. But by your good fortune you have developed a special loving attitude toward Me, by which you have obtained Me." (*SB* 10.82.44)

And they prayed to Him,

āhuś ca te nalina-nābha padāravindaṁ
yogeśvarair hṛdi vicintyam agādha-bodhaiḥ
saṁsāra-kūpa-patitottaraṇāvalambaṁ
gehaṁ juṣām api manasy udiyāt sadā naḥ

"Dear Lord, whose navel is just like a lotus flower, Your lotus feet are the only shelter for those who have fallen into the deep well of material existence. Your feet are worshiped and meditated upon by great mystic *yogīs* and highly learned philosophers. We wish that these lotus feet may also be awakened within our hearts, although we are only ordinary persons engaged in household affairs." (*SB* 10.82.48)

And to the wives of the *brāhmaṇas* who left their homes to come to meet Him, Lord Kṛṣṇa instructed:

śravaṇād darśanād dhyānān
mayi bhāvo 'nukīrtanāt
na tathā sannikarṣeṇa
pratiyāta tato gṛhān

"It is by hearing about Me, seeing My Deity form, meditating upon Me, and chanting My names and glories that love for Me develops, not by physical proximity. Therefore please go back to your homes." (*SB* 10.23.33)

Whether in the material world or the spiritual world, the basic principle of association is loving service—following the master's instructions, pleasing the loved one.

But in our efforts to develop loving service, we need help. And thus we turn to the words and examples of Śrīla Prabhupāda, Śrī Caitanya Mahāprabhu, and their moonlike followers for guidance and inspiration, and we pray to them for their mercy.

At the beginning of this book I prayed to Jayānanda Prabhu with a haiku:

Prabhupāda's full moon
Beams upon my heart's lotus—
Guru's service blooms

In conclusion, we offer the same prayer to all the moonlike devotees mentioned in the book—and to all the moonlike followers of Śrīla Prabhupāda, now and forever.

Hare Kṛṣṇa.

Appendixes

Glossary

abhidheya The system of devotional service meant for developing our loving relationship with Kṛṣṇa.
abhiṣeka A ceremonial bath performed in the worship of a deity or the coronation of a king.
Absolute Truth The ultimate source of all that exists.
ācārya One who teaches by personal example. *Ācāryas* in the pure Vaiṣṇava line instruct people and initiate them into the Supreme Lord's devotional service.
A.C. Bhaktivedanta Swami Prabhupāda The founder-*ācārya* of ISKCON and foremost preacher of Kṛṣṇa consciousness in the Western world.
Ālālanātha (Alarnath) Also known as Brahmagiri, a sacred site about fourteen miles from Jagannātha Purī, also on the coast, where, in Satya-yuga, Lord Brahmā worshiped Lord Nārāyaṇa, who then described in detail the form of a deity Brahmā should carve and worship.
ānanda Bliss, happiness.
Anupama The younger brother of Rūpa Gosvāmī.
ārati A standard ceremony of worship with offerings of lamps, fans, incense, flowers, water, and other items, similar to the custom of greeting a guest to one's home, especially at night (*ā-rātrikam*).
arcanaṁ The process of Deity worship.
āśrama (ashram) 1. The hermitage of a sage or teacher.
2. In the *varṇāśrama* social system, the four spiritual orders of life: *brahmacārī* (celibate student), *gṛhastha* (householder), *vānaprastha* (retired), and *sannyāsa* (renounced).
aṣṭa-kālīya-līlā Kṛṣṇa's eightfold daily pastimes.
āṭā Stone-ground whole-wheat flour.
audārya Magnanimity.
bābājī A renounced person fully dedicated to hearing and chanting about Kṛṣṇa and residing in Vraja, Gauḍa-maṇḍala, or any other holy place. *Bābājīs* are beyond the *varnāśrama* system.
Baladeva Vidyābhūṣaṇa A prominent eighteenth-century *ācārya* in the Gauḍīya Vaiṣṇava *sampradāya*. He studied under Śrīla Viśvanātha Cakravartī and composed *Śrī Govinda-bhāṣya*, the

Gauḍīya commentary on *Vedānta-sūtra*, directly inspired by Śrī Govindajī Himself.

Balarāma (Baladeva, Balabhadra) Kṛṣṇa's first plenary expansion, who appears in *kṛṣṇa-līlā* as Kṛṣṇa's elder brother, the son of Vasudeva and Rohiṇī.

Bhagavad-gītā "The Song of God," the book in which the Supreme Lord, Kṛṣṇa, explains the science of *yoga*, giving essential teachings on progressive spiritual life and pure devotion to God, spoken five thousand years ago to His friend Arjuna moments before the great battle at Kurukṣetra. Vyāsadeva included the *Bhagavad-gītā* in the *Bhīṣma-parva* section of the *Mahābhārata*.

Bhāgavata Purāṇa *Śrīmad-Bhāgavatam*.

bhajana 1. Loving devotional service to the Supreme Lord. 2. A devotional song in glorification of the Lord.

bhajana-kuṭīra A cottage, hut, or similar place for performing one's devotional service.

bhakta A devotee of the Supreme Lord.

bhakti Devotional service to the Supreme Lord. *Bhakti* in practice is the prime means of achieving spiritual success, and perfected *bhakti*, pure love of God, is the ultimate goal of life.

Bhakti-rasāmṛta-sindhu Literally, "The Ocean of the Pure Nectar of Devotional Service," Rūpa Gosvāmī's textbook on the principles and cultivation of devotional service (*bhakti*), both in practice and in perfection.

Bhaktisiddhānta Sarasvatī Ṭhākura An *ācārya* in the Brahma-Madhva-Gauḍīya Vaiṣṇava *sampradāya*, the founder-*ācārya* of the Gauḍīya Maṭha, and the spiritual master of His Divine Grace A.C. Bhaktivedanta Swami Prabhupāda.

Bhaktivinoda Ṭhākura An *ācārya* in the Brahma-Madhva-Gauḍīya Vaiṣṇava disciplic succession, the spiritual master of Gaurakiśora dāsa Bābājī, and the father and grand spiritual master of Bhaktisiddhānta Sarasvatī Ṭhākura.

bhakti-yoga The spiritual process of linking to the Supreme Lord through pure devotional service.

bhāva Mood; emotion; ecstasy in love of God. Various kinds of *bhāva* join together as the components of *rasa*, or *prema*.

bhāva-bhakti The stage of devotional service after *sādhana-bhakti* and before *prema-bhakti*; the preliminary stage of love of Godhead.

Bhīma (-sena) The second and strongest of the five Pāṇḍava brothers, a great fighter and punisher of wrongdoers. In the Battle of Kurukṣetra he fulfilled his vow to kill Duryodhana and all the Kaurava brothers.

Bhīṣma (-deva) The son of Śāntanu and Gaṅgā. He is one of the Twelve Mahājanas, great authorities on Vedic knowledge. As the elder of the Kuru warriors, he led Duryodhana's forces in battle until he was felled by the arrows of Arjuna. He passed away gloriously at his own chosen moment in the presence of Kṛṣṇa.

BHISMA Bhaktivedanta Information Services and Mailing.

bhoga Foodstuffs meant to be offered to the Deity.

Brahmā The first finite living being in the material creation. He was born from the lotus growing from the navel of Garbhodakaśāyī Viṣṇu. At the beginning of creation, and again at the start of each day of his life, Brahmā engineers the appearance of all the species and the planets on which they reside. He is the first teacher of the *Vedas* and the final material authority to whom the demigods resort when belabored by their opponents.

brahmacārī In the *varṇāśrama* system, a celibate male in the student stage of spiritual life, receiving education at the residence of a spiritual master.

Brahmagiri See *Ālālanātha*.

brāhma-muhūrta The hour and a half just before sunrise, the most auspicious time of the day for spiritual practices.

Brahman Absolute Truth.

brāhmaṇa (brahmin) A member of the intellectual class, which consists mainly of teachers and priests and is one of the four occupational divisions in the *varṇāśrama* social system.

Caitanya-caritāmṛta A major work on Caitanya Mahāprabhu's life and teachings, written by Kṛṣṇadāsa Kavirāja Gosvāmī.

Caitanya Mahāprabhu The original Supreme Personality of Godhead, Kṛṣṇa, acting in the guise of His own devotee. He advented Himself in 1486 at Māyāpur, West Bengal, and introduced *saṅkīrtana*, the congregational chanting of the holy names, as the *yuga-dharma* for the present age. He propounded the sublime philosophy of *acintya-bhedābheda-tattva*, the inconceivable simultaneous oneness and difference between the Lord and His energies, and taught the pure worship of Rādhā and Kṛṣṇa.

Candrāvalī One of the principal *gopīs* of Vraja and the leader of the right-wing *gopīs*, who are transcendental rivals of Rādhārāṇī.

caraṇāmṛta The water that has bathed the feet of the Supreme Lord or His devotee. One honors *caraṇāmṛta* by sipping it and sprinkling it on one's head.

chakra "Wheel," or "disk." A wheel-like vortex through which the energy of life flows, often associated with the seven energy centers of the body.

Dāmodara Kṛṣṇa, who was bound at the waist (*udara*) with rope (*dāma*) by Mother Yaśodā as a punishment for stealing butter.

darśana "Viewing"; an auspicious audience with a deity or holy person.

deity An authorized worshipable form of God, a demigod, or a devotee. The Lord and His devotees are manifested in such forms, which may be made of stone, wood, metal, earth, paint or ink, sand (drawn upon the ground), or jewels, or conceived of in the mind.

demigods Pious finite living beings endowed with the intelligence and influence necessary to administrate the material universe on behalf of the Supreme Lord. Lesser demigods reside in Svarga, and their king is Indra. They govern under the direction of higher demigods, who reside on higher planets.

dhāma A domain where the Supreme Lord personally resides and enjoys eternal pastimes with His loving devotees.

dharmaśālā A building, often in a holy place, where pilgrims and mendicants can find simple accommodation.

dhoti A long piece of cotton or silk cloth worn on the lower part of the body by men of Vedic culture.

dīkṣā-guru The spiritual master who connects one with the Supreme Lord through the process of initiation. A disciple has only one *dīkṣā-guru* but may have any number of *śikṣā-gurus*, instructing spiritual masters.

Diwali (Dipāvalī) Festival observed on the New Year's Day of the Hindu calendar, the day on which Lord Rāmacandra returned from a fourteen-year exile.

Dvaipāyana Vyāsa The empowered compiler of the *Vedas*. A different *vyāsa*, "editor," appears at the end of each Dvāpara age, when understanding of the *Vedas* becomes confused. The current Vyāsa, Kṛṣṇa Dvaipāyana, is an incarnation of the Supreme Lord. The *Vedānta-sūtra* and *Mahābhārata* are his personal compositions, and the culmination of his literary effort is *Śrīmad-Bhāgavatam*.

Dvārakā The eternal abode in which Kṛṣṇa fully displays the royal opulence of God. While on earth, Kṛṣṇa resettled the entire population of Mathurā in the city of Dvārakā, which He manifested on the ocean, near the coast of the Ānarta province (Gujarat).

Ekādaśī The spiritually auspicious eleventh day after the full moon and the new moon, meant for increasing one's devotion to Lord Hari, Kṛṣṇa, by fasting from at least grains and beans and increasing one's devotional activities, especially the chanting of the Hare Kṛṣṇa *mahā-mantra*.

Gāndharvikā A name for Śrīmatī Rādhārāṇī, referring to Her consummate expertise as a singer. (The name Gāndharvikā is derived from the Gandharva planet, which is filled with celestial beings who sing beautifully.)

Gāndharvikā-Giridhārī Rādhā, the expert singer, and Kṛṣṇa, the lifter of Govardhana Hill.

Gaṅgā (-devī) The Ganges, the sacred river that flows from the peaks of the Himalayas to the Bay of Bengal. Due to contact with the toe of Lord Viṣṇu, the supreme pure, she purifies and delivers from sin anyone who comes in contact with her waters.

Gauḍa-maṇḍala-bhūmi The places in Bengal where Lord Caitanya stayed.

Gauḍīya Maṭha The Kṛṣṇa conscious institution founded by Bhaktisiddhānta Sarasvatī Ṭhākura.

Gauḍīya-sampradāya A branch of the Brahma-Madhva-sampradāya founded by Śrī Caitanya Mahāprabhu for inundating the world with pure devotion to Rādhā and Kṛṣṇa.

Gauḍīya Vaiṣṇavas Followers of Lord Caitanya.

gaura-līlā Pastimes of Lord Caitanya.

Gaurāṅga Lord Caitanya, who has a golden (*gaura*) body (*aṅga*—limbs).

Gaura-Nitāi Lord Caitanya (Gaura) and Lord Nityānanda (Nitāi).

Gaura-pūrṇimā The appearance day of Lord Caitanya.

Gāyatrī A sacred *mantra* that *brāhmaṇas* chant silently three times a day—at sunrise, noon, and sunset—to attain the transcendental platform; the Vedic *mantra* that delivers one from material entanglement.

Giridhārī Kṛṣṇa, the lifter of Govardhana Hill.

Giri Govardhana See *Govardhana*.

Girirāja "The king of mountains," another name for Govardhana Hill.

Gītā See *Bhagavad-gītā*.

Godhead The Absolute Truth, the Supreme Reality, progressively realized initially as the impersonal, all-pervasive oneness; more fully as the Supersoul within the heart of every living being; and ultimately as the all-opulent Supreme Person.

Goloka The planet (*loka*) of cows (*go*). The eternal abode of the Supreme Lord in His original form of Kṛṣṇa. It is situated above all the other Vaikuṇṭha planets and has three sections: Vṛndāvana, Mathurā, and Dvārakā. There is also a heavenly Goloka in the material world.

Gopal Jiu The family deity of Śrīpāda Gour Govinda Swami.

Gopīnātha Kṛṣṇa, master of the *gopīs*; one of the original important deities of Vṛndāvana, worshiped by Madhu Paṇḍita.

gopīs Cowherd girls or women, especially Kṛṣṇa's young girlfriends in Vraja, who are His most intimate devotees.

Gopīśvara Mahādeva The deity of Lord Śiva in Vṛndāvana who protects the site of Kṛṣṇa's *rāsa* dance with the *gopīs*. He can grant one the qualification to enter the *rāsa* dance.

gośālā The place where cows are kept; a cowshed.

gosvāmī (goswami) One who controls his mind and senses. When capitalized, it may be a title of one in the renounced order of life or it may refer specifically to any of the Six Gosvāmīs of Vṛndāvana.

Govardhana A hill situated fifteen miles west of Mathurā city, considered to be an incarnation of Lord Viṣṇu. Kṛṣṇa lifted it and for seven days held it aloft as a huge umbrella to protect the residents of Vraja from a devastating storm caused by the jealous Indra. Also, the main village alongside the hill.

govardhana-śilās Stones from Govardhana Hill. On the basis of *Śrīmad-Bhāgavatam*, Lord Caitanya accepted Govardhana Hill as being nondifferent from Kṛṣṇa, and each of its stones as worshipable.

Govinda (jī) Kṛṣṇa, the Lord who gives pleasure to the cows, the earth, and everyone's senses; one of the original important deities of Vṛndāvana, worshiped by Rūpa Gosvāmī.

gṛhastha A member of the household order of life, the second stage in the *varṇāśrama* system.

guru A teacher or spiritual master.

gurudeva The spiritual master.

guru-kṛpā The mercy of the spiritual master.

gurukula "The *guru's* family"; a teacher's ashram or school where traditional education is given.

gurukulī A *gurukula* student or graduate.

Guru Mahārāja A form of address for one's spiritual master.

guru-niṣṭhā Faith in the spiritual master.

guru-paramparā See *paramparā*.

guru-pūjā Worship of the spiritual master with *ārati* and *kīrtana*.

guru-tattva The ontological truth of the identity and activities of the spiritual master.

halavā A dessert made of semolina (or other grain), ghee, sugar, and water.

Hanumān Lord Rāmacandra's faithful eternal servant, who has the body of a *kimpuruṣa*, a humanlike monkey.

Hare Kṛṣṇa mantra A sixteen-word prayer composed of the names Hare, Kṛṣṇa, and Rāma—Hare Kṛṣṇa, Hare Kṛṣṇa, Kṛṣṇa Kṛṣṇa, Hare Hare/ Hare Rāma, Hare Rāma, Rāma Rāma, Hare Hare. *Hare*, the personal form of God's own happiness, His eternal consort, Śrīmatī Rādhārāṇī; *Kṛṣṇa*, "the all-attractive one"; and *Rāma*, "the all-pleasing one," are names of God. The purport of the prayer is, "My dear Rādhārāṇī and Kṛṣṇa, please engage me in Your devotional service." The *Vedas* recommend the chanting of the Hare Kṛṣṇa *mantra* as the easiest and most sublime method for awakening one's dormant love of God. These names have been particularly recommended as the great chant for deliverance in this age.

Haridāsa Ṭhākura A great devotee of Śrī Caitanya Mahāprabhu, he is known as the *nāmācārya*, the master who taught the chanting of the holy names by precept and by his own example.

hari-kathā Narration, or discussion, of topics of Lord Hari, Kṛṣṇa.

hari-kīrtana Glorification of Lord Hari (Kṛṣṇa); singing or narrating the glories of the Supreme Personality of Godhead and His names, forms, qualities, and pastimes.

hari-nāma The holy name of Kṛṣṇa.

hari-nāma-saṅkīrtana Congregational chanting of the holy names of the Supreme Lord.

hari-pūjā Worship of Hari, Lord Kṛṣṇa.

Hastināpura The capital of the Kurus, located on the banks of the Gaṅgā, east of what is now Delhi.

hṛd-puṇḍarīka The heart lotus, which surrounds the soul—the consciousness—and sometimes opens and sometimes closes.

iṣṭa-goṣṭhī "Desirable association," the discussion of spiritual topics among devotees.

Jagannātha "Lord of the universe," an ancient deity of Kṛṣṇa installed along with deities of His brother, Balarāma, and His sister, Subhadrā, in the holy city of Purī on the coast of Orissa, where He was worshiped by Śrī Caitanya Mahāprabhu; any deity in the image of the one in Purī.

Jagannātha Purī See *Purī*.

Jahnu-saptamī Also known as Gaṅgā-saptamī; the seventh day of the waxing fortnight of the full moon in the month of Vaiśākha (April-May), the date on which the sage Jahnu drank all the water of the Ganges in one gulp and then released it, after which the Ganges became known as Jāhnavī, the descendent of Jahnu.

Jalāṅgī River near Māyāpur.

Janmāṣṭamī See *Kṛṣṇa Janmāṣṭamī*.

japa Quiet, meditative chanting of a mantra.

Jīva Gosvāmī One of the Six Gosvāmīs of Vṛndāvana and the greatest scholar in the Gauḍīya-sampradāya. His most important works are the *Ṣaṭ-sandarbha* and *Gopāla-campū*.

kalaśa Waterpot.

Kali (-yuga) "Quarrel"; the name of the fourth of four repeating ages (*yugas*) of universal time. In each Kali-yuga the world degrades into hypocrisy, dishonesty, and conflict. The present Kali-yuga began 5,000 years ago and will continue for another 427,000 years.

Kaṁsa The king of Bhoja and son of Ugrasena who usurped the throne of Mathurā. After sending many demons to Vraja to kill Kṛṣṇa and Balarāma, he finally brought the two brothers to Mathurā to be killed in a wrestling tournament, but Kṛṣṇa killed him instead.

Kāmyavana One of the twelve forests of Vṛndāvana, known to fulfill all desires and presided over by Vṛndādevī.

karatālas Hand cymbals used during *kīrtana*.

Karoli A town about 120 miles from Jaipur, in the state of Rajasthan.

Kārtika The Vedic month corresponding to October–November, in which Lord Dāmodara is worshiped.

kathā Sacred narrations.

kavirāja 1. A great poet.
2. An Ayurvedic physician, *vaidya*.

khādī Homespun cotton cloth.

kicharī A rice dish cooked with lentils and, often, vegetables.

kīrtana Glorification of the Supreme Lord; narrating or singing the names and glories of the Supreme Personality of Godhead—the primary devotional practice in the present Age of Kali.

kīrtanīyā A performer of *kīrtana*, often a lead singer.

Kṛṣṇa The original Supreme Personality of Godhead, who enjoys life as a youthful cowherd with His family and friends in Vṛndāvana and later as a heroic prince in Mathurā and Dvārakā.

Kṛṣṇa-Balarāma Kṛṣṇa, the Supreme Personality of Godhead, and Balarāma, His first plenary expansion, who appears in *kṛṣṇa-līlā* as His elder brother.

Kṛṣṇa book Śrīla Prabhupāda's summary study of the Tenth Canto of *Śrīmad-Bhāgavatam.*

Kṛṣṇa consciousness Awareness of one's eternal relationship with the Supreme Personality of Godhead; the process that enables one to return to the spiritual world; Śrīla Prabhupāda's condensed rendering of Rūpa Gosvāmī's Sanskrit phrase *kṛṣṇa-bhakti-rasa-bhāvitā matiḥ*, "to be absorbed in the mellows of executing devotional service to Kṛṣṇa."

Kṛṣṇadāsa Kavirāja Gosvāmī The author of *Śrī Caitanya-caritāmṛta.*

Kṛṣṇa Janmāṣṭamī The date, or *tithi*, of Kṛṣṇa's appearance in this world; the festival celebrating the anniversary of Kṛṣṇa's appearance.

kṛṣṇa-kathā Discussions about Kṛṣṇa.

kṛṣṇa-kīrtana The chanting of Kṛṣṇa's name and pastimes.

kṛṣṇa-līlā Kṛṣṇa's pastimes.

Kṛṣṇaloka Kṛṣṇa's eternal abode in the spiritual sky.

kṛṣṇa-prema Pure love for Kṛṣṇa, which is the perfection of life.

Kumbha-melā A spiritual fair (*melā*) held every twelve years at a place where millions of years ago drops from the pot (*kumbha*) of nectar churned by the demigods and demons fell. From all over India, millions of pilgrims and saintly persons seeking spiritual upliftment gather at the Triveṇī—the confluence of the three holy rivers Ganges, Yamunā, and Sarasvatī—at Prayāga, near the modern city of Allahabad. Taking bath at the Triveṇī at the astrologically auspicious time assures the worshiper liberation from the cycle of birth and death. The other three Kumbha-melās take place at Haridwar, Nasik, and Ujjain.

kuṇḍa A lake or pond; often refers to one of the sacred ponds in Vṛndāvana.

kuñja Bushes; grove; bower.

Kuntī (Pṛthā) One of King Pāṇḍu's two wives. With the help of various demigods, she became the mother of Karṇa, Yudhiṣṭhira, Bhīma, and Arjuna.

lakh One hundred thousand.

Lakṣmī (-devī) The eternal consort of the Supreme Lord Viṣṇu. She presides over the infinite opulences of Vaikuṇṭha, and her partial expansion dispenses opulences in the material world.

Lalitā (-devī) One of Śrīmatī Rādhārāṇī's principal direct expansions and most intimate friends. She is Rādhārāṇī's chief companion and, being slightly older than Rādhā, Her advisor on appropriate behavior.

Lalita-mādhava A drama by Rūpa Gosvāmī describing Kṛṣṇa's pastimes in Dvārakā and Mathurā and His devotees' ecstatic emotional love for Him.

lāphrā A preparation made from several vegetables boiled in water with spices.

līlā "Pastimes," the eternal activities of the Supreme Lord in loving reciprocation with His devotees. Unlike the affairs of materially conditioned souls, the Lord's *līlās* are not restricted by the laws of nature or impelled by the reactions of past deeds or subject to future reactions.

Madana-mohana Kṛṣṇa, who attracts and bewilders Cupid; one of the original important deities of Vṛndāvana, worshiped by Sanātana Gosvāmī.

Mādhavendra Purī The spiritual master of Īśvara Purī, whom Śrī Caitanya Mahāprabhu accepted as spiritual master. He introduced the mood of ecstatic love in separation—the mood of Śrīmatī Rādhārāṇī's feelings in separation from Kṛṣṇa—in what came to be known as the Gauḍīya-sampradāya.

mādhurya (-bhāva, -rasa) The mellow of devotional service to Kṛṣṇa in conjugal love, one of the five primary relationships with Kṛṣṇa.

Mādhurya Kaḍambinī A book written by Śrīla Viśvanātha Cakravartī Ṭhākura that describes the progressive stages of *uttama-bhakti* from *śraddhā* to *prema.*

mahājana A "great person," one who understands the Absolute Truth and acts accordingly; especially when capitalized, any one of the twelve great self-realized souls, authorized agents of the Lord, whose duty is to preach and exemplify the principles of devotional service for the benefit of the people.

Mahā-kumbha-melā A great Kumbha-melā held once every twelve Kumbha-melās, or 144 years. See *Kumbha-melā.*

mahā-mantra The great chant for deliverance: Hare Kṛṣṇa, Hare Kṛṣṇa, Kṛṣṇa Kṛṣṇa, Hare Hare/ Hare Rāma, Hare Rāma, Rāma Rāma, Hare Hare.

mahānta A Hindu religious leader who is the head or proprietor of a temple or monastery.

Mahāprabhu The supreme master of all masters; refers to Lord Caitanya.

mahā-prasāda The sanctified remnants of food offered directly to the Supreme Lord and left by Him for the benefit of His devotees.

Mahārāja "Great ruler," a term of address for kings, renounced holy men, and *brāhmaṇas*.

mahātmā A "great soul," a saint who has broad intelligence by dint of his full Kṛṣṇa consciousness.

mālā Garland, i.e. a strung circle of flowers, jewels, or beads.

māna An advanced development of *prema*, a type of transcendental jealous anger exhibited solely for Kṛṣṇa's pleasure by Śrīmatī Rādhārāṇī and other sweethearts of Kṛṣṇa.

mandira A temple; sometimes, more generally, any building or residence.

maṅgala-ārati In Deity worship, the first *ārati* of the day, performed an hour and a half before sunrise.

mañjarī 1. A *tulasī* flower, often offered in worship at the lotus feet of the Lord or strung into garlands to be placed around His neck.
2. A *gopī* who acts as an assistant to the more senior *gopīs*, or specifically as a maidservant of Śrīmatī Rādhārāṇī.

mantra "That which delivers the mind," a sacred invocation chanted to purify the mind and fulfill various aspirations.

mātā (-jī) "Mother"; a term of respect for a woman, sometime used as a form of address or added to a woman's name.

maṭha A temple of the Lord with an attached residence or ashram for *brahmacārīs* (celibate students) and *sannyāsīs* (renunciants); monastery.

Mathurā (-dhāma, -maṇḍala, -purī) The eternal abode in which Kṛṣṇa manifests Himself as the Lord of the Yādavas. During His descent to earth, Kṛṣṇa reclaimed Mathurā for the Yādavas by killing Kaṁsa and installing Ugrasena on the throne. Kṛṣṇa resided in Mathurā for thirty-three years before relocating the Yādavas to Dvārakā.

māyā Illusion; the illusion in which the conditioned souls are kept by the Lord's inferior, material energy, personified and overseen by the goddess Durgā, or Māyā.

Māyāpur A village in West Bengal, India, where Lord Caitanya appeared; the place of ISKCON's world headquarters.

mṛdaṅga A two-headed drum traditionally used in *kīrtana*.

nāmāparādha Offense to the holy name.

Nārada (Muni) One of the principal associates of Lord Nārāyaṇa. He travels throughout the spiritual and material worlds glorifying the Lord and preaching pure devotional service, and he reveals confidential information to various parties to advance the Supreme Lord's pastimes.

Narottama dāsa Ṭhākura A renowned sixteenth-century Vaiṣṇava spiritual master in the disciplic succession from Śrī Caitanya Mahāprabhu, most famous for his many devotional songs. He was the initiated disciple of Lokanātha Gosvāmī and studied under Jīva Gosvāmī and preached widely throughout India.

Navadvīpa (-dhāma) Lord Caitanya Mahāprabhu's eternal abode, non-different from Kṛṣṇa's Vṛndāvana abode. On earth, Navadvīpa is located in the district of Nadia, West Bengal.

nirjana-bhajana The solitary worship of the Supreme Lord in a secluded place.

Nityānanda The principal associate of Lord Caitanya, He is the incarnation of Lord Balarāma.

Nityānanda-trayodaśī The appearance day of Lord Nityānanda.

niyamāgraha Neglecting to follow rules and regulations (*niyama-agraha*), or following them fanatically, without understanding the purpose (*niyama-āgraha*).

Nṛsiṁha (-deva) The pastime incarnation of the Supreme Lord Viṣṇu as half-man half-lion. He appeared in order to deliver the saintly child Prahlāda from the persecutions of his demonic father, Hiraṇyakaśipu. When Hiraṇyakaśipu demanded of Prahlāda, "If your god is everywhere, is he also in this pillar?" Lord Nṛsiṁha burst out of the pillar and ripped Hiraṇyakaśipu apart.

Nṛsiṁha-caturdaśī The appearance day of Lord Nṛsiṁha.

Padyāvalī An anthology of verses compiled by Śrīla Rūpa Gosvāmī.

Pañca-tattva The Lord in five features: the original Supreme Personality of Godhead—Śrī Caitanya Mahāprabhu; His plenary portion—Nityānanda Prabhu; His incarnation—Advaita Prabhu; His energy—Gadādhara Paṇḍita; and His devotee—Śrīvāsa Ṭhākura.

paṇḍāl "Tent"; often refers to religious programs and lectures held under large tents.

Pāṇḍavas The five sons of Pāṇḍu. The three older Pāṇḍavas—

Yudhiṣṭhira, Bhīma, and Arjuna—were born to Pāṇḍu's wife Kuntī through the agency of the three demigods Yamarāja, Vāyu, and Indra. The other two sons, Nakula and Sahadeva, were born of Pāṇḍu's other wife, Mādrī, through the agency of the Aśvinī-kumāras.

paramparā Literally, "one after the other"; an authorized Vaiṣṇava disciplic succession; more ordinarily, a lineage passing down a tradition.

parikramā 1. Circumambulation of a sacred area, site, deity, or saintly person.
2. A journey, usually by foot, to various sites of pilgrimage.

prabhu "Master"; a term of respect for a devotee, sometimes used as a form of address or added to a devotee's name.

prabhu-datta deśa A place or country (*deśa*) for preaching given (*datta*) by the spiritual master or Lord (*prabhu*).

Prabhupāda 1. One whose position is representative of Prabhu (the Supreme Lord).
2. One who is situated at the feet of Prabhu.
3. One at whose feet are many *prabhus* (devotees); a term of highest respect used to designate or address an *ācārya*. See also *Śrīla Prabhupāda*.

prasāda (prasādam) The sanctified remnants of food or other items that have been offered to the Supreme Lord. By accepting Kṛṣṇa's *prasāda*, one can rapidly become purified and achieve pure love of God.

prāyaścitta Atonement for sinful acts.

prayojana Necessity, aim, objective; the ultimate goal of life: love of God (*prema*).

prema Pure ecstatic love of God.

prema-bhakti Devotional service to the Supreme Lord in pure love.

pūjārī A devotee who performs direct worship of a deity.

pukka Perfect; 100 percent.

Purañjana The hero of an allegorical story told by Nārada to King Prācīnabarhi to teach the folly of materialistic life.

Purī (Jagannātha Purī, Nīlācala, Nīlādri) A holy city in Orissa, on the Bay of Bengal, where Lord Jagannātha resides.

puṣpāñjali The ceremonial offering of flowers from folded palms to the Supreme Lord or His pure devotees.

puṣpa-samādhi A memorial in which the flowers worn by a departed spiritual master or saintly devotee are enshrined and worshiped.

Rādhā (-rāṇī, Rādhikā) The personification of Kṛṣṇa's original pleasure potency, from whom all His internal energies expand. She is His eternal consort in Vṛndāvana and the most exalted and beloved of His devotees.

Rādhā-Dāmodara Rādhā and Kṛṣṇa, bound at the waist with rope.

Rādhā-Giridhārī Rādhā and Kṛṣṇa, the lifter of Govardhana Hill.

Rādhā-Gokulānanda The Rādhā-Kṛṣṇa deities at Bhaktivedanta Manor, outside London.

Rādhā-Gopīnātha Rādhā and Kṛṣṇa, the master of the *gopīs*.

Rādhā-Govinda Rādhā and Kṛṣṇa, who gives pleasure to the land, cows, and senses.

Rādhā-Kālachandjī Rādhā-Kṛṣṇa deities in the ISKCON temple in Dallas, Texas.

Rādhā-kuṇḍa The bathing place of Śrīmatī Rādhārāṇī, a sacred pond near Govardhana Hill created by Rādhārāṇī and Her *gopī* companions. It is the supreme holy place of Vraja, especially worshipable for Gauḍīya Vaiṣṇavas. The seven major Gauḍīya Vaiṣṇava temples of Vṛndāvana also exist there, as well as *bhajana-kutīras* of many Gauḍīya Vaiṣṇava *ācāryas*. Rādhā-kuṇḍa is the site of the most intimate loving affairs of Śrī Śrī Rādhā-Kṛṣṇa, and Her waters are considered nondifferent from Rādhārāṇī Herself and bestow love of Godhead.

Rādhā-Rādhānātha 1. Rādhā and Kṛṣṇa, the Lord of Śrīmatī Rādhārāṇī.

Rādhā-Rāsabihārī The Rādhā-Kṛṣṇa deities at Hare Krishna Land, Juhu, India.

Rādhāṣṭamī The festival celebrating Rādhārāṇī's appearance day.

Rādhā-Śyāmasundara Rādhā and Kṛṣṇa, who has a beautiful blackish form.

Rādhe The vocative form of "Rādhā."

Rādhe-Śyāma A vocative form of "Rādhā-Kṛṣṇa," especially popular in Vṛndāvana.

Raghunātha dāsa Gosvāmī One of the Six Gosvāmīs of Vṛndāvana, born around 1494 CE in Bengal. His forefathers were all Vaiṣṇavas and very rich men. Raghunātha dāsa was a family man, but he had no attachment to his estate or wife and tried many times to run away from home. He finally managed to escape his father's vigilance and in 1517 CE went to Jagannātha Purī to meet Śrī Caitanya Mahāprabhu. He resided for most of his life at Rādhā-kuṇḍa and wrote three books, *Stava-mālā* (or *Stavāvalī*), *Dāna-carita*, and

Muktā-carita. His only concern was to engage in the service of the Lord, and he gradually reduced his eating and sleeping to almost nil. The *Gaura-gaṇoddeśa-dīpikā* (186) states that Raghunātha dāsa Gosvāmī was formerly the *gopī* named Rasa-mañjarī and that sometimes it is said that he was Rati-mañjarī.

Rāma (-candra) The incarnation of the Supreme Lord as a perfect, righteous king, born as the son of Daśaratha and Kauśalya. Rāma is also a name of Lord Kṛṣṇa, meaning "the source of all pleasure," and a name of Lord Balarāma and of Lord Paraśurāma.

Rāmacandra Kavirāja A disciple of Śrīnivāsa Ācārya and the most intimate friend of Narottama dāsa Ṭhākura, who acknowledged his love for him in his songbook *Prārthanā*.

Ramaṇa-reti The area in Vṛndāvana where Kṛṣṇa and Balarāma performed Their childhood pastimes and where ISKCON's Kṛṣṇa-Balarāma temple is located.

Ranganiketan "House of Colorful Arts," a group of Manipuri singers, dancers, musicians, martial artists, choreographers, and artisans.

rasa Transcendental taste, or mellow; the boundless pleasure enjoyed in one of the five primary relationships with Kṛṣṇa: reverence, servanthood, friendship, parental affection, and conjugal love.

rāsa (-līlā, dance) Kṛṣṇa's divine dance with the *gopīs*, the grand celebration of their conjugal love.

ratha A cart or chariot, used during religious festivals to carry the deities.

Ratha-yātrā The yearly festival celebrated throughout the world—especially in Purī—in which Lord Jagannātha; His brother, Balarāma; and His sister, Subhadrā, are taken out from their usual place of residence and pulled through the streets on elaborate carts. In Purī they travel from the Nīlācala temple to the Guṇḍicā temple, which represents Vṛndāvana.

ṛṣi A Vedic sage. The first *ṛṣis* were the "seers" of the Vedic hymns, who perceived the eternal *mantras* in their meditation and passed them on to human society.

Rūpa Gosvāmī One of the Six Gosvāmīs of Vṛndāvana and the prime authority on the science of *rasa*, loving exchanges with God, which he expounded in his *Bhakti-rasāmṛta-sindhu* and *Ujjvala-nīlamaṇi*. He was also an eminent playwright and poet. Many Gauḍīya Vaiṣṇavas consider themselves *rūpānugas*, followers of Rūpa Gosvāmī.

sabjī A vegetable or vegetable dish.

Śacī (-devī, -mātā) The mother of Lord Caitanya Mahāprabhu and wife of Jagannātha Miśra of Navadvīpa.

sac-cid-ānanda "Eternal existence, knowledge, and bliss," the constitutional nature of the Supreme Lord and of the finite living beings. The Supreme Lord's *sac-cid-ānanda* nature is always manifest, whereas that of the *jīvas*, the minute living entities, is covered by material illusion when they turn away from the Lord.

sadācāra Clean habits, adherence to scriptural rules governing proper behavior—for example, no illicit sex, no intoxication, no meat-eating, no gambling; rising early in the morning, bathing thrice daily.

sādhana Practices for achieving pure devotional service; more generally, the means for achieving any goal.

sādhana-bhakti Devotional service in practice, performed with the senses, by which ecstatic love for the Supreme Lord is awakened.

sādhu A saintly person.

sakhī Girlfriend. Often refers to Śrīmatī Rādhārāṇī's intimate girlfriends, who assist Her in Her service to Kṛṣṇa.

śālagrāma-śilā A deity of Lord Nārāyaṇa in the form of a small black stone marked with *cakras* and other symbols. These *śilās*, obtained only from one location on the river Gaṇḍakī and typically worshiped by *brāhmaṇas* in their homes, can each be recognized by unique markings as a specific incarnation of the Lord.

samādhi 1. Fully matured meditation, the last of the eight steps of the *yoga* system taught by Patañjali. A perfected devotee of the Supreme Lord also achieves *samādhi.*
2. The tomb where the body of a spiritually advanced soul is laid after his departure from this world.

samādhi-mandira The structure accommodating the tomb of a spiritually advanced soul.

sambandha One's original relationship with the Lord.

sampradāya A school of philosophy or religion. According to the *Padma Purāṇa*, there are four authorized Vaiṣṇava *sampradāyas*, founded by Lord Brahmā, the goddess Lakṣmī, Lord Śiva, and the four Kumāra sages. In Kali-yuga these schools have been reestablished by the *ācāryas* Madhva, Rāmānuja, Viṣṇu Svāmī, and Nimbārka. The *sampradāya* of Lord Caitanya Mahāprabhu is officially connected with the Madhva line but incorporates the teachings of all four *sampradāyas*.

Sanātana Gosvāmī One of the Six Gosvāmīs of Vṛndāvana, the older brother and *śikṣā-guru* of Rūpa Gosvāmī and author of *Śrī Bṛhad-bhāgavatāmṛta.*

sanātha "With a fitting master"; one who is protected.

Sāndīpani (Muni) The celebrated sage residing in Avantī (modern Ujjain) who was Kṛṣṇa and Balarāma's *guru* and taught Them the sixty-four traditional arts in sixty-four days.

saṅkīrtana 1. Congregational chanting of the names and glories of Kṛṣṇa—the *yuga-dharma*, or prime means for spiritual success, in the Age of Kali.
2. The transmission of the Lord's glories through literature; book distribution.

sannyāsa The renounced order of life, the final stage in the *varṇāśrama* system.

sannyāsī A man in the renounced order. *Sannyāsīs* take a vow of lifelong celibacy.

Sanskrit The oldest language in the world; the language of the *Vedas.*

śāstra Revealed scripture; an authorized textbook on any subject.

sat-saṅga Association of the devotees.

sāttvika Characterized by the mode of goodness (*sattva*).

siddhānta The ultimate conclusion of any philosophical proposal or system.

śikhā A tuft of hair at the back of the head, marking one as a devotee of Kṛṣṇa.

śikṣā-guru An instructing spiritual master.

śilā Stone.

Śiva A special expansion of the Supreme Lord, who is uniquely neither God nor *jīva*, but "almost God." He is God (Viṣṇu) in contact with the material nature. He energizes the material creation and, as the presiding deity of the mode of ignorance, controls the forces of destruction.

śiva-liṅga A rounded stone symbolizing Lord Śiva's creative potency, often worshiped by Śaivites.

Six Gosvāmīs Direct followers of Śrī Caitanya Mahāprabhu who systematically presented His teachings and excavated holy places in Vṛndāvana.

śloka A Sanskrit verse.

snāna-yātrā The public bathing ceremony of Lord Jagannātha.

Śrī A name for Lakṣmī, the goddess of fortune, the eternal consort of the Supreme Lord Nārāyaṇa. Also, a term of respect used before the names of deities, revered texts, respectable persons, and sacred objects.

Śrīdhara Svāmī The author of the earliest extant Vaiṣṇava commentaries on the *Bhagavad-gītā* and *Śrīmad-Bhāgavatam*, he taught pure Vaiṣṇava philosophy and worshiped Lord Nṛsiṁhadeva. Lord Caitanya declared that anyone who wants to write a commentary on *Srīmad-Bhagavatam* must follow Srīdhara Svāmī's.

Śrīla "Endowed by the goddess of fortune," a respectful title used by Gauḍīya Vaiṣṇavas for their spiritual masters.

Śrīla Prabhupāda See *A.C. Bhaktivedanta Swami Prabhupāda* and *Bhaktisiddhānta Sarasvatī Ṭhākura.*

Śrīmad-Bhāgavatam The "beautiful story of the Personality of Godhead," also known as the *amala-purāṇa*, the completely pure, "spotless *Purāṇa*," which teaches unalloyed devotional service to Kṛṣṇa, the original Supreme Personality of Godhead.

Śrīmān "Having the favors of the goddess of fortune," an honorific title preceding the name of a respected male. It also means "very beautiful."

Śrīmatī The female form of the title Śrīman.

Śrīnivāsa Ācārya A chief follower of the Six Gosvāmīs of Vṛndāvana, disciple of Gopāla Bhaṭṭa Gosvāmī.

Śrīpāda "His Holiness." A respectful title used by Gauḍīya Vaiṣṇavas for *sannyāsīs, gurus, ācāryas.*

Śrīvāsa-aṅgana The place in Māyāpur where Lord Caitanya inaugurated the *saṅkīrtana* movement and performed His nocturnal *kīrtanas* with His eternal associates.

Śrīvāsa Ṭhākura An intimate associate of Lord Caitanya, he is the incarnation of Nārada Muni in *gaura-līlā*. Lord Caitanya's *saṅkīrtana* movement began in his courtyard, and his altar was the site of the *mahā-prakāśa* pastime, in which Lord Caitanya exhibited His ecstatic mood as the omnipotent, omniscient Supreme Lord for twenty-one consecutive hours.

Subhadrā Kṛṣṇa's sister, also known as Yogamāyā, the internal potency of the Supreme Lord; the wife of Arjuna and mother of Abhimanyu.

Sudāmā One of the principal cowherd boyfriends of Lord Kṛṣṇa.

Supersoul Paramātmā, an expansion of the Supreme Lord that pervades the universe and dwells in the heart of every living entity.

Supreme Personality of Godhead The Supreme Lord Kṛṣṇa (and His direct expansions).

svāmī (swami) One who controls his senses; title of one in the renounced order of life.

Śyāmānanda Paṇḍita One of the great Vaiṣṇava *ācāryas* who lived in Vṛndāvana after the time of Śrī Caitanya. He received the direct mercy of Rādhārāṇī in Vṛndāvana, was tutored in the *bhakti-śāstras* by Jīva Gosvāmī, and delivered countless souls, especially in Orissa.

Śyāmasundara A name of Kṛṣṇa meaning "blackish" (*śyāma*) and "beautiful" (*sundara*).

tattva Truth, reality. A metaphysical principle; a philosophical topic, particularly as described in Vedic literature and elucidated by *ācāryas*. According to Baladeva Vidyābhūṣaṇa, Vedic knowledge categorizes reality into five *tattvas*, or ontological truths: *īśvara* (the Supreme Lord), *jīva* (the living entity), *prakṛti* (nature), *kāla* (eternal time), and *karma* (activity).

tilaka Auspicious markings, of sacred clay or other substances, applied on the upper part of the body, principally the forehead.

tithi Lunar day, measured in the Vedic calendar according to the phases of the moon. In Vedic culture important events such as the appearance or disappearance of exalted personages are recorded and celebrated according to the corresponding *tithi*.

tulasī The sacred plant most dear to Kṛṣṇa. *Tulasī* is an expansion of the *gopī* Vṛndā. Without the leaves of the *tulasī* plant, offerings of food and worship to Lord Viṣṇu are incomplete.

Unchagaon The village of Śrīmatī Lalitā-sakhī.

utsava Festival; an adjective referring to the small deities used for worship in such festivals.

vaidya Physician.

Vaikuṇṭha (-loka) "The place free from anxiety"; the kingdom of God, full of all opulences and unlimited by time and space.

Vaiṣṇava (Vaiṣṇavite) A devotee of the Supreme Lord Viṣṇu. Since Kṛṣṇa and Viṣṇu are different aspects of the same Supreme Person, devotees of Kṛṣṇa are also Vaiṣṇavas.

vaiṣṇava-aparādha An offense against a Vaiṣṇava.

vānaprastha Retired life, the third stage in the *varṇāśrama* social system, in which a man, sometimes together with his wife, gives up the *gṛhastha-āśrama* and visits holy places of pilgrimage or resides in a forest or holy place; a person in the *vānaprastha-āśrama*.

vāṇī Words, instructions, message.

vapuḥ Body, form.

Varāha (-deva) Lord Viṣṇu's incarnation as a huge boar, who killed the demon Hiraṇyākṣa and lifted the earth from the depths of the Garbhodaka Ocean.

varṇa Any of the four occupational divisions of the *varṇāśrama* social system: *brāhmaṇas* (teachers and priests), *kṣatriyas* (rulers and warriors), *vaiśyas* (farmers and businessmen), and *śūdras* (workers).

varṇāśrama (-dharma) The Vedic social system of four occupational divisions (*varṇas*) and four spiritual stages (*āśramas*).

Vāsudeva Datta The older brother of Mukunda Datta, who was the childhood friend of Śrī Caitanya Mahāprabhu. Vāsudeva Datta prayed to the Lord to let him bear the sinful reactions of all living entities in the universe, so they could be delivered.

Vedas The original revealed scriptures, eternal like the Supreme Lord, and thus authorless. Because in Kali-yuga the *Vedas* are difficult to understand or even study, the *Purāṇas* and epic histories, especially *Śrīmad-Bhāgavatam*, are essential for gaining access to their teachings.

Vedic Pertaining to the *Vedas* or, more broadly, following or derived from their authority.

Vidagdha-mādhava A seven-act play by Rūpa Gosvāmī describing the pastimes of Śrī Kṛṣṇa in Vṛndāvana.

vipralambha Separation (of lovers); the ecstasy of separation from Kṛṣṇa or His devotee(s).

vipralambha-kṣetra That place where intense pangs of separation from Kṛṣṇa are felt.

Viṣṇu The Supreme Lord in His opulent feature as the Lord of Vaikuṇṭha, who expands into countless forms and incarnations, some for the creation and maintenance of the material universes.

Viśvanātha Cakravartī A prominent seventeenth-century Gauḍīya Vaiṣṇava *ācārya* in the line of Narottama dāsa Ṭhākura, and a *śikṣā-guru* of Baladeva Vidyābhūṣaṇa. He wrote commentaries on the *Bhagavad-gītā* and *Śrīmad-Bhāgavatam* and on books by important followers of Śrī Caitanya Mahāprabhu.

Vraja (-bhūmi, -dhāma) The eternal place of Kṛṣṇa's cowherd pastimes, manifest on earth in the district of Mathurā.

Vraja-vāsīs The residents of Vraja, or Vṛndāvana.

Vṛndā (-devī) A direct *gopī* expansion of Śrīmatī Rādhārāṇī. She is the presiding deity of the Vṛndāvana forest, and her expansion is the *tulasī* plant. She and Paurṇamāsī make behind-the-scenes arrangements for Rādhā and Kṛṣṇa's daily pastimes.

Vṛndā-kuṇḍa The eternal home of Vṛndādevī, where she contemplates making arrangements for Rādhā and Kṛṣṇa's daily pastimes.

Vṛndāvana Kṛṣṇa's most beloved forest in Vraja-bhūmi, where He enjoys pastimes with the cowherd boys and the young *gopīs*; also, the entirety of Vraja.

Vyāsa (-deva) See *Dvaipāyana Vyāsa.*

Vyāsa-pūjā Worship of the compiler of the *Vedas*, Vyāsadeva; worship of the bona fide spiritual master as the representative of Vyāsadeva, on his appearance day.

vyāsāsana "The seat of Vyāsa," a special seat reserved for the spiritual master, the representative of Vyāsadeva.

walla One who does, makes, pulls, carries, sells, promotes (the noun it follows).

Yamunā The holiest of rivers, flowing through Vraja-bhūmi, in which Kṛṣṇa enjoyed many youthful pastimes.

Yāmunācārya Also known as Ālabandāru, he was born as a king and later became a great *ācārya* in the Śrī-sampradāya and the spiritual master of Rāmānujācārya.

yātrā A religious festival; a journey.

yoga "Yoking," a spiritual process for linking oneself with the Supreme. There are various kinds of *yoga*, including *karma-yoga* (the offering of the fruits of one's work for the pleasure of the Supreme), *jñāna-yoga* (the cultivation of spiritual knowledge of the soul and Supersoul), *aṣṭāṇga-yoga* (the eightfold process of meditation taught by Patañjali), and *bhakti-yoga* (pure devotional service to the Personality of Godhead).

yogī A practitioner of *yoga*.

yukta-vairāgya Befitting renunciation, in which one appropriately uses material sense objects in the service of the Supreme Lord, Kṛṣṇa.

Sanskrit Pronunciation Guide

Throughout the centuries, the Sanskrit language has been written in a variety of alphabets. The mode of writing most widely used throughout India, however, is called *devanāgarī*, which means, literally, the writing used in "the cities of the demigods." The *devanāgarī* alphabet consists of forty-eight characters: thirteen vowels and thirty-five consonants. Ancient Sanskrit grammarians arranged this alphabet according to practical linguistic principles, and this order has been accepted by all Western scholars. The system of transliteration used in this book conforms to a system that scholars have accepted to indicate the pronunciation of each Sanskrit sound.

VOWELS

a	ā	i	ī	u	ū	ṛ
ṝ	ḷ	ai	o	au		

CONSONANTS

Gutturals:	**ka**	**kha**	**ga**	**gha**	**ṅa**
Palatals:	**ca**	**cha**	**ja**	**jha**	**ña**
Cerebrals:	**ṭa**	**ṭha**	**ḍa**	**ḍha**	**ṇa**
Dentals:	**ta**	**tha**	**da**	**dha**	**na**
Labials:	**pa**	**pha**	**ba**	**bha**	**ma**
Semivowels:	**ya**	**ra**	**la**	**va**	
Sibilants:	**śa**	**ṣa**	**sa**		
Aspirate:	**ha**	Anusvara: **- ṁ**	Visarga: **ḥ**		

NUMERALS

0 1 2 3 4 5 6 7 8 9

The vowels are written as follows after a consonant:

ā i ī u ū ṛ ṝ e ai o au

For example: **ka kā ki kī ku kū**
kṛ kṝ kḷ ke kai ko kau

Generally two or more consonants in conjunction are written together in a special form, as for example: **kṣa tra**. The vowel **"a"** is implied after a consonant with no vowel symbol. The symbol *virāma* indicates that there is no final vowel.

THE VOWELS ARE PRONOUNCED AS FOLLOWS:

a — as in but
ā — as in far but held twice as long as **a**
i — as in pin
ī — as in pique but held twice as long as **i**
u — as in push
ū — as in rule but held twice as long as **u**

ṛ — as in rim
ṝ — as in reed but held twice as long as **r**
ḷ — as in happily
e — as in they
ai — as in aisle
o — as in go
au — as in how

THE CONSONANTS ARE PRONOUNCED AS FOLLOWS:

Gutturals
(pronounced from the throat)
k — as in kite
kh — as in Eckhart
g — as in give
gh — as in dig-hard
ṅ — as in sing
ñ — as in canyon

Palatals
(pronounced with the middle of the tongue against the palate)
c — as in chair
ch — as in staunch-heart
j — as in joy
jh — as in hedgehog

Cerebrals
(pronounced with the tip of the tongue against the roof of the mouth)
ṭ — as in tub
ṭh — as in light-heart
ḍ — as in dove
ḍh — as in red-hot
ṇ — as in sing

Dentals
(pronounced like the cerebrals but with the tongue against the teeth)
t — as in tub
h — as in light-heart
d — as in dove
dh — as in red-hot
n — as in nut

Labials
(pronounced with the lips)
p — as in pine
ph — as in up-hill

Semivowels
y — as in yes
r — as in run
l — as in light

b — as in **b**ird
bh — as in ru**b-h**ard
m — as in **m**other

v — as in **v**ine, except when preceded in the same syllable by a consonant, then as in s**w**an

Sibilants

ś — as in the German word *sprechen*
ṣ — as in **sh**ine
s — as in **s**un

Aspirate

h — as in **h**ome

Anusvara

ṁ — a resonant nasal sound as in the French word *bon*

Visarga

ḥ — a final h-sound: aḥ is pronounced like aha; iḥ like ihi.

There is no strong accentuation of syllables in Sanskrit, or pausing between words in a line, only a flowing of short and long syllables (the long twice as long as the short). A long syllable is one whose vowel is long (**ā, ī, ū, ṝ, e, ai, o, au**) or whose short vowel is followed by more than one consonant. The letters **ḥ** and **ṁ** count as consonants. Aspirated consonants (consonants followed by an **h**) count as single consonants.

Abbreviations

Books of His Divine Grace A.C. Bhaktivedanta Swami Prabhupāda:

Bg—*Bhagavad-gītā*
Cc—*Śrī Caitanya-caritāmṛta*
SB—*Śrīmad-Bhāgavatam*

Other books:
BaU—*Bṛhad-āraṇyaka Upaniṣad*
BnP—*Bṛhan-nāradīya Purāṇa*
Brs—*Bhakti-rasāmṛta-sindhu* by Śrīla Rūpa Gosvāmī
SGm—*Sāvaraṇa-Gaura-mahimā* by Narottama dāsa Ṭhākura
Vk—*Vilāpa-kusumāñjali* by Raghunātha dāsa Gosvāmī

Index of Verses

General Index

A

AAR conference, 36, 39
Abhidheya, 21
Abhirāma Gopāla (dāsa), 252
Abhirāma Ṭhākura (dāsa), xvi, 252–258
  detachment of, 254
  service mood of, 257
  service to devotees by, 253, 256–257
Abhiṣeka, 26, 132
Absolute Truth, 203, 299
Ācārya, xvii, 15, 24, 35, 42, 45–46, 121, 140–143, 163
Adbhuta Hari (dāsa), 122
Advaita Ācārya (dāsa), 189
Africa, 11, 165–167
Africans, 144
Ahmedabad, 119
Aindra (dāsa), xxvi, 189
Alachua, 98, 155
Ālālanātha, 25
Alarnath, 25–27
Allahabad, 19
Ambarīṣa (dāsa), 108
America, 16, 23, 90, 109, 125, 147, 172, 196, 199
Amoghalīlā (dāsa), 154, 158, 252, 254, 256
Ananta dāsa Bābājī, 220
Ananta-śānti dāsa, 221
Anupama, 74
Anuttama (dāsa), 158
Ārati, 192
Arcanaṁ, 210
Arcā-vigraha dāsī, xvi, 206–250, 263, 283, 289
  as a balanced devotee, 223
  as a perfectionist, 207
  career as an artist, 208–209
  chanting rounds by, 211, 242
  death of her husband, 208
  desire to hear about Kṛṣṇa by, 244
  early childhood of, 207–208
  extraordinary service to Giriraj Swami by, 233
  Eye Opener, The, by, 212, 219
  faith in *guru* of, 230
  first meeting with devotees, 209
  initiation of, 210
  last service by, 239
  mentality and integrity of, 240
  on performing devotional service, 211, 215
  painting deities by, 218–220
  passing away of her mother, 207–208
  position in the spiritual world of, 232
  preaching of, 240–241
  service to devotees by, 212–213, 234, 249
  spontaneity of, 210
  surrender of, 216, 230
  taking care of Giriraj Swami's health by, 213
  travels to Sinai desert by, 208
Āśrama, xxv, 142
Aṣṭa-kālīya-līlā, 189

O

P

W

Y

Z

His Divine Grace A. C. Bhaktivedanta Swami Prabhupāda

His Divine Grace A. C. Bhaktivedanta Swami Prabhupāda appeared in this world in 1896 in Calcutta, India. He first met his spiritual master, Śrīla Bhaktisiddhānta Sarasvatī Gosvāmī, in Calcutta in 1922. Bhaktisiddhānta Sarasvatī, a prominent religious scholar and the founder of the sixty-four-branch Gauḍīya Maṭha, liked this educated young man and convinced him to dedicate his life to teaching Vedic knowledge. Śrīla Prabhupāda, who at that time was known by his given name Abhay Charan, became his student, and eleven years later, in 1933, his initiated disciple.

At their first meeting Bhaktisiddhānta Sarasvatī requested the young man to broadcast Vedic knowledge through the English language. In the years that followed, Śrīla Prabhupāda wrote a commentary on the *Bhagavad-gītā*, assisted the Gauḍīya Maṭha in its work, and, in 1944, started *Back to Godhead*, an English fortnightly magazine. Single-handedly, he wrote the articles, typed and edited the manuscripts, checked the galley proofs, and even distributed the individual copies. Once begun, the magazine never stopped; it is still being published, now in over thirty languages.

Recognizing Śrīla Prabhupāda's philosophical learning and devotion, in 1947 the Gauḍīya Vaiṣṇava Society honored him with the title "Bhaktivedanta." In 1950, at the age of fifty-four, Śrīla Prabhupāda retired from married life, adopting the *vānaprastha* (retired) order to devote more time to his studies and writing. He traveled to the holy city of Vṛndāvana, where he lived humbly in the historic Rādhā-Dāmodara temple and for several years engaged in deep study and writing. After accepting the renounced order of life (*sannyāsa*) in 1959, he began work on his life's masterpiece: a multivolume translation of and commentary on the eighteen-thousand-verse *Śrīmad-Bhāgavatam*.

In 1965, at the age of seventy, after publishing three volumes of the *Bhāgavatam*, Śrīla Prabhupāda came to the United States to fulfill his spiritual master's mission, enduring a torturous two-month journey on a freighter and suffering two heart attacks on the way. When he arrived in New York City, he was practically penniless. Only after nearly a year of great difficulty—in July of 1966—did he manage to establish the International Society for Krishna Consciousness. Before his passing away on November 14, 1977, he had guided the Society and seen it grow to a worldwide confederation of more than one hundred ashrams, schools, temples, institutes, and farm communities.

In the twelve years between his arrival in the US and his departure from this world, with a vigorous schedule of translating, writing, and lecturing, Śrīla Prabhupāda circled the globe fourteen times and visited six continents. His books, highly respected by scholars for their clarity, depth, and authority, have been translated into over fifty languages, and the Bhaktivedanta Book Trust, established in 1972 to publish his work, has become the world's largest publisher in the field of Indian culture, religion, and philosophy.

The Author and Contributors

Giriraj Swami was born Glenn Phillip Teton, the only son of a respected Chicago lawyer who was later appointed judge. In March of 1969, while studying at Brandeis University in Boston, he met His Divine Grace A.C. Bhaktivedanta Swami Prabhupāda, the founder-*ācārya* of the International Society for Krishna Consciousness, and considered that he learned more from Śrīla Prabhupāda in five minutes than he had learned in his twenty years of academic education. After graduating from Brandeis *cum laude*, Glenn took formal initiation from Śrīla Prabhupāda and was given the spiritual name "Giriraj das." Giriraj quickly became a leading member of the Boston center. He was then given the opportunity to go to India with Śrīla Prabhupāda and helped establish his mission there.

In 1972 Prabhupāda appointed Giriraj president of ISKCON Bombay and trustee of the Bhaktivedanta Book Trust. Since then, he has made many significant contributions to Śrīla Prabhupāda's mission, most notably overseeing all aspects of the development of Hare Krishna Land in Juhu, Bombay. He was instrumental in the acquisition and development of the Bhaktivedanta Ashram in Govardhana, and, more recently, led the development of the Kirtan Ashram for renounced women, the Bhaktivedanta Hospice, and the Vrindavan Institute of Palliative Care, all in Vṛndāvana. Through all his efforts, Giriraj Swami has become renowned for the austerities he has accepted, his loyalty and dedication to Śrīla Prabhupāda's mission, his ability to raise funds and cultivate important members of society, and his care for devotees around the world.

In the year following Śrīla Prabhupāda's departure in 1977, Giriraj das was awarded the renounced order of life and appointed president of ISKCON's board of trustees in India. In 1982 he was made a member of ISKCON's Governing Body Commission, the ultimate managing authority for the movement, and he went on to oversee the Society's activities in Bombay, Mauritius, South Africa, Spain, Portugal, Sri Lanka, and Pakistan.

Giriraj Swami has also taught at the Vrindavan Institute for Higher Education and continues to lecture and to give presentations at *japa* retreats and workshops around the world.

Presently based in Carpinteria, California, Giriraj Swami is now focusing on one of Śrīla Prabhupāda's main personal instructions to him—to write. He is the author of *Watering the Seed* and is working on several publications, including books about death and dying in the Vedic tradition, his search for a spiritual master and his early days in the Boston temple, his travels with Śrīla Prabhupāda in India, and Śrīla Prabhupāda's monumental efforts in Bombay.

Bhakti Bhṛṅga Govinda Swami is a disciple of His Divine Grace A.C. Bhaktivedanta Swami Prabhupāda and a preacher, renunciant priest, and initiating *guru* in the International Society for Krishna Consciousness. He joined the Kṛṣṇa consciousness movement in 1971 in Buffalo, New York, and ever since has served in the US, Canada, India, Europe, and especially Russia and Central Asia, where he has provided guidance and leadership to devotees struggling against hostile government authorities to maintain their religious freedom and practices. A renowned *kīrtanīyā*, Govinda Swami has for the last ten years led a group of Kazakhstani musicians around the world, entertaining and enlightening audiences and promoting the chanting of the holy names. In Vṛndāvana in the late eighties and early nineties, he helped care for his two friends Buddhimanta dāsa and Arcā-vigraha dāsī as they prepared to leave their bodies in Kṛṣṇa consciousness.

Bhūrijana dāsa met His Divine Grace A.C. Bhaktivedanta Swami Prabhupāda in 1968 at the first ISKCON temple, on Second Avenue in New York City, and was initiated by Śrīla Prabhupāda later that year. He helped pioneer the Kṛṣṇa consciousness movement in Japan and Hong Kong and was instrumental in developing ISKCON's educational system—working in primary education and curriculum development, conducting teacher training courses, and establishing and teaching in the Vrindavan Institute for Higher Education.

Bhūrijana dāsa has written several books, including *The Art of Teaching*, *Surrender Unto Me* (a study of the *Bhagavad-gītā*), *Studying Śrīmad-Bhāgavatam*, *My Glorious Master* (a memoir of his time with Śrīla Prabhupāda), *Unveiling His Lotus Feet* (a study of the first four cantos of *Śrīmad-Bhāgavatam*), and *Japa: Nine Keys from the Śikṣāṣṭaka to Improve Your Japa.* He is currently writing two more volumes of his *Bhāgavatam* study and continues to teach—in Vṛndāvana and in Perth, Australia.

Bhakta Carl Herzig, PhD, is the younger brother of Tamal Krishna Goswami. He is a professor of English in Davenport, Iowa, where he teaches courses in sacred poetry, the *Bhagavad-gītā*, and other related topics, and leads students on service-learning trips to Vṛndāvana. He has written and helped edit several books, including those by ISKCON authors Giriraj Swami, Lokanath Swami, Mukunda Goswami, Hari-śauri dāsa, Aindra dāsa, Kalakaṇṭha dāsa, Rādhā-caraṇa dāsa, and Tamal Krishna Goswami.

Ekavīra dāsa received initiation from Bhakti Tirtha Swami in 1992 and was among the first devotees to assist with the development of the Institute for Applied Spiritual Technology. He served for nine years as president of the Gita Nagari temple and was one of Bhakti Tirtha Swami's primary caregivers until Mahārāja's departure in 2005. Ekavīra is a certified Holistic Health Consultant and a member of the GBC Devotee Care Committee.

Guṇagrāhī dāsa Goswami joined ISKCON in Buffalo, New York, in 1969. He was initiated by His Divine Grace A.C. Bhaktivedanta Swami Prabhupāda two years later and accepted *sannyāsa*, the renounced order of life, in 1983. He has served as president of the Buffalo, San Diego, and New York temples and is currently ISKCON's zonal secretary for Argentina and Uruguay. He travels extensively in the US and abroad developing Kṛṣṇa conscious centers, teaching, counseling, and leading *kīrtana*.

Guru-bhakti dāsī, MD, was born in Fiji, completed her medical training in India, and in 1986 received initiation from Tamal Krishna Goswami in Houston, Texas. There, she is Director of Outreach and a member of the Houston Vaiṣṇavas Care team and serves the deities and devotee community as *pūjārī*, teacher, cook, and physician. Guru-bhakti was the primary caregiver for Tamal Krishna Goswami—most intensively in 1999 during his bout with cancer—and continues to maintain an active private medical practice.

Kuntīdevī dāsī joined the Kṛṣṇa consciousness movement in South Africa in 1985 and there became a full-time traveling *saṅkīrtana* devotee. In 1991 she accompanied Mother Arcā-vigraha to India to care for her in the final stage of her life. After Arcā-vigraha's passing three years later, Kuntīdevī taught in the Bhaktivedanta Gurukula, then moved to Bombay, where she began her service as secretary and research assistant for

Giriraj Swami, whose ashram in Carpinteria she has managed since 1999.

Māyāpur dāsa, a native of Dubrovnik, Croatia, joined ISKCON in 1993. Two years later he met Sridhar Swami, and for the next ten years he served in India, first as a traveling book distributor, then as Sridhar Mahārāja's personal assistant until Mahārāja's passing from this world in 2004. He is currently back in Croatia leading *kīrtana* programs.

Rasikendra dāsa, born in Singapore to South Indian parents, holds a PhD in Aerospace Engineering. In 1995 he was initiated by Tamal Krishna Goswami in Dallas, Texas, where he assisted Mother Kīrtidā in serving the Dallas temple's presiding Deities, Śrī Śrī Rādhā-Kālachandjī. He and his wife, Padadhūli dāsī, helped care for Kīrtidā in their home when she moved to Dallas in 2001 for the final months of her life. They currently reside in Houston, where Rasikendra is employed as an engineer and the couple serves the ISKCON temple deities and devotees.

Ṛtadhvaja Swami, a disciple of His Divine Grace A. C. Bhaktivedanta Swami Prabhupāda, joined ISKCON in 1975 and ten years later accepted the renounced order of *sannyāsa*. He first served in Winnipeg, Canada, and then moved to Florida, where over the next eleven years he served as *saṅkīrtana* and *bhakta* leader, Gainesville temple president, regional secretary, servant and secretary to Hridayānanda dāsa Goswami, and *gurukula* teacher and headmaster. Since 1998 he has been preaching in China and elsewhere around the world.

In 1999, when Tamal Krishna Goswami became ill with cancer, he asked Ṛtadhvaja Swami to be part of his support staff during and after his surgery. During the many hours they spent together, they developed an intimate friendship that continued to deepen in the years before Tamal Krishna Goswami's passing in 2002.

Sārvabhauma dāsa, a native of Southern California, was active in the Transcendental Meditation movement before meeting Kṛṣṇa devotees in Los Angeles in the late 1970s. He joined the Dallas ISKCON temple in 1981 and received initiation from Tamal Krishna Goswami a year later. In 2007 he wrote Kīrtidā dāsī's biography, *Servant of Love: the Saintly Life of Kīrtidā Devī.* He also contributed a chapter on death and dying in the Hindu tradition to the anthology *Ultimate Journey: Death and Dying in the World's Major Religions* (2008) and co-authored "Lord Krishna and the Animals" in *A Call to Compassion: Religious Perspectives on Animal Advocacy from a Range of Religious Perspectives* (2011). His blog, "Spirit Soul with Sarva," is a regular feature in the *Houston Chronicle.*

Vraja-līlā dāsī, an early pioneer of Kṛṣṇa consciousness in West Africa, met Bhakti Tirtha Swami in 1979, accepted initiation from him a year later, and was one of Mahārāja's primary caregivers until his departure in 2005. She has served as executive director of the Institute for Applied Spiritual Technology, co-president of the Gita Nagari temple, and trainer and mediator for ISKCON Resolve. Currently based in Gita Nagari, Vraja-līlā facilitates workshops on emotional care and is a caregiver and a member of the GBC Devotee Care Committee.